THE SCHOOLS HISTORY PROJECT

· S·H·P ·

OFFICIAL TEXT

SHP
HISTORY
YEAR 9

DALE BANHAM

IAN LUFF

DYNAMIC LEARNING

HODDER
EDUCATION
AN HACHETTE UK COMPANY

This book is dedicated to: Frank and Alma, two remarkable people who generously shared their experiences with us; and Russell Hall and Mick Batten, two teachers who made a difference.

Thanks to all the Suffolk schools that have trialled our work, and to Kim, Aidan, Caitlin, Amanda, James and Anna for their love and support.

The Schools History Project

Set up in 1972 to bring new life to history for students aged 13–16, the Schools History Project continues to play an innovatory role in secondary history education. From the start, SHP aimed to show how good history has an important contribution to make to the education of a young person. It does this by creating courses and materials which both respect the importance of up-to-date, well-researched history and provide enjoyable learning experiences for students.

Since 1978 the Project has been based at Trinity and All Saints University College Leeds. It continues to support, inspire and challenge teachers through the annual conference, regional courses and website: http://www.schoolshistoryproject.org.uk. The Project is also closely involved with government bodies and awarding bodies in the planning of courses for Key Stage 3, GCSE and A level.

Acknowledgements

p.2 Allen Guttman, Olympics data from *The Olympics: A History of the Modern Games* (University of Illinois, 2002); **Section 1** Michael Alexander and Sushila Anand, extracts from *Queen Victoria's Maharajah: Duleep Singh 1838-93* (Weidenfeld & Nicolson/Phoenix Press, 2001); **p.45** Edward Luce, extracts based on information from *In Spite of the Gods: The Strange Rise of Modern India* (Little, Brown, 2006); **Section 2 p.58** Siegfried Sassoon, lines from 'Aftermath' from *Collected Poems 1908–1956* (Faber & Faber, 1984), reproduced by permission of Barbara Levy Literary Agency; **p.63** Robert Graves, extract from *Goodbye to All That* (Jonathan Cape, 1929); **p.64** Hugh Quigley, extract from *Passchendaele and The Somme: A Diary of 1917* (Methuen, 1928); **pp.76–77** Max Hastings, extracts (adapted) from *Overlord: D Day and the Battle for Normandy 1944* (Michael Joseph, 1984); **p.79** Frederick Taylor, extract (adapted) from *Dresden: Tuesday, 13 February, 1945* (Bloomsbury, 2005); **pp.90–91** Michihiko Hachiya, extracts from *Hiroshima Diary* (University of North Carolina Press, 1955); **Section 4 p.144** Richard Pankhurst, extract (adapted) from *Sylvia Pankhurst: Artist and Crusader, an Intimate Portrait* (Paddington Press, 1979); Rosemary Taylor, extracts from *Walks Through History: Exploring the East End* (Breedon Books, 2001); **pp.149–151** Andrew Rosen, extracts (adapted) from *Rise Up, Women!: Militant Campaign of the Women's Social and Political Union, 1903–14* (Routledge Kegan & Paul, 1974); **p.155** Donald McRae, extract (adapted) from *In Black & White – The Untold Story of Joe Louis and Jesse Owens* (Simon & Schuster UK, 2002); **p.161** Abel Meeropol, *Strange Fruit,* song lyrics (1936); **p.174–175** Nelson Mandela, from speech from the dock in 1964 from *Speeches that Changed the World*, edited by Simon Sebag Montefiore (Quercus Publishing, 2007); **p.182** F.W. de Klerk, extract, 'Great Speeches of the 20th century: An ideal for which I am prepared to die: Nelson Mandela, April 20 1964' from *The Guardian* (23 April 2007), copyright Guardian News & Media Ltd 2007, reproduced by permission of the publisher; **Section 5 p.192** David Kynaston, extract (adapted) from *Austerity Britain, 1945-51* (Bloomsbury, 2008); **p.201** Nelson Mandela, from speech in Trafalgar Square in 2005 from *Speeches that Changed the World*, edited by Simon Sebag Montefiore (Quercus Publishing, 2007); **Section 6** Robert Winder, information from *Bloody Foreigners* (Little, Brown, 2004); **p.219** Benjamin Zephaniah, 'The British' from *Wicked World* (Puffin Books, 2000).

Every effort has been made to trace all copyright holders, but if any have been inadvertently overlooked the Publishers will be pleased to make the necessary arrangements at the first opportunity.

Although every effort has been made to ensure that website addresses are correct at time of going to press, Hodder Education cannot be held responsible for the content of any website mentioned in this book. It is sometimes possible to find a relocated web page by typing in the address of the home page for a website in the URL window of your browser.

Hachette UK's policy is to use papers that are natural, renewable and recyclable products and made from wood grown in sustainable forests. The logging and manufacturing processes are expected to conform to the environmental regulations of the country of origin.

Orders: please contact Bookpoint Ltd, 130 Milton Park, Abingdon, Oxon OX14 4SB. Telephone: +44 (0)1235 827720. Fax: +44 (0)1235 400454. Lines are open 9.00–5.00, Monday to Saturday, with a 24-hour message answering service. Visit our website at www.hoddereducation.co.uk.

© Dale Banham and Ian Luff 2009
First published in 2009 by Hodder Education,
An Hachette UK company
Carmelite House, 50 Victoria Embankment, London EC4Y 0DZ

Impression number   16   15   14
Year   2023   2022   2021

Typeset in 12/14 pt Palatino Light
Layouts by Fiona Webb
Artwork by Art Construction, Jon Davis, Peter Bull, Steve Smith, Richard Duszczak, Tony Randell and Patricia Ludlow
Printed and bound in Dubai

A catalogue record for this title is available from the British Library

ISBN 978 0 340 90739 9
Teacher's Resource Book ISBN 978 0 340 90740 5

Contents

Key features of *SHP History*

Before you start using this book here is a guide to help you get the most out of it.

Enquiry This book is full of enquiry questions to investigate. Some short enquiries will only take one lesson. Other longer ones – the depth studies – may spread over a number of weeks.

Quick history These are overviews that sum up long periods in a short activity.

Banner This introduces the enquiry and sums up what you are going to focus on.

Activities These help you to build your enquiry step by step.

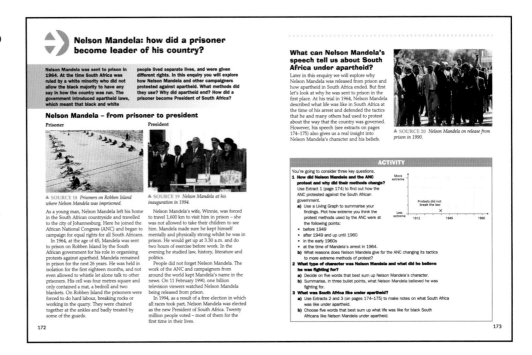

Big Story At the end of each section is a Big Story page that sums up the section and connects it with what has already been studied, or with what is going to be studied.

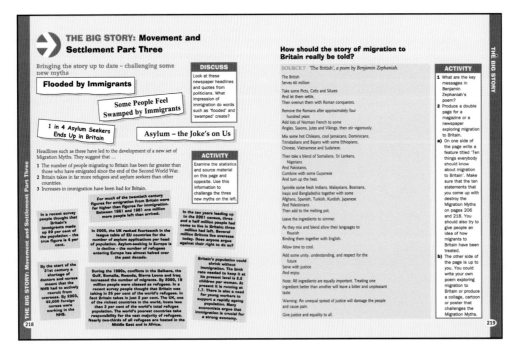

Themes Each section focuses on one thematic story. This section focuses on Movement and Settlement. You will probably have started this theme in Year 7 and continued it in Year 8.

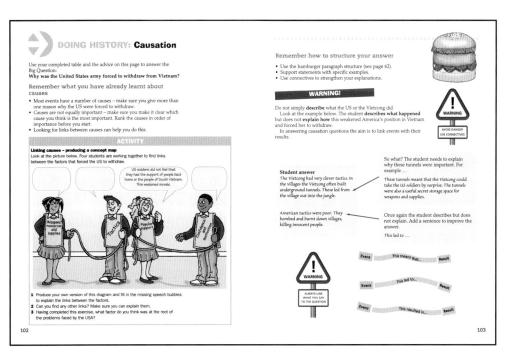

Doing History Each time you meet a new concept or process we recap the key ideas like this. If you want to get better at history this is what you focus on.

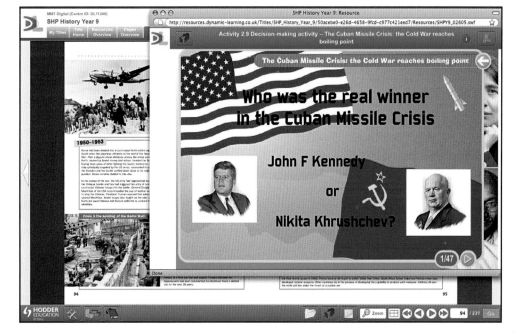

Dynamic Learning An interactive version of this textbook including on-screen activities and ICT-based investigations to help you.

What can the Olympics tell us about the key events and changes of the twentieth century?

The modern Olympics started in 1896. Since then, with a couple of exceptions, the Games have been held regularly every four years. Each Olympics reflects what the world is like at the time they take place. In this unit you will use the Olympics as a window on the twentieth century. What can the Games tell us about the major political events of the last 100 years? What can the Olympics tell us about the social, cultural and technological changes that have taken place since 1896?

PICTURE PUZZLE

1 Each of the pictures on page 3 is taken from an Olympic Games that took place in the twentieth century. Use the clues in the pictures to place the Games in chronological order.
2 For each picture try to answer as many of the following questions as possible. Do not worry if you cannot answer all the questions at this stage. Use the table on the right and the clues in the picture to help you.
   • **Who** is in the picture?
   • **Where** are the Olympics taking place?
   • **When** did these Olympics take place?
   • **What** is happening in the picture?
   • **Why** was this event important?
   • **How** useful is this source? What does it tell us about life at the time?
3 Try to solve the extra puzzles in the yellow boxes on page 3.

NUMBER PUZZLE

1 The Olympic Games are usually held every four years. Why were they not held in 1916, 1940 and 1944?
2 Why do you think the number of athletes competing in the Games fell in 1904, 1932, and 1956? CLUE – This has nothing to do with politics … think geography!
3 In 1980 and 1984, lots of countries boycotted the Games. Why did they refuse to attend?

The Olympics 1900–2000. ▶

Year	Place	Male athletes	Female athletes
1900	Paris, France	1066	11
1904	St Louis, USA	548	6
1908	London	1998	36
1912	Stockholm, Sweden	2447	57
1920	Antwerp, Belgium	2527	64
1924	Paris, France	2939	136
1928	Amsterdam, Netherlands	2681	290
1932	Los Angeles, USA	1204	127
1936	Berlin, Germany	3652	328
1948	London	3677	385
1952	Helsinki, Finland	5349	518
1956	Melbourne, Australia	2958	384
1960	Rome, Italy	4785	610
1964	Tokyo, Japan	4903	683
1968	Mexico City, Mexico	5845	781
1972	Munich, Germany	6595	1299
1976	Montreal, Canada	4938	1251
1980	Moscow, USSR	4835	1088
1984	Los Angeles, USA	5429	1626
1988	Seoul, South Korea	6941	2476
1992	Barcelona, Spain	6648	2715
1996	Atlanta, USA	6797	3523
2000	Sydney, Australia	6582	4069

Why did the sprinter who came second win the gold medal?

What can you tell by looking through an Olympics window?

Why did this individual annoy Hitler?

What happened for the first time at this Olympics?

Why did armed gunmen enter the Israeli team's base in the Olympic village?

Why did Tommie Smith and John Carlos remove their shoes before stepping on to the medal podium and why are they saluting in this way?

Every picture tells a story

ACTIVITY

1 Use the Olympics Scrapbook on pages 4–6 to check your answers to the picture puzzles on pages 2 and 3.

2 Why were these five Olympic Games so important? For each Games, explain in no more than 50 words what they tell us about the world in the twentieth century.

1928: AMSTERDAM

WOMEN COMPETE FOR THE FIRST TIME IN TRACK AND FIELD EVENTS

The modern Olympics were the idea of Pierre de Coubertin, a French educator. De Coubertin and many of his colleagues on the International Olympic Committee (IOC) believed that athletics was not 'ladylike' and that athletic exercise was damaging to women. In Athens in 1896 there had been no events for women. In the **1900 Paris Olympics** women took part in the Olympics for the first time. However, they were only allowed to compete in golf and tennis. In 1912 this was extended to swimming.

It was not until the **1928 Amsterdam Olympics** that women were allowed to compete in track and field athletics events for the first time. Even then, the number of events that they could take part in was limited. They were only allowed to participate in the 100 m, 800 m, 4 x 100 m

relay, discus and high jump. After the women's 800 metres there were complaints that the competitors looked too exhausted. Women were not allowed to run races of more than 200 metres again until the **1964 Tokyo Olympics**.

Things took a long time to change. Even in the **1980 Moscow Olympics**, only

18 per cent of the athletes were women. Today women compete in a number of sports such as football and weightlifting that in 1980 were reserved only for men. However, male athletes still outnumber female athletes.

In Section 4 of this book you will explore how women had to campaign for equal rights in sport and in politics.

SPORT AS PROPAGANDA

The **1936 Olympics** were perhaps the most infamous of them all. They were used by Hitler and Goebbels as propaganda to promote the Nazi regime. The idea of the Olympic torch relay was introduced. The torch was lit in Olympia and carried to Berlin by a relay of thousands of runners. At the Olympic stadium, against an elaborate backdrop of Nazi banners and symbols, it was used to light the Olympic flame during the opening ceremony.

Hitler believed that the Olympics would show that the German Aryan race was superior to all other races. However, a black American, Jesse Owens, became the hero of the games by winning four gold medals. In Section 3 of this book you will explore Hitler's racist beliefs and the way he changed life in Germany.

Black Power Protest at Olympics

The photograph shows the American athletes Tommie Smith and John Carlos (first and third in the 200 metres) giving the Black Power salute at the Olympic Games in Mexico in 1968. They wanted to raise awareness of the inequality that existed in America and to express their pride in being black Americans. As part of their protest, they removed their shoes to symbolise black poverty. They were thrown out of the Olympics as a result of their protest.

In Section 4 of this book you will find out more about how black Americans protested about the way they were treated in the United States.

TERRORIST ATTACK ON ISRAELI ATHLETES

Just before dawn on the eleventh day of the Olympics, a small gang of Palestinian terrorists climbed the fence of the Olympic village. The terrorists were members of the Black September organisation. They made their way to where the Israeli team were staying, killed two Israelis and took nine hostages. The masked gunmen threatened to kill the Israeli hostages unless 200 Palestinian prisoners held in Israel were released.

After a day of negotiations the terrorists were allowed to take the hostages to the airport where they expected to be flown out of the country. The security forces launched a rescue attempt. In the gunfight that followed five of the terrorists, a German policeman and all of the hostages were killed.

Since 1972 terrorism has remained a threat at all Olympics. Security was raised for the Games that followed Munich. However, at the **1996 Atlanta Olympics** a bomb exploded on 27 July, which left one person dead and more than one hundred injured. The bomb was set by an American terrorist, Eric Robert Rudolph, who claimed that he had planted the bomb to protest against the

American government allowing abortion. In Section 2 of this book you will learn more about how terrorism has developed.

FASTEST MAN ON EARTH FAILS DRUG TEST

Many people thought that they had witnessed one of the greatest sporting performances of all time in 1988 when Ben Johnson, the Canadian sprinter, won the 100 metres in a world record time of 9.79 seconds. At the press conference that followed Johnson was asked what meant more, the record or the medal. He replied

'They can break my record, but they can't take my gold medal away.'

However, his medal was taken away. Johnson tested positive for anabolic steroids and was stripped of both his world record and his gold medal. The second place American athlete, Carl Lewis, was awarded the gold medal.

The substance used by Johnson was stanozolol, which increases muscle bulk, strength and power. It was a sign that sport was now so big that competitors were willing to risk everything to win. Johnson was one of a number of competitors who were disqualified from the Games because of drug scandals.

Johnson was not the first athlete to use drugs to try and improve performance. As sport became more global and professional the stakes got higher and higher. Some athletes began to look to drugs as a way of gaining an advantage over their rivals. Rumours of widespread drug taking first emerged in the 1952 Winter Olympics. In the **1960 Rome Olympics** a Danish cyclist died. His post-mortem showed that he had taken amphetamines. Drug testing was introduced at the **1968 Mexico Olympics**. At the **1976 Montreal Olympics** seven weight lifters, including a number of gold medal winners, were disqualified for using anabolic steroids.

You will consider whether drug taking is the main threat to future Olympics at the end of this introductory section.

Every number tells a story

Pierre de Coubertin, the founder of the modern Olympics, thought that they would promote peace and understanding between countries, and improve the physical and moral stature of young athletes. De Coubertin hoped that the Olympics would be free from politics. However, politics has always been part of the Olympics. The Olympics were soon affected by the major conflicts and political events of the twentieth century.

ACTIVITY

Use the information on this page to check your answers to the number puzzle on page 2.

Political conflict

The Olympics did not take place in 1916 because of the First World War and there was a gap of twelve years between the 1936 Olympics and the next Games in 1948 because of the Second World War. These two conflicts also explain why Germany and her allies were not invited to the 1920 and 1948 Olympics.

The boycotts of the 1980 and 1984 Olympics reflect the bad relations that existed between the United States and the Soviet Union during the early 1980s as a consequence of the Cold War. In 1979 the Soviet Union invaded Afghanistan and as a result America and a number of other nations boycotted the 1980 Moscow Olympics in protest. In retaliation the Soviet Union and some of her allies in Eastern Europe boycotted the Los Angeles Olympics four years later. In Section 2 of this book you will examine the major conflicts of the last 100 years.

Changes in technology

However, the Olympics can tell us about more than just politics. The table on page 2 shows that the number of athletes competing in the games fell significantly in 1904 and 1932 when the Olympics were held in America. This is a reflection of transport and technology at the time. In 1904 European athletes faced a long boat ride, followed by a slow 1000-mile train ride. Of the 548 athletes who took part, 432 were American. Numbers participating fell again in 1956 when the Olympics were held in Australia. This shows that long-distance travel was nowhere near as simple or straightforward as it is now. By the time the Olympics were held in Australia again, in 2000, technology had moved on and air travel was far quicker and easier.

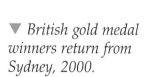

▼ *British gold medal winners return from Sydney, 2000.*

From Athens to Athens: exploring change and continuity

What changed and what stayed the same between the 1896 and 2004 Athens Olympics?

The first modern Olympics were held in Athens in 1896. Greece was chosen because it was where the Ancient Olympics had started in 776 BC and where they were held for hundreds of years. In 2004 the Olympic Games returned to Greece. Comparing the 1896 and 2004 Games can reveal a great deal about how the world changed during the twentieth century. However, it is not just the changes that interest historians. It is also what stays the same. Remember to look for evidence of continuity as well as change when you compare the two Games.

1896: Athens – The First Modern Olympics

- Fourteen nations took part
- 245 athletes participated
- Only male athletes were involved
- Nine sports (track and field athletics, gymnastics, cycling, fencing, weightlifting, wrestling, swimming, tennis and shooting)
- 43 events (none open to women)
- The games lasted ten days
- The USA won the most athletics events
- Greece won most medals overall (47)
- All athletes were unpaid and had to find their own accommodation
- The swimming events were held in the Aegean Sea. In the 1200 m event the nine competitors were taken out to sea by boat and left to swim back to shore, struggling against 12-foot waves
- The events were reported in newspapers and were well attended. More than 100,000 spectators lined the route of the marathon, which was won by a Greek athlete, Spiridon Louis, in 2 hours 58 minutes
- James Connolly, the American triple jump champion, had to raise the funds for the trip to Greece himself. He then had to endure a sixteen-day boat trip to Naples in Italy, eventually arriving in Greece one day before he competed in the triple jump
- Every winner was presented with a silver medal and an olive branch
- The 100 metres was won by Thomas Burke, from the USA, in a time of 12.0 seconds

1 Look at the picture of the 1896 Olympics in Athens below. Compare it to the pictures of the 2004 Athens Olympics opposite. What similarities and differences can you see?
2 Read the information boxes on each Olympics. What are the main changes that took place between the Athens games in 1896 and the Athens games in 2004?
3 What do these changes tell us about how life changed during the twentieth century?

8

The 2004 Athens Olympics

- 201 nations took part
- 10,625 athletes (4,329 women, 6,296 men) competed in the Games. They were housed in an Olympic village
- Many of the athletes were professional sportsmen and women
- 28 sports
- 301 events (133 open to women)
- The events were contested on 37 different sites
- The Games lasted 17 days
- 45,000 people were responsible for security at the Games

- 21,500 journalists
- Popularity of the Games soared to new highs as 3.9 billion people had access to the television coverage
- The United States won the most gold medals
- The cost of the Games was estimated to be 7.2 billion euros. Lots of this money was spent on state-of-the-art venues. The Olympic stadium, for example, was designed with a retractable glass roof
- The 2004 Summer Paralympics were also held in Athens: 4000 athletes took part
- The men's 100 metres was won by Justin Gatlin from the USA in a time of 9.85 seconds
- The marathon was won by Stefano Baldini from Italy in a time of 2 hours and 10 minutes

What is the biggest danger facing future Olympics?

Sport as big business?

As you have seen, the Olympics have changed a great deal since 1896. Many people are concerned that sport has become too much like big business and that the Olympics are in danger of becoming too commercialised.

ACTIVITY

1 Use the information on pages 10–11 to explain when and why the Olympics became commercialised.
2 Do you think that commercialisation is the biggest danger facing future Olympics? Place the following potential threats in order of importance and explain your choices.
   • Drugs
   • The Olympics becoming too commercialised
   • Terrorism
   • Political boycotts

1900: PARIS – THE OLYMPICS IN A PARK!

In the 1900 Paris Olympics many of the sporting contests took place in the Bois de Boulogne, the city's largest park. Races were held on the grass because the French authorities did not want to disfigure the park with a cinder running track. Swimming and diving events took place in the River Seine. The Games did not receive much publicity and the crowds watching the events were small. These Olympics remind us of how much sport has changed. Today sport is big business. During the twentieth century the Olympics became more and more commercialised and leading athletes became wealthy and famous.

1948: London – The 'Make Do and Mend' Olympics

These Olympics were the first to be held after the Second World War. Britain had very little money to spend on the Games and the 1948 Olympics have been called the 'make-do-and-mend Games'.
• Transport was provided on London buses
• RAF camps, nurses' hostels and local schools provided the accommodation for the athletes. Term ended early for some local schoolchildren as their classrooms were turned into bedrooms for the athletes
• When the cycling event went into the evening, spectators were invited to circle the track in their cars, with headlights full on so that the racing could be completed
• The athletics events were held in Wembley Stadium (as well as football and hockey finals). It cost just £89,000 to prepare the stadium. Some changes had to be made. The greyhound track that encircled the football pitch had to be made suitable for athletics events
• The Empire pool (built in 1934) was used to hold the swimming events. It held 8000 people and there was still black-out paint on the glass roof from the Second World War
• Food for athletes was rationed (although athletes were put on the largest allowance). Meat, eggs and butter were scarce and some athletes ate whale meat (which was not rationed) to try to get enough protein
• Many athletes competed in home-made kit and some training methods were very different from today. Emil Zatopek, the 5000 and 10,000 metres champion, prepared for the Olympics by running with his wife on his back!
• Security was provided by bobbies on the beat (mainly by local policemen patrolling on foot)

1960: ROME – TV TAKES OVER

The Rome Olympics were the first Games to be televised across the world. Over 100 television channels broadcast both live and recorded footage of the Games to eighteen countries across Europe as well as to the United States, Japan and Canada. CBS-TV paid $660,000 to film the Games. Footage from Rome was flown to New York so that it was ready for 'prime-time' broadcasts.

Some people on the International Olympic Committee (IOC) hated the idea of commercialisation. However, the IOC could no longer ignore the potential for huge sums of money to be made from the Games. By the time of the **1976 Montreal Olympics** ABC were paying $25 million for the rights to broadcast the Games. The introduction of TV coverage also increased the interest of big business. Soon companies were making deals with athletes to wear their brand of shoes or to use their sports equipment.

1984: LOS ANGELES – RECORD PROFITS

The Los Angeles Games were the first to be staged without government financing. Big business took over and, despite the boycott by the Soviet Union and her allies, the Games made a $223 million profit. $130 million was raised from 30 corporate sponsors. ABC paid $225 million for the television rights and there were also 43 companies licensed to sell 'official' Olympic products. The Mars Bar was the official snack food of the Games and McDonald's sold the official Olympic burger. For the **1996 Atlanta Olympics**, NBC paid $456 million to televise the Games and received $600 million back in advertising revenue.

2012: THE OLYMPICS RETURN TO LONDON

- Total cost = £9 billion
- Cost of the building programme = £7 billion
- Cost of staging all the events = £2 billion
- Cost of the athletes' village is expected to be £1 billion. The village will provide accommodation for over 17,000 athletes and officials
- Cost of security = £1.2 billion
- A new 80,000 seat Olympic Stadium will be built to hold the athletics events
- A new venue to host the swimming events is also being built. The building will cost an estimated £300 million and will hold 17,500 spectators. The roof of the building has been designed to resemble a wave
- The Olympic Park will have its own power station

Winners or losers? Why do people argue about who gained and who lost from the British Empire?

Understanding empires is an important part of understanding history. The British Empire was the biggest the world had ever known. You have already explored how and why this empire grew and its impact across the world. In this section you will explore why the British Empire is so controversial. Why do people still argue about the impact the Empire had on people living at the time?

How was the British Empire portrayed at the end of the nineteenth century?

On 22 June 1897 a spectacular procession wound its way through the streets of London. Soldiers marched proudly to stirring music provided by military bands. Crowds lined the route and waved thousands of tiny Union Jacks as they cheered.

Behind the smart soldiers came an open carriage carrying a very old woman dressed soberly and waving gently to the crowds. Her face wore a warm smile and, despite considerable frailty, she seemed to be enjoying the occasion.

The grand old lady in the carriage was Queen Victoria who had been on the British throne for 60 years. During Victoria's reign the British Empire had grown significantly. By 1897 Queen Victoria ruled over the biggest empire in world history. The British Empire covered close to a quarter of the world's land surface. Over 400 million people lived under some form of British rule, nearly one in four of the world's population.

This glittering procession was the main feature of the celebrations organised to mark Queen Victoria's Diamond Jubilee. The Diamond Jubilee saw much rejoicing and great ceremonies and displays. Throughout Britain and across the Empire there were parades, speeches, plays, balls, street parties, shows and concerts. In Britain there were widespread feelings of satisfaction and pride.

Behind Queen Victoria's carriage rode 50,000 soldiers – many of whom were Indian – and scores of Indian princes dressed in the rich, colourful clothes of that subcontinent.

During Victoria's reign, the Indian subcontinent (which then included all of what are now the countries of India, Pakistan and Bangladesh) was viewed as 'the jewel in the Crown' of the British Empire. Victoria had been granted the title 'Empress of India' by the British Parliament in 1877.

DISCUSS

- Why might Queen Victoria have wanted Indian princes and Indian soldiers to take part in the procession?
- Do you think that the Victorians viewed the British Empire as a good or a bad thing?

'The greatest force for good the world has ever seen'?

We are all British gentlemen engaged in the magnificent work of governing an inferior race.

Governor General Mayo, British ruler of India 1869–1872

A single shelf of a good European library is worth the whole native literature of India and Arabia.

Lord Macaulay, British politician, and adviser to a British Governor General of India

The British Empire is the greatest force for good the world has ever seen.

Lord Curzon, Viceroy of India 1899–1906

ACTIVITY

1 Look at the statements on the left from British politicians. How did Victorians view:
a) The Empire – did they think it was a good thing?
b) India – did they think that the Indian people were winning or losing from being part of the Empire?

2 Look at the extract from a school textbook published in 1904. What did the author want children to think about:
a) the Empire?
b) India?

Since 1870 every child in Britain had received an education up to the age of eleven and it was considered important that they learnt about Britain's Empire. In those days children were rarely encouraged to think for themselves. They were made to learn information off by heart from textbooks and were not encouraged to question that information.

Other races should be grateful for British control. We are simply superior in every way to the people we have made part of our empire. British rule has brought order and economic progress to countries that were extremely backward.

Victorian teacher

THE WORLD AND ITS PEOPLE
A New Geography Reader with special reference to the British Empire

Why has Europe become so great? Why have its peoples left behind all other nations in the race for power and wealth? Chiefly because they have been active, clever and eager to learn. They have not been content to sit down and wait with folded hands for good things to come to them; they have always been trying hard to improve their lot.

From these shores thousands of Englishmen, Scotsmen, Irishmen and Welshmen have gone forth to the outermost parts of the earth, and have founded an empire which is a hundred times more extensive than the mother islands.

While Europe and the New World have constantly advanced in knowledge skill and wealth, Asia has either been standing still or falling back. With the exception of Japan, which has adopted Western ideas, the nations of the East are now unable to advance with the times, except under the direction of Europeans.

As you can see, the Victorians had a very positive view of empire. They certainly saw the British Empire as a good thing and believed that the people they ruled over in places such as India were gaining from being part of the British Empire.

However, you saw in Year 7 and Year 8 that empires can be very controversial. They bring out strong emotions both at the time they exist and much later as historians begin to form views about them.

At the time of an empire's existence some people gain from that empire – possibly through trade or employment. Others lose as their interests come into conflict with those of the empire's. Remember also that historians argue about empires. They excavate the past to find evidence to support their arguments.

Historian A

Empire was basically the exploitation of one race by another for the purpose of gaining wealth. Lasting damage was often done to the cultures and economies of the countries that were taken over and became part of an empire.

Spanish Empire

Historian B

Roman Empire

British Empire

It is true that there were many unacceptable things done in the name of empire but we cannot judge the past by the standards of the present. Many of the countries and individuals taken over did benefit in at least some ways from becoming part of an empire.

Slavery

Building skills

Taxes

Trade

Exploitation

Education

ACTIVITY

Think back to what you have already learnt about empires in history.

1 What impact did the Roman and Spanish Empires have on people living at the time? Did **everyone** gain from those empires?

2 Look at the arguments put forward by the two historians on the left. Which interpretation do you agree with?

3 Which rocks could each historian use to support his argument?

4 Can you think of other pieces of evidence that each historian could use to support his point of view?

5 Why do people disagree about whether empires are a good or a bad thing?

Was Duleep Singh a winner or a loser from the British Empire?

It is time to start arguing about the British Empire. You will start by exploring the life of one individual. The case of Maharajah Duleep Singh is a powerful story of one man's direct contact with the British Empire. Whether Duleep Singh gained or lost from the Empire is still a subject of hot debate. Sometimes, gain and loss is not quite so clear cut. People like Duleep Singh may not have found it easy to decide if they had been winners or losers from coming into contact with the British Empire. As you will see Duleep Singh's own views changed over time.

Stage 1: Early years, 1838–1846

- Duleep Singh was born on 4 September 1838. At the time of Duleep Singh's birth, the British were already firmly established in India. They controlled many of its states directly and influenced the rulers of many others by bribery, trade and the threat of military force.
- Duleep Singh's father, Maharajah Ranjit Singh, ruled the Punjab. The Punjab was a wealthy and powerful independent state situated in a key position on the Indian subcontinent. Ranjit was a fearsome warrior and a strong ruler. The British themselves had no wish to tangle with his experienced army and signed a friendship treaty with him.
- Ranjit Singh died in the summer of 1839. Now the young Duleep Singh found himself at the heart of a power struggle for the throne.
- In 1843 Duleep Singh's mother and uncle managed to gain him enough support to become Maharajah. He was the last survivor of Ranjit's sons but was only five years old.
- Duleep's uncle was stabbed and shot in the head by Sikh army leaders. The Sikh army declared war on the British.
- The British were victorious and forced Duleep Singh to sign the Treaty of Lahore in 1846. The little boy wore a picture of Queen Victoria around his neck and did not seem at all unhappy to sign. Duleep was taken away from his Sikh sirdars (teachers) and began a British-style education.

▲ *Maharajah Duleep Singh, 1854.*

TREATY OF LAHORE

- The richest part of the Punjab will be given to the British
- The rest of the country will be governed by the Maharajah when he comes of age
- Until the Maharajah comes of age his council of distinguished Sikhs will rule for him from the city of Lahore
- A British official and large British army will be based in Lahore

▲ SOURCE 1 *The Treaty of Lahore.*

1 On the following pages you will learn more about the life of Duleep Singh.

As you find out more about his fascinating story use a Living Graph to show:

a) Duleep Singh's thoughts. Does he think he is gaining or losing from the British Empire?

b) Your thoughts. Is Duleep Singh a winner or a loser in the British Empire?

2 You will also be asked to explain the reasons for drawing particular sections of the Living Graph in the way you have.

A Living Graph has been started on the right. However, you may disagree with the point of view put forward here. Think carefully about what happened to Duleep Singh between 1838 and 1846 and use the advice provided to start your own graph.

If you are producing a big graph as a group, you can record your explanations on the graph. Alternatively, you could record longer explanations on a separate piece of paper. Use the advice box to help you.

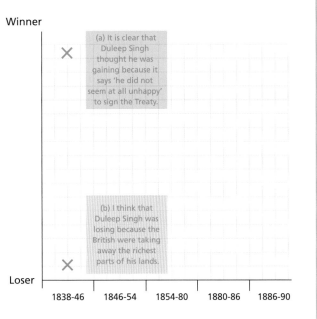

Winner

(a) It is clear that Duleep Singh thought he was gaining because it says 'he did not seem at all unhappy' to sign the Treaty.

(b) I think that Duleep Singh was losing because the British were taking away the richest parts of his lands.

Loser

| 1838-46 | 1846-54 | 1854-80 | 1880-86 | 1886-90 |

ADVICE BOX

Tip 1 Think carefully about how certain you can be about what someone else was thinking in the past.

• Is there enough evidence for the student to be so sure that Duleep Singh thought he was gaining from the British Empire? Use a traffic lighting system to show how certain you are as you read Duleep Singh's story and plot his thoughts. Using green (like the student has above) indicates that you are very sure about what he was thinking. Use amber or red to show that you are less certain.

• Also think very carefully about the language you use in your explanation. The student has stated their explanation with the phrase 'It is clear that'. Can you think of a better way to start your explanation?

Tip 2 Consider both sides of the story. Structure your explanation by using the word 'however' as a link between opposite views.
Example:

The Maharajah was promised the right to rule once he had grown up. This shows that the British seemed to have some respect for Punjabi rights. **However**, *the British took the richest part of the Punjab for themselves; this shows that they could easily take whatever they wanted.*

Stage 2: Under British control in the Punjab, 1846–1854

- Duleep's mother was taken from him by the British for fear that she would use the young boy in plots against them. She had been involved in such plots – once planning to murder Sir Henry Lawrence, the British government's representative in Lahore.
- A revolt broke out against the British in 1849. A brief but hard-fought war ended in victory for the British army. The Sikh army had been shattered at the Battle of Gujrat. The British army was in control of the Punjab and occupied Lahore.
- Meanwhile, Duleep Singh's British-style education continued and he spent a great deal of time with British people such as Sir Henry Lawrence who took him to firework displays and horse races.
- Duleep Singh signed the Treaty of Bhyrowal in March 1849. Duleep signed the treaty 'with alacrity', which means he seemed willing to sign.
- Indian advisers to Duleep Singh urged him to sign, telling him any show of hesitation might lead to a less favourable treaty. These advisers had been told by Henry Eliot (Secretary to the British government of India) that they would keep their personal lands and wealth only if the Treaty was signed.

TREATY OF BHYROWAL, 1849

- Maharajah Duleep Singh is forced to give up all claims to the rule of the Punjab for himself and his future heirs
- All property of the state of the Punjab will pass to the British in payment for the war
- The Koh-i-noor diamond (at the size of a pigeon's egg, one of the largest in the world) shall be given by Maharajah Duleep Singh to the Queen of England
- His Highness is promised £50,000 per year providing he remains loyal to the British and lives where told by the British ruler of India
- The Maharajah shall be treated with respect

▲ SOURCE 2 *Treaty of Bhyrowal, 1849.*

SOURCE 3 *From* Queen Victoria's Maharajah *by Alexander and Ward.*

The new Governor General of India, Lord Dalhousie, thought that Duleep Singh signed so willingly because:

'He does not care two pence about it himself – he will have a good and regular amount of money without income tax all his life and will die in his bed like a gentleman.'

ACTIVITY

1 Look carefully at the reasons Lord Dalhousie gives above for Duleep Singh's 'willingness' to sign the Treaty. Do you agree with his point of view? What in your opinion might explain Duleep Singh's apparent willingness to sign the Treaty?

2 To what extent does Duleep Singh's willingness to sign the Treaty show that *he thought* he was gaining from the British? Add to the Living Graph you started on page 17. Remember to think carefully about the extent to which you can draw firm conclusions about what Duleep Singh was thinking.

3 In this time period was Duleep Singh gaining or losing from the British in *your* view? Add to your Living Graph and explain your answer using the same structure you used before.

Stage 3: An English country gentleman, 1854–1880

- At the start of this period Duleep Singh's friends were all the sons of British gentlemen with whom he rode, raced and hunted. These boys were all regular churchgoers and despite their friendship with Duleep they teased him as being 'a heathen'. Duleep, at the age of twelve, declared that he wished to become a Christian.

- In 1854 at the age of fifteen, just before he left India, Duleep Singh was allowed by the British to change his religion from Sikhism to Christianity. He was the first Indian prince to do so.

- Duleep Singh was taken to England in 1854 for fear that his presence in any part of India would provoke a rebellion in the Punjab.

- In July 1854 Duleep Singh was presented to Queen Victoria. She took an immediate liking to him – as her diary entries and letters show.

- Duleep Singh was a frequent guest of Queen Victoria during his teens and early twenties. Queen Victoria thought so highly of Duleep Singh that in 1866 she became godmother to his first child, Prince Victor Singh. Victoria also allowed her own eldest son – the Prince of Wales – to become a very close friend of Duleep Singh.

- In 1864, Duleep married Bamba Muller, the Christian daughter of an Abyssinian lady and a German merchant. Duleep fell in love with Bamba after seeing her teach a large, disciplined class of students.

- Duleep Singh bought a huge country house in Suffolk with a lot of land for himself and his new bride in 1865. He did this with a loan of £105,000 from the British government at a low rate of interest. He lived the luxurious life of a rich country gentleman and entertained the very highest ranks of the English aristocracy in fine style and at great expense.

SOURCE 4 *Extracts from Queen Victoria's diary and letters.*

1 July 1854 He is extremely handsome and speaks English perfectly, and has a pretty, graceful and dignified manner. He was beautifully dressed and covered with diamonds.

6 July 1854 He speaks English remarkably well and seems to prefer doing so, more than his own language, which he thinks he will forget. He regrets India not being nearer to enable more Indians to come here 'as it would open their eyes'.

22 August 1854 The Maharajah carried little Prince Leopold, who is so fond of him, in his arms. We left the Maharajah shaking him warmly by the hand and wishing him many happy returns for his birthday when he will be 16 and would have been old enough to rule if we had not had to take the Punjab.

ACTIVITY

1 Look carefully at the picture on page 20. What factors might explain the considerable changes in Duleep Singh's appearance since the picture painted in 1854 (page 16)?

2 Look carefully at the extracts from Queen Victoria's letters and diary. Is there any evidence that allows us to infer Duleep Singh's attitude at the time. Does he think he is gaining or losing from the British Empire? Remember to add to your Living Graph and explain your answer.

3 In this time period was Duleep Singh gaining or losing from the British in your view? Add to your Living Graph, remembering to structure your supporting explanation very carefully.

▼ **SOURCE 5**
Elveden shooting party hosted by Duleep Singh.

Stage 4: Still loyal? 1881–1886

- British agriculture began to struggle as cheap imports of crops started to arrive from the prairies of North America. The incomes of farmers and great landowners such as Duleep Singh began to fall. Many of Duleep's farms were left vacant.
- By 1881 Duleep Singh was beginning to build up large debts. His income from the British and from his land was no longer sufficient to maintain his lavish lifestyle in addition to supporting a wife and six children.
- When Duleep Singh asked the British government of India for more money it refused – telling him to sell his Elveden estate in favour of a smaller house in London. This made him furious.
- Duleep Singh claimed that his kingdom of the Punjab was bringing the British government over £1,000,000 per year. He also claimed to have lost private family land in India worth £120,000 per year, to say nothing of the priceless Koh-i-noor diamond that had once been his but that had been given to Queen Victoria. Duleep Singh had been promised £50,000 per year, yet he was being given only £25,000 to live on – and he was paying £5,000 of this in interest on the loan he had been given to buy Elveden. £25,000 was a small sum for a leading aristocrat at the time. Duleep Singh was hurt and furious.
- In 1882 Duleep Singh wrote to *The Times* in an attempt to gain the sympathy of the public for his cause. He demanded the income from his lost private estates in the Punjab and an increase in the money paid to him by Britain in return for agreeing, through loyalty towards Queen Victoria, not to enforce his 'right' to rule the Punjab.
- The attempt to gain sympathy failed. The British government refused to offer Duleep Singh more money. Duleep Singh became a Sikh once again and set off for India.

ACTIVITY

Add to your Living Graph. Consider:
- To what extent have Duleep Singh's views changed by 1886? Does he think he is gaining or losing from the British Empire? Remember to add to your Living Graph and explain your answer.
- In this time period was Duleep Singh gaining or losing from the British in your view? Remember to structure your explanation very carefully.

- In 1886 Maharajah Duleep Singh was arrested on his way to India. He was beside himself with rage. He wrote:

'I shall have no alternative but to transfer my allegiance to some other European power, who, I daresay, will provide for my maintenance.'

▶SOURCE 6 *Duleep Singh in 1882.*

Stage 5: England's proud enemy, 1886–1888

- Duleep Singh was bursting with hurt pride and frustration after his arrest and continuing money worries. He blamed not the Queen but her government officials who were responsible for running India. He was determined now to hurt the nation that he felt was unjustly keeping his rightful property and wealth from him. He based himself in Paris and laid his plans.
- Duleep Singh contacted the Russian ambassador in Paris in July 1886 offering his services to the Russian Emperor. This was a great cause of worry to the British as the Russians had many times shown ambition to rule India. If Duleep Singh really could cause a rebellion of Sikhs in the Punjab with Russian support then Britain's Empire in India would certainly have been at risk.
- Fortunately for Britain, Russia had troubles of its own at this time and was in no hurry to upset Britain. In fact, relations between the British and the Russians were at their warmest for many generations. In addition to this the Russians were suspicious of Duleep Singh.
- Duleep Singh prepared two proclamations (public written statements designed to create support in India) for newspaper publication in the Punjab. The first publicly stated that he no longer recognised the 1846 Treaty of Lahore by which he had ceased to be ruler of the Punjab. The second was an appeal to the princes and people of India to support his cause by giving him money.
- Whilst in Paris, Duleep Singh socialised with many enemies of Britain including the brothers Patrick and James Casey who were involved with an Irish rebel organisation, the Fenians. This organisation had killed British government officials and had planted bombs in London.
- Using Patrick Casey's passport, Duleep Singh went to Russia in 1887 without an official invitation. He was ignored and succeeded only in spending more money. By the later part of the year he was offering his clothes for sale to raise money, having become the father of another child by Ada Wetherill, the daughter of a British working-class man. His wife in England, the Maharanee, died very soon after, having been ill for some time.
- Duleep Singh was still trying to create a Sikh rebellion against the British in the Punjab but without Russian help the plan did not get off the ground. In fact, during 1887 many of the very Indian princes Duleep Singh was counting on to help him rebel against the British were in London helping to celebrate Queen Victoria's Golden Jubilee.
- Duleep Singh's resentment against Britain remained strong as shown in his letter to the Prince of Wales – who had only written to offer sympathy on the death of the Maharanee.

SOURCE 7 *Extract from Duleep Singh's letter to the Prince of Wales.*

Under other circumstances I should have felt grateful but while your illustrious mother proclaims herself sovereign of a throne and an empire both of which have been acquired by fraud and of which Your Royal Highness hopes one day to become the emperor, these empty words of sympathy become an insult.

Signed Duleep Singh Sovereign of the Sikh Nation and Proud Implacable Foe of England.

ACTIVITY

Add to your Living Graph. Consider:
- Does Duleep Singh think he is gaining or losing from the British Empire? Remember to add to your Living Graph and explain your answer.
- In this time period was Duleep Singh gaining or losing from the British in *your* view? Remember to structure your explanation very carefully.

Stage 6: Illness, apology and death, 1890–1893

- In 1888 Duleep Singh, accompanied by his new wife and family returned to Paris. They were running out of funds and had become an embarrassment to the Russian Tsar who still hoped to remain on good terms with the British Empire.
- In 1890 Duleep Singh suffered a stroke and, after a frantic carriage drive around Paris in search of his doctor, found himself partially paralysed. This finally broke his hopes of a Sikh rebellion. He was penniless and helpless.
- After emotional apologies to the Queen and the Prince of Wales, Duleep Singh was allowed to return briefly to England. He met the Queen in France, a meeting that was recorded by the Queen herself in a letter to her daughter: *I asked him to sit down and almost directly he burst into a most violent and terrible fit of crying, almost screaming. And said 'Pray excuse me and forgive my faults', and I answered 'They are forgotten and forgiven'.*
- On 22 October 1893 Duleep Singh, Maharajah of Lahore, died in Paris of an apoplectic fit. Neither the Queen nor the Prince of Wales attended the funeral although both sent splendid wreaths. Duleep Singh was buried at the small Christian church of Elveden in Suffolk on the estate the Maharajah had once owned and loved so well. Sikh visitors are often seen at the graveside.

When I was researching this book I was standing at Duleep Singh's graveside deep in thought when a small family of British Asian people arrived. The father of the family stood alongside me and we spoke. He explained that he was of the Sikh faith and had come to visit the grave from respect. I asked if he felt that Duleep Singh had been treated badly by the British.

He replied 'No'.

I then mentioned the loss of the Koh-i-noor diamond and a kingdom, followed by a life in exile. The visitor to the grave replied:

'Yes, but that's what empires do, don't they?'

ACTIVITY

Complete your Living Graph. Consider:
- At the end of his life did Duleep Singh think he had gained or lost from the British Empire?
- In the time period 1890–1893, was Duleep Singh gaining or losing from the British in *your* view?

▼ SOURCE 8
Duleep Singh's grave.

22

Producing a balanced argument

Pulling it all together – how should Duleep Singh's story be told?

ACTIVITY

To what extent do you agree with the visitors to Duleep Singh's grave? How would you have responded to the question:

Was Duleep Singh treated badly by the British?

Use your completed Living Graph and the advice box below to help you plan your answer.

ADVICE BOX

Try and give a balanced answer. Think of your answer as having three parts.

Step 1 Use the left hand to record points that support the argument that Duleep Singh gained from the British Empire. You can make a maximum of five points.

Step 2 Use the right hand to record points that support the argument that Duleep Singh lost from British rule.

Step 3 Use your head to weigh up the points and reach an overall judgement.

How is Duleep Singh remembered?

At the end of the last century a magnificent statue of Duleep Singh was placed in the centre of Thetford, the town closest to the Elveden estate and one that benefited from many gifts from Duleep Singh in his lifetime. Prince Charles unveiled the statue.

▼ **SOURCE 9** *An inscription on the statue of Duleep Singh.*

'BRINGING HISTORY AND CULTURE TOGETHER'

THIS PLAQUE COMMEMORATES THE OFFICIAL UNVEILING OF THIS MONUMENT BY HRH THE PRINCE OF WALES, K.G.K.T., ON 29 JULY 1999.

IN 1843 MAHARAJAH DULEEP SINGH SUCCEEDED HIS FATHER TO THE THRONE OF THE SOVEREIGN SIKH KINGDOM OF PUNJAB. HE WAS DESTINED TO BE ITS LAST RULER.

IN 1849, FOLLOWING THE CLOSELY FOUGHT ANGLO-SIKH WARS, THE BRITISH ANNEXED THE PUNJAB. DULEEP SINGH WAS COMPELLED TO RESIGN HIS SOVEREIGN RIGHTS AND EXILED. IT WAS AT THIS TIME THAT THE KOH-I-NOOR DIAMOND, LATER INCORPORATED INTO THE CROWN JEWELS, PASSED TO THE BRITISH AUTHORITIES.

DULEEP SINGH EVENTUALLY CAME TO BRITAIN AND SETTLED AT THE ELVEDEN ESTATE IN SUFFOLK. HE WAS A CLOSE FAVOURITE OF QUEEN VICTORIA AND BECAME A PROMINENT LOCAL FIGURE IN EAST ANGLIA.

LATER IN HIS LIFE HE ANNOUNCED HIS INTENTION TO RETURN TO HIS BELOVED PUNJAB BUT WAS NOT ALLOWED TO DO SO. HE DIED IN PARIS ON 22 OCTOBER 1893 HAVING RE-EMBRACED THE SIKH FAITH AND WHILST STILL ENGAGED IN A STRUGGLE TO RECLAIM HIS THRONE.

TO THIS DAY THE SIKH NATION ASPIRES TO REGAIN ITS SOVEREIGNTY.

DEG TEG FATEH

ACTIVITY

1 The inscription on the left has been very carefully worded. Can you pick out phrases that seem to:
- criticise the actions of the British
- praise Duleep Singh?

2 Working in a group, rewrite the plaque several times changing as few words as possible in order to make it:
a) criticise the British more strongly
b) contain no criticism of the British
c) make Duleep Singh seem like a Sikh hero.

3 How does Duleep Singh's story help us understand why people still argue about the British Empire?

24

How typical were the experiences of Duleep Singh?

As you have seen Duleep Singh had a very mixed experience of the British Empire. However, he came from a privileged background in India. What about the majority of the Indian people? Were they winners or losers of the Empire? Did they have a similar bitter-sweet experience of life under the British?

ACTIVITY

Look at the brief summaries of lives of Indian people or groups who experienced British rule in India. For each individual or group fill in a section of an 'experience chart' like the one below or use the 'two hands' approach you used for Duleep Singh. When your class or your group has finished be prepared to share your judgements and the reasons for them in an open discussion. Then turn to page 29 to make use of the views you have formed.

Name of person	Positive experiences under and resulting from British rule	Negative experiences under and resulting from British rule	Indian person's likely overall judgement – what would they have thought at the time?	My overall judgement
1. Dadabhai Naoroji				

Case Study 1: Dadabhai Naoroji, the businessman politician

Born in 1825 the son of a priest, Naoroji graduated from a college established by the British in Bombay. He later became the first Indian professor of that college. In 1855 he came to England to work for the first Indian company to be established here. By 1859 he had set up his own Indian cotton company in Britain.

Naoroji helped set up the Indian National Congress and led it a record three times. In 1892, he became the first Asian to become a British MP, standing for the British Liberal Party. His race was brought into the election debate by the British Prime Minister who questioned whether a black man was a suitable candidate to stand for Parliament in Britain.

Naoroji did not oppose British rule. He believed that the British Empire had both a positive and negative impact on India. He praised Britain's contribution to education, its preservation of law and order, its establishment of a railway system and its development of valuable products such as tea and silk.

However, he did not like Britain's slowness in sharing power with native Indians. In particular, he disapproved of the British tax burden on people living in the countryside who were desperately poor. He accused Britain of not causing but failing to prevent mass starvation at times. Naoroji left Britain in 1907 and retired back to India where he died in 1917.

Case Study 2: Kumar Shri Ranjitsinhji, the cricketer

Kumar Shri Ranjitsinhji was born the son of a nobleman in 1872 in the Indian province of Kathiawar. Ranji, as he later became known, started going to the Rajkumar College at the age of eight with many Indian princes, and was introduced to cricket by the British headmaster. In 1888, at the end of his schooling in India, Ranji was sent to England to attend Cambridge University where he showed a lot of promise at cricket.

By the age of twenty Ranji was a regular in the Trinity College cricket team and was playing so well that he became a strong candidate to play for the England test cricket team. At first Ranji was left out of the test team because one of the selectors believed that Ranji had no right to be selected for England, as he was not born in England. Despite this Ranji went on to represent England fifteen times in test matches, averaging 44 runs per match.

Ranji returned to India in 1905 to start moving towards taking his place as the ruler of his province. He became the Maharajah Jam Seheb of Nawanagar on 10 March 1907. The responsibilities of ruling restricted Ranji's opportunities to continue playing cricket in England.

Case Study 3: Dr Bhimrao Ambedkar, the untouchable

Ambedkar was born on 14 April 1891 in Mhow. He belonged to the 'untouchable' caste considered so low among Hindus that all contact with them was forbidden. His father and grandfather served in the British army. In those days, the British government ensured that all the army personnel and their children were educated and they ran special schools for this purpose. This ensured a good education for Ambedkar, which otherwise would have been denied to him as an untouchable.

Ambedkar experienced caste discrimination right from childhood. The family settled when his father left the army and Ambedkar was enrolled in the local school. Here, he had to sit on the floor in one corner of the classroom and teachers would not touch his notebooks. In spite of these hardships, Ambedkar continued his studies and passed his exams. In 1912, he graduated in Political Science and Economics from Bombay University and was awarded a scholarship to continue his studies in New York. There he attained a degree in Master of Arts and a Doctorate in Philosophy. From America, Ambedkar travelled to London to study economics and political science.

Ambedkar returned to India when the Maharajah of Baroda appointed him as his political secretary. But no one would take orders from him as an untouchable. Ambedkar then returned to Bombay in November 1917. There he started a newspaper, called the *Dumb Hero*, which campaigned for rights for his fellow untouchables.

In September 1920, Ambedkar went back to London to complete his studies. He became a barrister and got a Doctorate in Science. After completing his studies in London, Ambedkar returned to India where he continued to try and improve the lives of those treated as outcasts in Indian society. In 1927, he led the Mahad March at the Chowdar Tank at Colaba, near Bombay, to give the untouchables the right to draw water from the public tank.

When India gained independence from British rule in 1947, Ambedkar joined the new government as Law Minister and played a leading role in drafting the new Indian Constitution.

Over 80 per cent of Indians lived and worked on the land during the period when the British ruled India. Land was kept in the hands of large landowners, who acted as tax collectors for the British. Famine hit British India on many occasions and the rural areas bore the brunt of the suffering. It is estimated that during the late Victorian period famines killed between 12 and 29 million Indians.

When a drought hit farmers of the Deccan plateau in 1876 there was a net surplus of rice and wheat in India. But the man in charge of India, the Viceroy, Lord Lytton, insisted that nothing should prevent the export of grain to England. In 1877 and 1878, as millions of Indian peasants began to starve, a record 6.4 million hundredweight of wheat was exported. To make matters worse, Lytton was determined to continue collecting taxes – money that he used to help fund a war in Afghanistan.

In the north-western provinces (Oud and the Punjab), which

had brought in record harvests in the three years leading up to the drought, over 1.25 million people died. In many districts, the only way that people could get help was through hard labour. Those who could no longer work were turned away from the labour camps.

From 1896 to 1902, seven years of almost uninterrupted drought brought crop failure, famine and disease to India. In western and central India thousands of square miles of agriculture and pasture lands were turned into barren deserts. Whilst back in Britain, people flocked onto the streets to celebrate Queen Victoria's Diamond Jubilee, many millions died in another part of the Empire in a tragedy that has largely been forgotten. In 1901, *The Lancet* estimated that 19 million people had died

as a result of starvation and disease. This was the equivalent of half the population of Victorian England.

Once again, massive grain exports to England continued during the famine whilst little help was given to the local population. As the source below shows, conditions in the 'relief camps' that were established were often appalling.

The 1951 census, the first since the end of British rule in India, revealed that life expectancy for the Indian people was just 32 years. Less than one in seven of India's population could read or write.

SOURCE 10 *Louis Klopsch (of the* Christian Herald*) visited a relief camp in Gujarat in 1900.*

The heat was intense; the thermometer indicated 108 degrees. A hot, blinding sandstorm filled our eyes and nostrils with dust. Cholera had broken out a short time before and 2400 famine sufferers had died within a few days. There were no disinfectants, hence the awful, sickening, disease-spreading stench. Millions of flies were permitted undisturbed to pester the unhappy victims. In the entire hospital I did not see a single decent garment, nothing but rags and dirt.

Case Study 5: Lascar sailors

Many Indians from desperately poor agricultural areas rode on the British-built railways to the coast. There they were taken on as sailors on British merchant ships for a fraction of the wage paid to a white sailor. The British merchant navy was the biggest trading navy in the world and was always in need of sailors. On arrival in Britain after their voyage, the Lascar sailors would be paid off and left to fend for themselves. Those who were lucky were able to gain work on another ship possibly going back to India. Those who couldn't find another ship were often found living rough in the dock areas. They were often harshly discriminated against and signs saying 'No Lascars' were a common sight in London's docklands.

Case Study 6: Life in the cities

Until 1911, Kolkata or Calcutta was the capital of the British Raj. It had been inhabited for well over a 1000 years before the British came but began to expand when used as the British East India Company's trade base in Bengal. Richard Wellesley was responsible for a lot of building in the city between 1791 and 1805. The city was split into two distinct areas: in one the white people lived in comfort; in the other (known as the black town) native Indian people lived in conditions that even by the standards of the 1850s were considered shocking slums. Kolkata became a major industrial centre under the British and remains so to this day. Under British rule, investments were made in railways, infrastructure and communications, largely to facilitate British industries and trade.

ACTIVITY

1 Use the table or notes you have taken to place each case study on the line below. Duleep Singh has already been placed on the line but you may want to change his position!

2 Look at your final line. How does this help explain why people still argue about the impact of the British Empire on India?

Did India lose or gain from the British Empire?

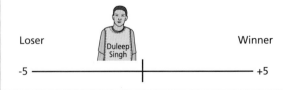

Loser   Winner

-5 ————————————————————— +5

DOING HISTORY:
Diversity and Interpretations

The impact that the British Empire had on India still causes a lot of controversy and debate amongst historians. One reason is the **diversity** of people's experiences.

> **Remember**
>
> • People's lives are different even if they live in the same country in the same period of history.

Whether or not people living in India benefited from British rule depended on a number of factors. For example:

• where they lived (did they live in the countryside or the town?)
• when they lived
• whether they were rich or poor.

Can you think of any other factors?

You have also seen how difficult it is to tell if someone is gaining or losing from an empire. The experiences of individuals such as Duleep Singh varied during his lifetime. Remember:

• People's experiences vary during their lifetime. We need to try and look at the whole experience rather than just concentrating on one specific episode.
• The diversity of people's experiences means that historians can **select** from the past to support their own point of view.
• Their interpretation of the past may depend on where they have looked for evidence. They may have **chosen** to use one case study or a particular part of someone's life to support their version of the past.

Remember the two historians arguing about empires on page 15? How would they use the evidence you have looked at in this enquiry to support their arguments?

Historian A

Individuals did not benefit from British rule. Duleep Singh had his land stolen from him and he died in poverty. Lasting damage was done to the Indian economy. Look at all the people who died as a result of famine.

Historian B

It is true that there were many unacceptable things that happened but we cannot judge the past by the standards of the present. Many individuals did benefit from becoming part of an empire. Naoroji and Ambedkar received a good education thanks to British rule. The Indian economy benefited from the British investment in railways and new buildings.

ACTIVITY

The two historians have started to debate whether British rule benefited India. Continue the debate. Develop more arguments to support either Historian A or Historian B. Make sure you give specific examples from pages 16–28 to support your arguments.

THE BIG STORY: Empire Part Three

Why is the British Empire so controversial? (1)

ARGUMENT 1: Impact on people living at the time

The impact that the British Empire had on people living at the time is very controversial. As you have just seen, some people believe that British rule benefited India; other people would argue that it had a very negative impact on many people's lives. The impact of the British Empire on other colonies is just as controversial. Look at the map below. It summarises some of the stories from other parts of the Empire that you explored in Year 8.

You may have already looked at other empires in Years 7 and 8, for example, the Roman Empire, or the Spanish Empire. One of the key questions you would have asked was: 'How did it affect people?'. You saw that there were winners and losers from empires and that people still argue about the overall impact of these empires.

> **ACTIVITY**
>
> Produce a summary box for India to complete the map. Aim for a balanced summary.

▼ SOURCE 11 *The British Empire at its height: the end of the nineteenth century.*

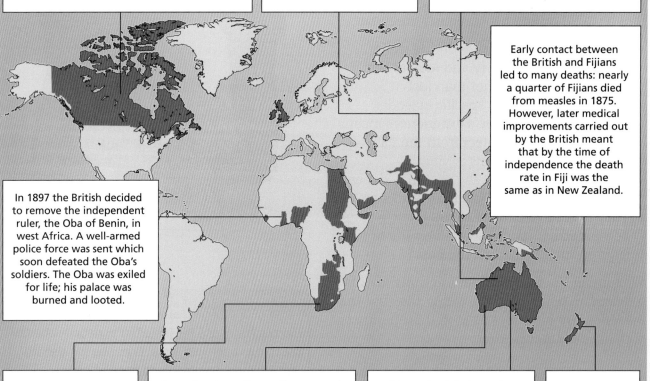

Canada, Australia, New Zealand and South Africa, all dominated by white settlers from Britain, had become 'dominions' by the early twentieth century. This meant that they ruled themselves as independent countries, but with the British monarch at their head and their foreign policy decided from London.

In India...

Throughout most of the Empire British sports like cricket, football and rugby were taken up. The first Aboriginal cricket team from Australia toured England in 1868 although it was many years before native peoples competed on equal terms.

Early contact between the British and Fijians led to many deaths: nearly a quarter of Fijians died from measles in 1875. However, later medical improvements carried out by the British meant that by the time of independence the death rate in Fiji was the same as in New Zealand.

In 1897 the British decided to remove the independent ruler, the Oba of Benin, in west Africa. A well-armed police force was sent which soon defeated the Oba's soldiers. The Oba was exiled for life; his palace was burned and looted.

In Africa missionaries such as David Livingstone spread Christianity and European ideas.

Soon after Australia was first mapped by Captain James Cook, the British government decided to use the new colony as a place to send criminals. Between 1787 and 1868, when it stopped, 160,000 British convicts were 'transported' to Australia.

Many Aboriginal peoples in Australia were killed by settlers and lost the right to live on their ancestors' lands because these lands were turned into cattle and sheep ranches.

Maoris in New Zealand lost lands to the British settlers.

THE BIG STORY: Empire Part Three

ARGUMENT 2: The end of Empire

In 1900 Britain ruled over a huge empire that contained a quarter of the world's population. Today the story is very different.

The Incredible Shrinking Empire!

▼ SOURCE 12 *The British Empire at the start of the 21st century.*

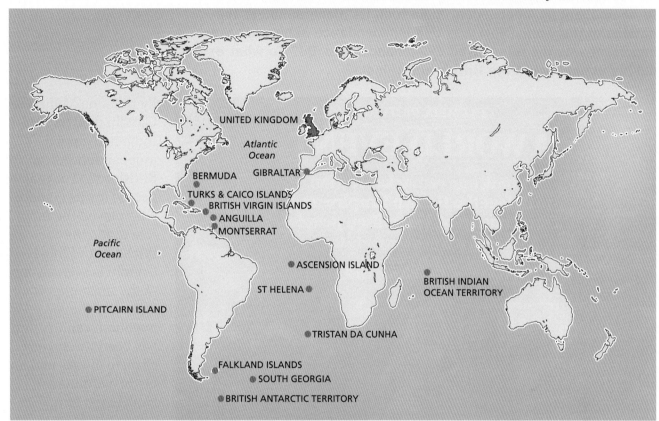

After the Second World War, the British Empire quickly shrunk as its colonies gained independence. India and Pakistan were the first to gain independence in 1947. Over the next 50 years they were followed by other colonies in a process known as 'decolonisation'.

This is another controversial story that causes debate and argument. Why did the British Empire shrink so rapidly? Were the British forced out of the colonies they controlled or did they leave voluntarily? How was independence achieved and how has it shaped the world we live in today?

You will have an opportunity to explore these key questions during the second part of this chapter. The main focus will be on how India achieved independence (see pages 32–45). However, you will also examine two shorter case studies that examine how British rule ended in Kenya and Hong Kong (see pages 47–51).

The end of Empire: how important was Gandhi's role in ending British rule in India?

At midnight on 14 August 1947, the British Union flag was lowered for the last time in India. Nearly 200 years of British rule had come to an end and an independent India took its place amongst the nations of the world. How was this independence achieved? How important was the role played by Mohandas Gandhi? To what extent did his actions force the British out of India?

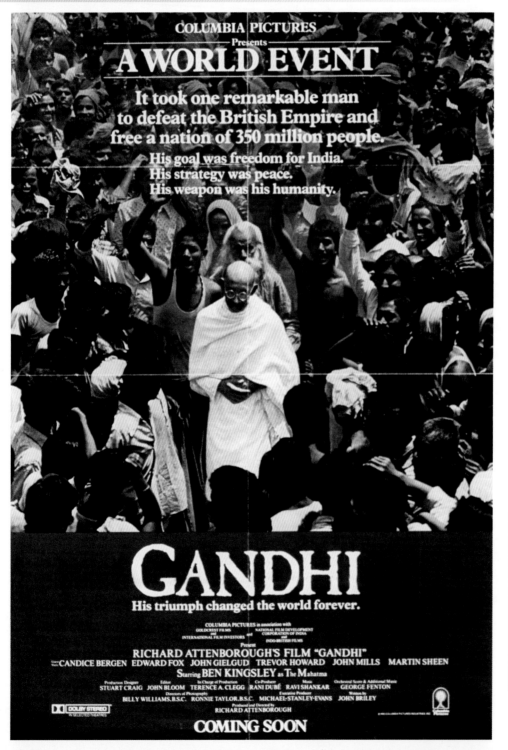

By the time Mohandas Gandhi died in 1948 India had gained independence from British rule. For many people it was Gandhi who played the main role in forcing the British out of India. Gandhi is seen as one of the most important figures of the twentieth century and has been the subject of many books and an Oscar-winning Hollywood film.

DISCUSS

Look at this poster designed to promote the film *Gandhi*. What impression does it create of Gandhi's role in forcing the British out of India?

DOING HISTORY:
Dealing with iceberg questions

The film poster on page 32 states that it took 'one remarkable man' to defeat the British Empire.

However, you have already seen from your study of history in Year 7 and 8 that:

- Most events have a number of causes.
- These causes are often linked.

Gandhi was clearly remarkable but he did not defeat the British Empire on his own. It would be dangerous to answer the question **'How important was the role played by Mohandas Gandhi in ending British rule in India?'** by only concentrating on Gandhi's actions. Think of it as an iceberg question. There is more to it than meets the eye! Look at the question carefully. You have to explore the extent to which Gandhi's actions forced the British out. To do this properly you must look at the role played by other factors as well. You must assess how important Gandhi's role was compared to other factors.

ACTIVITY

Extended writing
How important was the role played by Mohandas Gandhi in ending British rule in India? The ThreatOmeter activities on pages 34–40 will help you to understand the key events. You should then use the advice below to help you to write your answer.

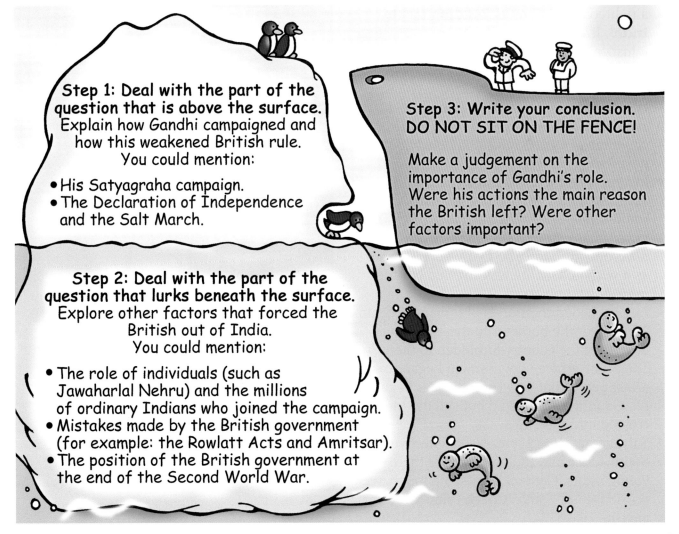

Step 1: Deal with the part of the question that is above the surface. Explain how Gandhi campaigned and how this weakened British rule. You could mention:

- His Satyagraha campaign.
- The Declaration of Independence and the Salt March.

Step 2: Deal with the part of the question that lurks beneath the surface. Explore other factors that forced the British out of India. You could mention:

- The role of individuals (such as Jawaharlal Nehru) and the millions of ordinary Indians who joined the campaign.
- Mistakes made by the British government (for example: the Rowlatt Acts and Amritsar).
- The position of the British government at the end of the Second World War.

Step 3: Write your conclusion. DO NOT SIT ON THE FENCE!

Make a judgement on the importance of Gandhi's role. Were his actions the main reason the British left? Were other factors important?

Who was Mohandas Gandhi and what did he believe in?

Background

- Mohandas Gandhi was born in India in 1869. His parents were rich and sent him to England to study law.
- In England he become a fully qualified barrister (lawyer able to present cases in the highest courts).
- He practised law in South Africa, which was itself part of the British Empire. Whilst there he led a campaign to maintain voting rights for Indians living in South Africa, after the government there sought to abolish those rights.
- He lived a life designed to be a model of simplicity and non-violence. He abandoned Western clothes in 1906 – preferring instead to dress in a simple cloth wrapped around his body. He was a strict vegetarian and ate only fruit and nuts.

What was Gandhi's idea of 'Satyagraha'?

- **Satyagraha** can be translated as 'firmness in a righteous cause' or as **'holding fast to truth'**. It was a **non-violent** way of resisting injustice.
- Gandhi used Satyagraha against the South African government. It involved mobilising large numbers of people in a non-violent campaign of non-cooperation. In practice it could mean a mass refusal to do what a government wished.
- In 1907 Gandhi urged Indians living in South Africa to refuse to register their names or to submit their fingerprints as required by the government. It proved impossible for the government to force so many people to act as it wished. Gandhi was arrested but the protest went on.
- In 1908 he led thousands of Indians in South Africa over the border into the Transvaal – an area of the country forbidden to them. The South African government began to arrest people but very soon the jails began to fill. Gandhi was arrested but still the Indians crossed into the Transvaal.
- Satyagraha proved remarkably effective in South Africa and Indians retained their voting rights. General Smuts, the tough, no-nonsense, South African Prime Minister, gave in.

Was Gandhi a threat to British power in India?

In 1915 Gandhi arrived in British India and joined the Congress Party. The party wanted more power to be given to the Indian people. However, it had always tried to achieve its aims by quiet discussion rather than by public protests. The British authorities in India commissioned the Bombay police force to investigate Gandhi and assess the threat he posed to British rule.

Their conclusion was that Gandhi was a harmless eccentric who posed no real threat. It was easy to see why they dismissed him as no threat. The tiny figure dressed in a loin cloth seemed eccentric to Indians as well as to Westerners. How could he possibly be any sort of real threat to the British Raj in India – an organisation 158 years old supported by 250,000 soldiers of the Indian army, numerous Indian princes and the might of the British government itself?

How wrong they were – this apparently odd and harmless figure was to prove the biggest thorn in the side of the British authorities for the next 32 years! Why did the campaigns of Mohandas Gandhi prove so difficult for the British to deal with in India?

ACTIVITY

The story of Gandhi's campaign against British rule has been divided into five stages. At the end of each stage you must draw a copy of the 'GandhiThreatOmeter' below. You will adjust its needle according to your assessment of the level of risk Gandhi poses to the British authorities. Every time you adjust the needle to a position give a brief explanation of your reasons for doing so.

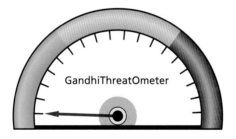

DISCUSS

At present, the GandhiThreatOmeter is set at the assessment carried out by the Bombay police in 1915. Gandhi is seen as a fairly harmless eccentric. Do you agree with the assessment made at the time? If you think the authorities underestimated Gandhi, change the reading and explain your reasons for doing so.

Stage 1: Gandhi's first moves

- When Gandhi arrived in India, the First World War was at its height. At first he ignored this. He addressed the British Viceroy of India but shocked him by declaring shame at having to speak in English whilst in India. He also verbally attacked the rich Indian princes who were loyal to – and benefited greatly from – British rule. Many princes were deeply offended and walked out.

- He then began a Satyagraha campaign to help poor Indian peasants in the district of Bihar. This was more a protest against conditions than against the British, but it did involve Gandhi encouraging Indians to refuse to pay taxes.

- In 1917, surprisingly, Gandhi joined a campaign organised by the British Viceroy to persuade ordinary Indians to join the army and help the British on the battlefields of France against the Germans. He personally toured the Indian district of Kheda in support of the campaign.

- Gandhi at this time appears to have believed that, although the British Empire was far from perfect, it had by and large been a force for good in India. He therefore saw the duty of every Indian to help the Empire in its hour of need. Many thousands of Indians fought and died in the service of the British Empire.

Stage 2: Gandhi turns against British rule

The end of the First World War seemed to hold great promise for India. She had been invited to the Versailles Peace Conference as a separate power in her own right. Also, towards the end of the war, the Montagu Declaration had promised increased participation in the government and justice system of India for Indian people. However, this promise was dashed by two events in the immediate period after the war: the **Rowlatt Acts** and the **Amritsar Massacre**.

The Rowlatt Acts

In wars, the individual rights of citizens such as free speech and the right to hold protest meetings are often temporarily suspended to give the impression that the whole country is united. Indians accepted this during the First World War but after the war the British government passed two Acts of Parliament known as the Rowlatt Acts.

These Acts said that the rights of Indians to free speech and protest would not be fully restored even though the war had ended. Gandhi saw this as unjust and became an increasingly active member of the Indian National Congress. The INC helped to organise protests all over India.

> **ACTIVITY**
>
> Adjust your 'GandhiThreatOmeter' and give your reasons for choosing the new needle position.

The Amritsar Massacre

In the north-western city of Amritsar the protests turned violent. Two banks were attacked and three members of staff were murdered. An English woman was pulled from her bicycle and assaulted. In response, British soldiers forced every Indian passing that point to crawl on his belly and endure the abuse and jibes of the soldiers (see photo right).

The British also banned all public meetings in Amritsar. On 13 April 1919 thousands of unarmed Indians ignored this order and crowded into an area known as the Jallianwala Bagh (below right). General Reginald Dyer, the soldier in charge of British forces in Amritsar, marched his soldiers to the meeting. The meeting was peaceful and made up of men, women and children. Despite this, Dyer ordered his troops to line up facing the crowd and to open fire. No final warning was given to the protesters.

SOURCE 13   *The scene at Jallianwala Bagh was described to the British Parliament by Winston Churchill, Secretary for War (the politician in charge of the army).*

'When fire had been opened upon the crowd to disperse it, it tried to run away. Pinned up in a narrow place with hardly any exits, and packed together so that one bullet would drive through three or four bodies, the people ran madly this way and the other. When the fire was directed upon the centre, they ran to the sides. The fire was then directed to the sides. Many threw themselves down on the ground, then the fire was then directed down on the ground. This was continued for eight to ten minutes, and it stopped only when the ammunition had reached the point of exhaustion. Finally, after 379 persons had been killed and when most certainly 1200 or more had been wounded, the troops, at whom not even a stone had been thrown, swung round and marched away.'

The British forces made no attempt to help the wounded. To make matters worse, at the official inquiry into the massacre, Dyer stated that he did not regret his actions and one British newspaper even made an appeal for money to be given as a gift to the General.

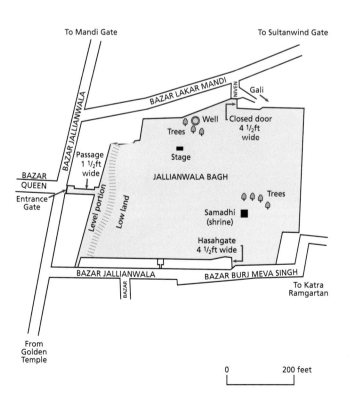

Reactions to Amritsar

After Amritsar, Gandhi lost any remaining respect he may have had for British rule. He branded the British government as 'satanic' (acting on behalf of the devil). He was not alone. **Jawaharlal Nehru** and other talented members of the Indian National Congress reacted in a very similar way. Many Indians were now set on ending British rule in India. They were now fully behind the quest for **swaraj** – or self-government.

What methods of protest did Gandhi use?

- Gandhi immediately returned to the British all the medals and honours he had been given as a reward for his recruitment campaign in the war.
- He encouraged non-cooperation with British rule. Many Indians renounced titles and honours; lawyers refused to work for the British. Students boycotted the schools and universities set up by the British.
- He then openly encouraged Indians not to buy – and indeed to burn – any British-made cloth. This cloth was imported in vast quantities to India to provide customers for British cotton and wool mills. The result was that Indian mills were often driven out of business. Gandhi encouraged home spinning and weaving to deprive the British of their customers. The peaceful, simple spinning wheel became a symbol of Satyagraha. It became the badge of the Indian National Congress and Gandhi lost no opportunity to be photographed with such a wheel.

- Above all, thousands of educated Indians from the cities began to spread Gandhi's message of non-cooperation.
- Gandhi's name was now known throughout India and literally millions waited for the news of his next move.

Gandhi remained firmly committed to non-violence. When a mob broke this rule and caused deaths, Gandhi fasted for five days and called off his campaign for fear that India would explode into violence. The British took advantage of this pause in the campaign to arrest him.

ACTIVITY

Adjust your 'GandhiThreatOmeter' and give your reasons for choosing the new needle position.

Stage 3: The Declaration of Independence and the Salt March

After his arrest Gandhi was sentenced to six years in prison. In January 1924, having served less than two years in prison, Gandhi was released through ill health. On his release he worked hard in the Indian National Congress to allow its many groups to work together. In particular, the power of Gandhi's personality enabled Hindus and Muslims to cooperate – this was in direct opposition to the wishes of the British who felt India was easier to control when its two main religious groups were arguing.

In Congress Gandhi brought about a vote to declare immediate self-rule for India – whatever the British might say or do. Under its young President, **Jawaharlal Nehru**, Congress passed the historic idea and became officially committed to ending British rule in India. At a solemn ceremony in 1930, **Jawaharlal Nehru** unfurled the Indian tricolour flag for the first time and made a historic speech.

On 12 March 1930, Gandhi began a march to the sea beach at Dandi. There it was possible to pick up salt from the beach – a simple action yet one that would challenge the hugely unpopular British law that taxed salt and forbade Indians to avoid this tax by making their own salt. Gandhi and 78 followers marched for 24 days and covered 241 miles.

Photographers recorded Gandhi picking up salt from the beach. Gandhi was arrested and very soon 100,000 Indians following his example had been arrested by the British. The jails of India were at bursting point and Indians were becoming aware that even the great military power of the British could not arrest them all.

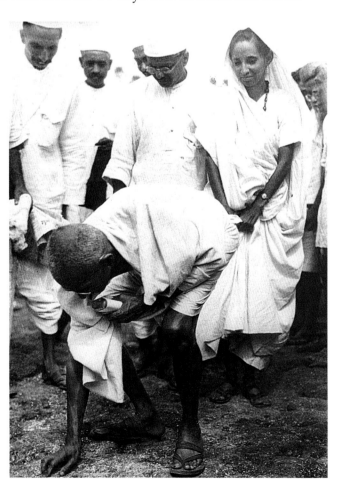

SOURCE 14 *Extract from Jawaharlal Nehru's speech, 26 January 1930.*

We believe that it is the inalienable right of the Indian people, as of any other people, to have freedom and to enjoy the fruits of their toil and have the necessities of life so that they may have opportunity for growth.

We believe also that if any government deprives a people of these rights and oppresses them, the people have further right to alter it or to abolish it. The British government of India has not only deprived the Indian people of their freedom but has ruined India economically, politically, culturally and spiritually.

ACTIVITY

Adjust your 'GandhiThreatOmeter' and give your reasons for choosing the new needle position.

Stage 4: Reform is not enough

Gandhi was released from prison in time to take part in a British-run conference on the future of India. The conference was held in Britain and Gandhi proved very popular with the British working classes of the East End of London when he refused to stay in a plush hotel but stayed in a social service community hall in a very poor London neighbourhood.

By 1935 the British had promised two things they thought to be of great significance for those hoping to see India become self-governing. The British hoped these would reduce the pressure being created by Gandhi and the Congress.

Gandhi was not impressed even though he saw that the measures would do some good. He believed that the measures did not go far enough.

Stage 5: The 'Quit India' Movement

In September 1939, the British Viceroy – Lord Linlithgow – took India into war against Germany without consulting one single Indian Nationalist leader. The leaders of the Indian National Congress were furious at Britain's arrogant treatment of India. Despite this they stopped short of condemning the war outright – realising that Nazi Germany and Fascist Italy were greater evils than British arrogance.

Nothing less than a firm promise to leave India as soon as possible would now do for the leaders of Congress. By 1942 the Japanese were at the Indian border. Britain's only hope of keeping the Japanese out was the continued loyalty of the Indian army. In this atmosphere the INC was determined to force concessions from the British. In August 1942, urged by Gandhi, it passed the controversial 'Quit India' motion. This demanded that the British promise to leave India immediately. Gandhi felt that Indian soldiers would fight more fiercely to protect their own independent India.

The British disagreed and arrested all of the leaders of the INC. Riots followed but most of the Indian army and Indian police stayed loyal – Britain's Indian army did hold off the Japanese whilst Gandhi and Nehru were held in jail.

ACTIVITY

Adjust your 'GandhiThreatOmeter' and give your reasons for choosing the new needle position. Do this for stage 4, then stage 5.

- The main provinces of India could hold elections and govern themselves after 1937 (but central government decisions would still be taken by the British)
- Major Indian services were to become half Indian by the following dates:

Indian Civil Service	1939
Indian Police	1949
Indian Army	1952

Independence at last!

Gandhi had been released from prison on grounds of ill health on 1 May 1944. Nehru and the other leaders were released in 1945.

In June 1945 and against all expectations the British Labour Party won the British general election. The leaders of this party had long been in favour of Indian independence. In addition, Britain was near bankruptcy and its principal financial supporter, the USA, was strongly disapproving of the idea of empire. Now it was not a question of 'if' the British would quit India but 'when'.

In March 1947, Lord Louis Mountbatten was sworn in as the last Viceroy of India. His mission was clear: make it possible for Britain to withdraw from India by 1948 – at the latest – with the minimum of unrest and violence. British rule in India was about to end.

Why was Gandhi, the man of non-violence, assassinated by a fellow Hindu so soon after Indian independence?

Gandhi was a Hindu but he preached tolerance and equality for all religions in the new India. This made him a target for those less tolerant. Gandhi was fully aware of this and had been a target for an attempted assassination on 20 January 1948. A bomb had been thrown at him during his usual ecumenical (mixed religion) evening prayers. Gandhi had continued his prayers unperturbed. Such is true courage.

In the following days, Gandhi refused to accept police protection. He knew the risks: some militant Hindus saw his love of non-violence as an obstacle preventing revenge against alleged violent acts by members of other religions. Gandhi was attempting, as always, to prevent a cycle of violence from developing.

On 30 January 1948 – four days after the first real Independence Day – Gandhi was late for prayer as a result of a conference with the new deputy Prime Minister of India. Gandhi had sought no such title and wished only to be punctual with those who wished to share prayer with him. A young Hindu from Poona pushed forward to join those wishing to touch Gandhi. He caught Gandhi's attention by calling 'Father, Father'.

Gandhi turned, and the young man fired three shots into his heart.

DISCUSS 1

Try this:

> Take a flower. Smell it. Feel it. Look at it closely. Destroy it. Tear it. Pound it. Tread on it.
> ... Now put the flower back together. Can you? Will you ever be able to? Can anybody?

What on earth has this got to do with Gandhi's belief in non-violence?

DISCUSS 2

1 Look at the picture on the right from Gandhi's funeral. What can we learn from this picture about how Gandhi was viewed in India at the time?

2 What impact do you think Gandhi's tragic death had on his reputation?

Why was India partitioned and how did this shape the world we live in today?

In 1947, Lord Louis Mountbatten was sworn in as the last Viceroy of India. His mission was clear: make it possible for Britain to withdraw from India as quickly as possible and with as little violence and bloodshed as possible. As you will see this was no easy task. His solution was to partition India. In this enquiry you will explore the short-term and long-term consequences of this decision.

Lord Mountbatten's problems, 1947

1 Some areas of India were dominated by one religious group.

2 Members of each religion often distrusted each other and rumour often caused savage mob violence.

3 Muslims and Hindus were not used to working together. Ever since 1906 the British had allowed them to elect separate representatives in even the smallest communities. This had been done partly to prevent the views of the Muslim minority from being swamped – but also the British knew that a divided community would be far easier to rule.

4 The Indian National Congress was dominated by Hindus. By 1946 most Muslims trusted the rival Muslim League (led by Mohammed Jinnah) to represent their interests.

5 The wealth of India was very unevenly distributed and much of the population lived in desperate poverty whilst some small sections held fabulous wealth.

6 Some areas were quite evenly split between religions. The Punjab, for example, was very evenly split between Muslims and Sikhs.

7 India's population was split into three main religious groups: Hindus, Muslims and Sikhs. Hindus were by far the largest group with nearly 80 per cent of the population.

8 The British armed forces consisted of many men who had signed up for the duration of the war only. They were impatient to go home and mutinies began to break out in 1946. Mountbatten couldn't do without these troops until India gained independence but he was increasingly worried about their loyalty.

9 The Muslim League had done well in the elections of 1940 and was determined that Muslim areas should not form part of the new India but should rule themselves in a separate country called 'Pakistan' (land of the pure).

10 Nehru and Gandhi, leaders of the Congress Party, believed that all religions should remain in the new India. They were opposed to the idea of Pakistan but could not persuade the Muslim League to agree with them.

11 Some provinces of India were far richer in terms of good soil or resources than others. If the country were to be divided these rich provinces – such as the Punjab – would cause much unrest.

12 Britain was nearly bankrupt after the Second World War. The Prime Minister was in a desperate hurry to get out of India.

13 A Muslim day of protest in August 1946 had led to mass religious violence; 15,000 dead Hindus and Muslims were left rotting in the streets. If this kind of violence were ever to spread across India millions might die.

ACTIVITY

Look at the situation cards on this page and opposite.
- Which cards would be improved by the solution of partition?
- Which would be unaffected by partition?
- Which would be made worse by partition?
Discuss in pairs. Does partition seem a reasonable solution in the circumstances?

Should India be partitioned (divided into two nations)?

As negotiations dragged on, one issue dominated the discussions. Should India be split into two nations: one containing a clear majority of Muslims and the other a majority of Hindus? Gandhi and Nehru were fiercely against this plan but they could not persuade the Muslim leader, Jinnah, to come around to their point of view. Jinnah was terrified that if Muslims joined India they would be so outnumbered by Hindus that they would have almost no say in how the country was ruled. He also felt that they would be defenceless if religious violence flared.

By the summer of 1947 Mountbatten could see no alternative to partition, and Gandhi and Nehru too were beginning to accept the idea. On 3 June 1947 all sides agreed that India would be partitioned with Indian states voting on which new country they would join. Some areas would be split with some sections going to India and some to the new Pakistan. Even after partition, 40 million Muslims remained in India and 8 million Hindus remained in the new Pakistan.

Why did so many Indians migrate in the months after independence and what was the result?

At midnight on 14 August 1947, the British Raj came to an end. Nehru became Prime Minister of the Independent Dominion of India – a self-governing state within the British Commonwealth of nations. The new state of Pakistan also came into being led by Mohammed Jinnah.

Nehru looked optimistically to the future:

At the stroke of the midnight hour, when the world sleeps, India will awake to life and freedom. A moment comes, which comes but rarely in history, when we step out from the old to the new, when an age ends, and when the soul of a nation long suppressed finds utterance.

As Nehru spoke many families who now found themselves in a religious minority wrestled with a desperately important decision. Should they move across the new borders into mainly Muslim Pakistan or mainly Hindu India?

Some five million Hindus and Sikhs left Pakistan in the first few months of independence. This number was matched by Muslims heading for Pakistan from India. Violence was horrific, particularly in the split Punjab. It seems likely that half a million Indians lost their lives during those terrible months.

How secure is the future for India?

As the 21st century unfolds, India is poised to become one of the world's great economic powers. With its population of 1.1 billion it is by far the world's largest democracy. Since 1947 Pakistan has split into two nations. To the east has emerged the nation of Bangladesh, to the west, Pakistan remains. Disputes over the border still exist between India and Pakistan and troops of both nations face each other in an uneasy truce in the divided province of Kashmir.

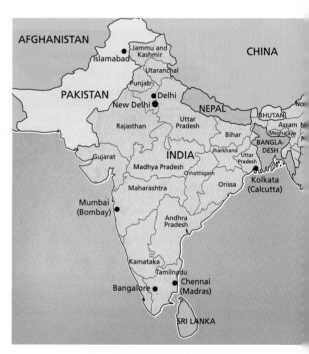

ACTIVITY 1

Revisit your opinion on partition – has that opinion changed now you have studied some of the **short-term** consequences of this decision?

ACTIVITY 2

1 Look carefully at the information above and the cards opposite.
Does your analysis suggest that India is on:
- the road to world status and wealth?
- the road to national break-up and/or increasing poverty?
- the road of doubt and uncertainty?

Make a large copy of the road diagram on the right.
Put each issue on the appropriate road it suggests for India.

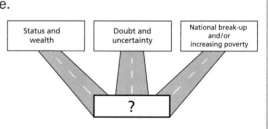

2 Revisit your opinion on partition – has that opinion changed now you have studied some of the **long-term** consequences of this decision?

1 The electricity supply to many Indian villages is very unreliable.

2 India has an average income per person of less than US$750 per year.

3 The Indian state broadcaster had only one TV channel in 1991 but by 2006 it had more than 150.

4 India badly needs to improve irrigation for poor farmers.

5 Most villages in India rely on money sent back from relatives living in cities. Agricultural plots are frequently too small to support a family.

6 Only 35 million Indians out of 470 million have job security. 21 of those 35 million work for the Indian government.

7 The Indian company Tata is one of the largest and most successful steel and vehicle making companies in the world. It owns Jaguar and Land Rover.

8 New crops and growing techniques mean that India now produces more than enough food to feed its population.

9 Many Indian companies are reluctant to employ workers since the law makes it very difficult to sack a bad employee.

10 India is world-famous for its technical and engineering expertise. It produces one million engineering graduates every year. Europe and the USA each produce fewer than 100,000.

11 Only 65% of Indians can read and write compared to 90% of Chinese people.

12 In 2006 almost 300 million Indians were still below the poverty line and unsure whether they could afford their next meal.

13 The poverty rate in India is dropping at 1% per year. In 2001 it was 26%.

14 India hopes to send a probe to the moon by 2010.

15 In India the state stores over a tonne of rice for every family below the poverty line but has no strong system to distribute this food.

16 India has fought three wars with neighbouring Pakistan since 1947. In 2002 India and Pakistan faced each other with a million soldiers along the disputed border of Kashmir.

17 Both India and Pakistan possess nuclear warheads and missiles to carry them. In 1998 India tested five nuclear bombs. The Pakistanis then tested six.

18 Many Indian Hindus still support the caste system where people are given a rank by birth. Caste or rank often decides who gets the best jobs.

19 Some new industries, such as ICT, do choose workers on merit rather than by caste. This trend is growing.

20 India imports over 70% of the oil it uses.

21 Pipelines for gas for India would need to come across the territory of Pakistan or Iran.

22 Many Indian Hindus will not even drink from the same well as somebody who is at the bottom of the caste system – an untouchable.

23 India's economy has grown at 75% per year since 2004.

24 India's Ministry of Railways is the second largest employer in the world. (The largest is China's army.)

25 India has some world-class roads linking its major cities.

26 India is very short of good roads across most of its territory.

27 India has been a democracy for its whole history apart from thirteen months in 1975–1976.

28 India is the world's largest democracy and has full electronic voting.

29 India has freedom of speech and an independent judiciary (court judges).

30 When an earthquake hit Pakistani Kashmir in 2005 the border was opened along the disputed line to let aid pass through.

31 China and Pakistan both border India. China is Pakistan's biggest arms supplier.

32 Since 2003 India and Pakistan have been engaged in serious peace talks over Kashmir.

33 China and India have two of the largest and fastest growing economies in the world. Each supplies the other with needed goods and services.

34 The USA has agreed to help India develop many nuclear reactors to help produce energy.

35 India's film industry is one of the largest in the world.

36 India has no official religion. All religions are tolerated.

37 There is a Hindu party with policies designed to make Hinduism the dominant religion in India.

38 India is predicted to have the world's largest population by 2032.

39 In 2001 average life expectancy was 65 years in India.

40 India has only 2.5 million tourist visitors a year, fewer than Dubai or Singapore. The UK has approximately 25 million visitors per year.

41 Fewer than 2% of Indian people own their own vehicles yet traffic congestion is horrific in the cities.

42 In terms of numbers infected, India is the second largest sufferer from HIV/AIDS in the world after South Africa.

THE BIG STORY: Empire Part Three (continued)

Why is the British Empire so controversial? (2)

The end of Empire: A controversial story

As you have seen, the end of the British Empire in India is controversial. The decision to partition India, made in 1947, has shaped the world we live in today and still causes heated arguments. The reasons why British rule in India ended are also controversial, with disagreements about what factors played the key role.

> **Protest** is the key. The British left because they were forced out by protest movements that wanted independence.

> **Pressure from other countries** was the vital factor. Britain needed the financial and military support of the United States. The US did not approve of Britain keeping a large empire.

> **Economics** is the most important factor. The British left because they were no longer making so much money from their colonies. Britain was bankrupt after the Second World War and it was becoming increasingly expensive to govern the colonies.

> **Changing political views in Britain** played the crucial role. Some politicians started to argue that Britain's colonies should be granted independence.

During the second half of the twentieth century many other colonies followed in India's footsteps and became independent. Why do you think this happened? Did the same factors that had played a role in India also play a role in other colonies?

ACTIVITY

1 Do you agree with how we have started to fill in the factors chart below for India? Change the percentage points we have awarded if you disagree. Remember to justify your scores as you complete the column on India.

2 Use the case studies on pages 47–51 to explore how British rule ended in Kenya and Hong Kong.

You need to:
- Identify the key factors that played a role in ending British rule.
- Rank these factors in order of importance. You can use the factor chart below to help you summarise your arguments. When you study Kenya and Hong Kong you may find that other factors come into play. You can add these to your table and give them a percentage score.

Factor	India	Kenya	Hong Kong
Protest	50 per cent because the protests led by Gandhi and the INC showed that the Indian people would no longer accept British rule		
Economics	10 per cent because …		
Pressure from other countries	20 per cent because …		
Changing views in Britain	20 per cent because the new Labour government that came to power in 1945 believed that India should be independent		
Other factors			

End-of-Empire Case Study 1:
Why did the British leave Kenya?

Background

The story began in the 1880s as the British built a railway across Kenya to connect land they controlled in the interior of Africa to the port of Mombasa on the Kenyan coast. The railway, and the soldiers sent to protect it, had a drastic effect on the Kenyan Kikuyu tribe who farmed the fertile highlands of central Kenya. Conflict with the soldiers and contact with European diseases had drastically reduced Kikuyu numbers. In Britain, people were encouraged to migrate to Kenya. Adverts such as this appeared in British newspapers:

Purchasers have expressed their utmost gratitude with these fine products and a continued supply is therefore to be most earnestly recommended.

SETTLE IN KENYA

BRITAIN'S YOUNGEST AND MOST ATTRACTIVE COLONY.

Low prices at present for fertile areas. No richer soil in the British Empire... secure the advantage of native labour to supplement your own effort.

Eventually a group of about 3000 Europeans farmed 12,000 square miles (31,089 square km) of fertile land in Kenya known now as the 'White Highlands' while 1,000,000 Kikuyu were left with only 2000 square miles (5,180 square km) of their former land. British settlers had good contacts in Parliament and managed to gain a dominant position over the Africans in Kenya. As you can see below left, society was divided along racial lines.

1 Black people were not allowed to own land in the 'White Highlands'. Instead they were restricted to far less fertile reserves of land.
2 Black Africans were allowed as 'squatters' on white land in the Highlands. This meant that they were allowed to farm and keep the crops grown on small pieces of white-owned land in return for working unpaid on the white farmers' tea or coffee crops.
3 Africans were made to pay taxes. To get the cash to pay these, Africans had no choice but to work for the white settlers.
4 All black Africans leaving their reserves were obliged to carry a pass. They frequently wore this in a metal container and called it the 'goat's bell'.

The system endured relatively unchallenged until the Second World War. The war had a big impact on Kenya. Many Kenyans of all tribes and races served with the British armed forces. In the course of their service they travelled far and wide – often to the nations of Western Europe. Meanwhile, in Kenya, white settler power in the government of Kenya grew as the British government was preoccupied with the war in Europe. More wealthy settlers began to invest in machinery which meant that black squatters were no longer needed to work on white-owned land. Many black squatters were expelled from their farms. A new British Governor took office in 1944. He promised to increase the proportion of black people in the Kenyan government but his changes were not planned to take effect for nearly ten years.

Mau Mau! 1952–1959

Gradually from 1950 a violent Kenyan national movement known as the Mau Mau began to gain widespread, although not total, support among Kikuyu tribesmen. Attacks began on white farms and white people. Many of these attacks involved terrible mutilations and atrocities. White communities replied with specially recruited commando units who were also prepared to use brutal methods.

By late 1952 the movement was so serious that the new British governor declared a state of emergency and sent for British troops. Information on Mau Mau members was very hard to come by. Police and soldiers were often met by a wall of silence from villagers and Mau Mau suspects alike. It was very difficult for troops serving the British – some of whom were Kikuyu tribesmen themselves – to tell who was a Mau Mau member and who was not.

In trying to defeat the Mau Mau the British appeared brutal to many ordinary Kenyans and to the rest of the world.

- To put down poorly armed Africans, the British used 12,000 soldiers supported by armoured cars and two squadrons of fighter jets. In addition to these troops, local part-time soldiers provided by the white settlers were used.
- Half of the population of Nairobi was sent to detention camps and movement in and out of the city was made very difficult indeed.
- Conditions in the camps and brutality by some guards led to the deaths of 20,000 suspects.
- Ten men were beaten to death at the Hola camp by drunken guards. The deaths were blamed on 'contaminated drinking water' until the real reason was revealed in Parliament in a blaze of bad publicity.

▲ SOURCE 15 *Troops inspect identity papers in Nairobi.*

DISCUSS

In the picture on the left you can see a Mau Mau suspect in contact with soldiers serving the British. Take the part of a black suspect and fill in the thought bubbles. One bubble should show the thoughts an actual Mau Mau member might have in the situation shown. The other bubble should show the possible thoughts of a non-Mau Mau member.

The Mau Mau, although never totally eradicated, were largely defeated as a real threat by 1959. By then circumstances had changed:

- The USA had made it clear to Britain that large empires were not to its liking. The British had borrowed huge amounts of money from the USA in the war so could not afford to ignore its wishes. Britain also depended on US support in the Cold War.
- The British Prime Minister, Harold Macmillan, declared himself in acceptance of the idea that Africans should gain independence in his famous 'winds of change' speech in 1960.
- By 1960 all European nations with the exception of Portugal, which was ruled by fascist army officers, were racing to leave their colonies in Africa.
- Britain had spent £60 million defeating the Mau Mau at a time of relative weakness for the British economy.

By 1961 Britain had had enough. In two conferences in London at the palatial Lancaster House the terms of independence were negotiated with Kenyan black nationalist leaders. In December 1963 Kenya became independent. The black nationalist leader Jomo Kenyatta became firstly Prime Minister then President of Kenya.

ACTIVITY

Now fill in your case study chart from page 46 for Kenya.

▼ SOURCE 16   *Kenyan independence, December 1963.*

End-of-Empire Case Study 2: Why did the British leave Hong Kong?

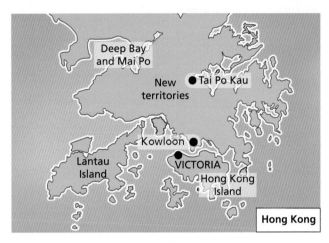

▲ SOURCE 17 *Map of Hong Kong.*

What were the British doing in Hong Kong?

In 1842 and 1860 the British fought two short, sharp wars against Imperial China. The wars were fought to ensure that the Chinese continued to accept a controversial British export grown in India, a powerful drug called opium. Today it is the raw material for making heroin! On both occasions British battleships quickly defeated Chinese war junks and forced the Chinese to give up **Hong Kong Island**, with its valuable harbour, along with **southern Kowloon** 'in perpetuity' (for ever).

In 1898 the population of Hong Kong Island was overflowing and the British negotiated a lease for 99 years on the **New Territories** and **Lantau Island**. By the terms of the lease this land would have to be handed back in 1997. What was known as Hong Kong was in fact two separate collections of areas with very different conditions of occupation.

Hong Kong became a vitally important naval base for the British. It also became a very important centre of trade and manufacturing. Regulations and taxes were few, which meant that Hong Kong goods were famous for their low prices. By 1980 Hong Kong with its six million people was exporting more than China, which had a population approaching one billion.

The end is nigh?

In 1982 the British Government began to talk to the government of China about the future of Hong Kong. The lease on the 'New Territories' was due to expire in 1997, meaning that they would have to be given back to China. The New Territories made up 92 per cent of the territory known as Hong Kong. Without them, Hong Kong Island and Kowloon, both of which did not have to be given back, would not be practical to run. There would simply not be enough space or resources to maintain the whole population on Hong Kong Island and Kowloon.

Mrs Thatcher's problem

By the 1980s China was showing every sign of insisting on its legal right to take the New Territories back. A clock was even mounted in Beijing's Tiananmen Square ticking down the moments to 1997! This seems to suggest that the Chinese were going to force Britain out of Hong Kong. The British position seemed weak and the law was clearly on the side of the Chinese government.

On the other hand six million citizens of Hong Kong viewed a Chinese takeover with real suspicion and often with dread. China was communist and run very differently to Hong Kong. It was run strictly by the Communist Party (the only political party allowed). This party believed that the government should run the economy and was therefore against private trade and manufacture.

Mrs Thatcher decides

Margaret Thatcher, the British Prime Minister in 1982, was feeling very confident after her victory over Argentina in the Falklands War and viewed the Hong Kong situation as very similar to that one: a small British colony was threatened by a larger non-democratic power. She effectively had a choice of four possible negotiating positions, each of which had disadvantages and advantages.

ACTIVITY 1

Look at the chart below.
1 In your groups, fill in the empty boxes with possible advantages and disadvantages. You may also add to the boxes that are already filled in if you wish.

2 Then take the part of the British. Which position would you adopt and why? Don't forget to consider the likely Chinese reaction to each possible choice. Be prepared to justify your decision.

Position	Advantage	Disadvantage
1 Simply hand over all of Hong Kong to the Chinese		*Could possibly lead to riots in Hong Kong*
2 Hand over Hong Kong but try to negotiate a special deal on how it would be run	*May allow Hong Kong's people to carry on their way of life and would allow Hong Kong to continue investing money for China*	
3 Hand over the New Territories but hold onto Hong Kong Island and Kowloon	*Legally correct*	
4 Refuse to hand over any of Hong Kong on the grounds that the people living there were against handover. Prepare to fight		*Could lead to war against a nuclear-armed country with the largest army on Earth*

In reality Mrs Thatcher initially wished to defend Hong Kong by force! On being persuaded by horrified British diplomats that Hong Kong could not be defended she allowed her negotiators to adopt position 2.

In December 1984 the British and Chinese governments signed a deal known as the 'Joint Declaration'. By its terms China would take over control of the whole of Hong Kong in 1997 but promised to allow its people to keep their way of life for at least 50 years. Hong Kong was to be known as a 'Special Administrative Region' of China. On 30 June 1997, 100 years to the week after Queen Victoria's Golden Jubilee, the Union Jack was lowered over Hong Kong. Britain's last economically significant colony had gone. The sun had finally set on the British Empire.

▲ SOURCE 18 *Hong Kong reverts to China, June 1997.*

ACTIVITY 2

Now fill in your case study chart from page 46 for Hong Kong.

51

Why has Britain been involved in so many conflicts over the last 100 years?

What can local war memorials tell us about the twentieth century?

War memorials are a common sight in most towns and villages in the United Kingdom. They tell us a great deal about twentieth-century conflicts. Visit your local war memorial. Are you surprised by the number of people from your local area who died fighting in conflicts during the twentieth century? Can you find out more about the people behind the names?

The twentieth century witnessed two global conflicts, the First World War and the Second World War. Britain was one of the key countries involved in both and their impact has had a lasting effect on this country and the world.

The First World War began in August 1914. Britain joined the war in support of Belgium and France, who were under threat of a German invasion. Five million people from Britain and the British Empire fought in the First World War. Over 700,000 of these men lost their lives. War memorials such as the one in the photograph (top right) are a common sight in our villages and towns. It is estimated that in total 20 million people died as a result of the war. France lost over one and a quarter million men, Germany nearly two million. Germany was eventually defeated in 1918.

In 1933 Adolf Hitler became leader of Germany. He re-built the German army and began to take over other countries in Europe. When the German army invaded Poland in September 1939, Britain declared war on Germany. By 1940, British towns and cities were under attack from the German air force. The Second World War was the most destructive war in history. This was 'total war'

fought against civilians as well as soldiers. At least 55 million people were killed. During the Second World War over 270,000 British soldiers and 60,000 civilians were killed.

The Cenotaph in London (above) commemorates all those soldiers who lost their lives in both the First and Second World War.

Why have new war memorials been built in the 21st century?

The contribution of men and women from Asia, Africa and the Caribbean who fought for Britain in the First and Second World Wars is often forgotten. In 2001, a commemorative gate appeared in London's Hyde Park Corner in honour of the overseas soldiers who fought for Britain in both wars. When we talk of 'Britain' fighting in these wars we really mean Britain and the countries that were then part of the British Empire. During both world wars Britain turned to the countries in her empire for support. All over the world, people offered their help.

During the First World War, battalions from the British West Indies Regiment served in France, Palestine, Egypt and Italy, suffering over 1,300 casualties. During the Second World War some 375,000 men and women from African countries served in the Allied forces. The Indian sub-continent (present-day India, Pakistan, Bangladesh and Sri Lanka) contributed 2.5 million servicemen and women – the largest volunteer army in history. Throughout the Empire, money was raised for tanks, aeroplanes and ambulances. Huge amounts of raw materials and food were exported to Britain to help supply her people and the war effort.

In 2007 a new war memorial was unveiled in Britain. The new National Armed Forces memorial in Staffordshire commemorates 16,000 men and women from the armed forces who have died on duty since 1945. It shows that since the end of the Second World War, British troops have continued to be involved in conflicts across the world. A brief summary of the main conflicts that Britain has been involved in since the end of the Second World War is provided on pages 54–55.

Why has Britain been involved in so many conflicts?

▲ *Memorial gates to Commonwealth war dead, Constitution Hill, London.*

▲ *Armed Forces Memorial at the National Memorial Arboretum, Staffordshire.*

ACTIVITY

1 Look for patterns. Think of conflicts that Britain was involved in before 1900. Why did Britain become involved?

Code	Reason
D	Defence from invasion
E	Empire – to defend or extend British territory overseas
A	To support an ally
R	Religion – to defend or spread Christianity
T	Trade (economic interests – to protect or expand trade routes and supplies of raw materials)
PK	Part of a UN peace-keeping force
UN	Part of UN fighting force

2 Look at the timeline on pages 54–55 showing some of the key conflicts of the last 100 years that Britain has been involved in. Use a code like the one in the table to show why Britain became involved.

You may want to use more than one code if you think there was more than one reason. For example, you could use the code 'A' for World War One. However, for World War Two you could use 'A' (support for Poland) and 'D' if you believe Britain was under threat of invasion.

3 Can you see any patterns? What have been the main reasons why Britain has been involved in conflict over the last 100 years? How does this compare to other periods of history?

Conflicts involving British armed forces overseas

1914–1918 The First World War	(You have an opportunity to study this conflict in greater detail on pages 56–67. The main focus will be on what motivated so many men from Britain to fight in the war.)

1939–1945 The Second World War	(You have an opportunity to explore this conflict in greater detail on pages 68–91. The main focus will be on the impact of the war on civilians, in particular the threat of bombing from the air.)

1945–1989 The Cold War	The Soviet Union and the United States came out of the Second World War as the two strongest countries in the world. After the war, rivalry quickly grew. Although there was never any direct fighting between them, the world lived in fear of another major conflict breaking out. By 1950 both the United States and the Soviet Union had nuclear weapons and the world lived with the fear that a third world war could destroy much of the planet.

(You will have an opportunity to study this conflict in more detail on pages 92–103.)

Britain sided with the United States throughout the conflict and allowed America to position military bases in the UK. However, apart from the Korean War, British forces were not actively involved in any Cold War conflict.

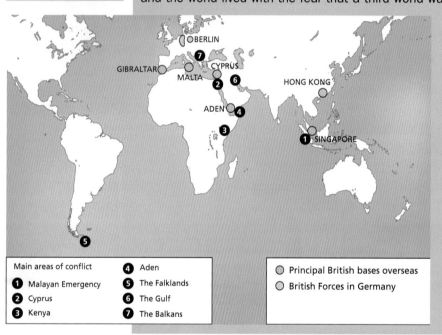

Main areas of conflict

1 Malayan Emergency
2 Cyprus
3 Kenya
4 Aden
5 The Falklands
6 The Gulf
7 The Balkans

○ Principal British bases overseas
○ British Forces in Germany

1950–1953 The Korean War	This was the first open military conflict of the Cold War. In 1945, Korea, after being liberated from Japanese occupation, was divided between a Communist-dominated north and an American-dominated south. In 1950 North Korean troops, supported by Chinese communist forces, invaded the south. Large numbers of American troops under the United Nations flag were sent to Korea. Other countries, including Britain, also sent military support. British casualties were 686 servicemen killed, 2,498 wounded and 1,102 reported missing.

1948–1966 Malaya	In 1948 a number of states that had been under British protection came together to form the Federation of Malaya. There was a communist rebellion against the federation. Britain sent forces to the area to support the Malay government in its fight against the Communists. In defending Malaysia, British and Commonwealth forces suffered over 300 casualties.

1952–1959 **Cyprus**	Britain had used Cyprus as a military base since the nineteenth century. Eighty per cent of the island's population were of Greek origin; the other 20 per cent were Turkish. The Greek majority wanted Cyprus to unite with Greece. When Britain refused to let this happen, an organisation called EOKA turned to terrorism against British forces and the Turkish minority. A civil war followed before a cease-fire was agreed in 1959. The bitterness between Greeks and Turks remained and the island was eventually partitioned.
1952–1960 **Kenya**	In British-controlled Kenya, white settlers dominated the government and owned the best land. The Kikuyu, Kenya's largest native tribe, began to organise resistance. Between 1952 and 1959 thousands of British troops were deployed in Kenya. (See pages 47–49.)
1956 **The Suez War**	The British, along with France and Israel, invaded Egypt after the Egyptian leader (President Nasser) seized control of the Suez Canal: a crucial trade route (particularly for oil). Britain and France had shares in the canal.
1963–1967 **Aden**	Aden was a key port at the southern end of the Red Sea. It had been controlled by Britain since the early nineteenth century. After the Second World War, Arab nationalists began demanding independence for Aden. In 1963 there was unrest within the country and attacks on British forces from across the border in Yemen. Fifty British troops were killed and 650 wounded in the four-year conflict. Eventually Britain withdrew and recognised Aden's independence within the People's Republic of South Yemen.
1982 **The Falklands** **War**	In April 1982, Argentina invaded the Falklands Islands (part of the British Empire since 1833). The ownership of the islands had been disputed by the two countries for a long time. The British quickly responded by sending troops to win back the island. The Falklands War ended with the formal surrender of the Argentine forces on 14 June. The conflict claimed the lives of 255 British and 665 Argentinian servicemen.
1991 **The Gulf War**	In 1990 Iraq invaded Kuwait. Britain sent 28,000 troops as part of a UN coalition force, primarily led by the United States, that defeated Iraqi forces and liberated Kuwait.
1990s **Yugoslavia**	Yugoslavia had been a communist republic since the Second World War. In the early 1990s the republic split up into separate independent states. In Bosnia-Herzegovina a civil war broke out when three separate groups (Serbs, Croats and Muslims) tried to gain control. It has been estimated that around 200,000 men, women and children were killed in the conflict. The British army played an increasingly prominent role in UN peace-keeping operations during the 1990s. In 1999 the British RAF took part in NATO bombing raids against Serbian forces. This was in response to Serbian attacks on the Albanian people of Kosovo.
2001 **The invasion** **of Afghanistan**	A large number of British troops formed part of a UN-backed international force, led by the United States, that invaded Afghanistan. This was in response to the attack on the World Trade Center in New York on 11 September 2001 (see page 104). The attack had been organised by members of al-Qaeda, a terrorist group that had bases in Afghanistan.
2003 **The invasion** **of Iraq**	In 2003 the US, Britain and some other countries attacked Iraq, without full authorisation by the UN Security Council, claiming that Saddam Hussein was capable of providing terrorist groups with chemical and biological weapons. Saddam's army was quickly defeated and eventually a new government was formed. However, there were also a growing number of attacks on US and British forces based in Iraq by groups opposed to foreign intervention.

A quick history of the First World War

The countdown to war

- **28 June 1914** Archduke Franz Ferdinand, the heir to the throne of Austria–Hungary, is assassinated by a Serbian terrorist.
- **28 July** Austria–Hungary, declares war on Serbia. Belgrade (in Serbia) is shelled.
- **29 July** Russia prepares for war against Austria–Hungary in order to help her ally, Serbia, defend itself against the attack.
- **1 August** Germany declares war on Russia, in order to help her ally, Austria–Hungary. It also starts to move its army towards France, Russia's ally.
- **3 August** Germany declares war on France and attacks through Belgium (at the time a neutral country). Britain orders Germany to withdraw from Belgium.
- **4 August** Germany does not withdraw from Belgium. Britain declares war on Germany to support Belgium and France.

The First World War begins

Other countries joined the war. In 1914 Turkey entered the war on the side of Germany. In 1917 the USA entered the war on the British side.

ACTIVITY

1. Produce a Living Graph like the one below to show the successes and failures of Britain and her allies during the war.
2. What was the key turning point that tipped the war in favour of Britain and her allies?

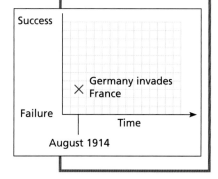

AUGUST 1914

Many people expected the war to be over quickly. Germany invaded France and Belgium but failed to capture Paris and the Channel ports. British and French troops managed to halt the German advance at the Battle of the Marne.

Both sides built trenches which, by the end of 1914, stretched from Switzerland to the English Channel.

DECEMBER 1914 STALEMATE

Both sides had huge armies and many factories to supply their forces with millions of guns, shells and bullets. Each side had massive guns that could shell the enemy and cause huge casualties. Both sides found it very difficult to advance. Trenches were defended by barbed wire and machine guns.

AUGUST 1915 GALLIPOLI LANDINGS

British forces, with many Australians and New Zealanders (ANZACS), landed at Gallipoli aiming to defeat Germany's ally, Turkey. The plan failed and many soldiers were killed.

FEBRUARY – DECEMBER 1916 THE BATTLE OF VERDUN

German forces attacked French forts at Verdun, hoping to wear down the French army. The French held out but 160,000 French soldiers lost their lives defending the town.

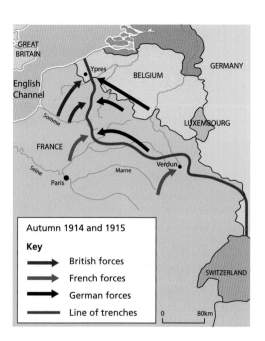

Autumn 1914 and 1915

Key

→ British forces
→ French forces
➜ German forces
— Line of trenches

0   80km

JULY – NOVEMBER 1916
THE BATTLE OF THE SOMME

The British launched a major attack against the German line. The main aim was to relieve the pressure on the French army and force the Germans to move troops away from Verdun. However, things did not go according to plan ...

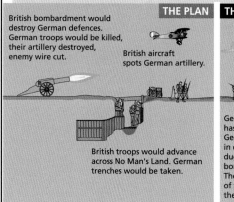

THE PLAN

British bombardment would destroy German defences. German troops would be killed, their artillery destroyed, enemy wire cut.

British aircraft spots German artillery.

British troops would advance across No Man's Land. German trenches would be taken.

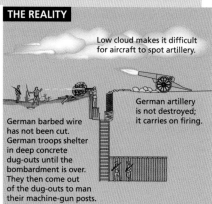

THE REALITY

Low cloud makes it difficult for aircraft to spot artillery.

German artillery is not destroyed; it carries on firing.

German barbed wire has not been cut. German troops shelter in deep concrete dug-outs until the bombardment is over. They then come out of the dug-outs to man their machine-gun posts.

The first day of the battle resulted in massive losses for the British Army. Casualty figures were over 60,000 (21,000 killed). By the end of the battle 8 km of land had been gained. Also, the attack relieved the pressure on the French at Verdun. Germany was forced to move troops to defend the line on the Somme. If these troops had been free to attack at Verdun the French may well have been defeated and knocked out of the war. However, over 400,000 British troops had been killed or wounded by the end of the battle.

JULY – NOVEMBER 1917
THE THIRD BATTLE OF YPRES

In 1917 there was a large-scale mutiny in the French army. The condition of the French army meant that it was important for the British to launch a major offensive to keep the German forces occupied.

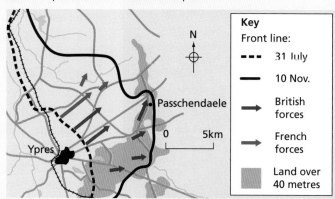

Key

Front line:

- - - 31 July

——— 10 Nov.

→ British forces

→ French forces

Land over 40 metres

0   5km

The Allies' aim was to capture the Passchendaele ridge. However, the Germans were determined to defend the ridge and were well prepared for the attack. For two years they had been building a line of concrete strong points. The situation was made even more difficult by the weather. Constant rain turned the area into a quagmire. The ridge was finally captured in November. By this point the British army had suffered nearly 245,000 casualties.

MARCH 1917
REVOLUTION IN RUSSIA

The Russian army was badly led and poorly supplied. By 1917 over one and a half million Russian soldiers had died fighting on the Eastern Front. This led to the overthrow of the country's leader, the Tsar. In November 1917, a communist government took over Russia and pulled the country out of the war.

SPRING 1918
THE GERMAN SPRING OFFENSIVE

The Germans attacked Allied forces on the Western Front in spring 1918. The Allies were forced to retreat but the Germans were unable to make a clear breakthrough.

AUTUMN 1918

The Allies, with support from newly arrived US troops, broke through German lines. The German army was pushed back and signed an armistice on 11 November 1918.

The First World War: why did soldiers carry on fighting in the trenches?

The way we remember the First World War today has been influenced by poems, films and novels. They often present a horrifying picture of life in trenches for British soldiers. If conditions really were so terrible why did soldiers volunteer? Why did they then carry on fighting? Your task is to explain what motivated British soldiers to fight in the First World War. You will need to consider a number of factors and support your explanation with specific examples from sources and statistics.

ACTIVITY

1 Interview family and friends. How similar is their image of the First World War to the one below on the left?
2 Read Source 2. How do poems such as this support the popular image of the First World War?
3 Can you find examples of films, TV programmes, novels or other poems that support this impression of the war?

The popular image – what do most people think life in the trenches was like?

When most people think of the First World War the image that comes into their head is probably very similar to the scene in the painting below.

Many films, novels and poems paint a picture of tired, *battle-weary soldiers* struggling to survive in *horrific conditions*. The popular image is of a pointless slaughter, as hundreds of thousands of *patriotic volunteers* are sent into battle by *stupid generals,* who live in luxury many miles from the front line. Meanwhile, the ordinary soldiers suffer from a *poor diet* and a lack of supplies. They spend most of their days in poorly built and *unhygienic* trenches *constantly being shelled or bombed,* surrounded by rats, lice and dead bodies. They are kept in line by *strict army discipline* – if they refuse to fight, they are 'shot at dawn'.

▼ **SOURCE 1** The Harvest of Battle *by CRW Nevinson painted in 1919.*

SOURCE 2 *An extract from 'Aftermath' by Siegfried Sassoon.*

Do you remember the
  dark months you held
  the sector at Mametz –
The nights you watched
  and wired and dug and
  piled sandbags on
  parapets?
Do you remember the
  rats; and the stench
Of corpses rotting in
  front of the front-line
  trench –
And dawn coming, dirty-
  white, and chill with a
  hopeless rain?
Do you ever stop and
  ask, 'Is it all going to
  happen again?'

What motivated men to sign up and fight?

In 1914 Britain only had a small army and it was soon clear that it would not be big enough to fight Germany and its allies. A recruitment campaign was established by Lord Kitchener. It was very successful. By the end of 1915 nearly two million men had signed up and there were more civilians training to be soldiers than ever before in British history. Why did so many men volunteer to fight?

Kitchener's recruitment campaign was based on four main aims:

1. To encourage patriotism – love of your country and your duty to fight for it.
2. To encourage heroism – to make you feel that you could share in the glory of a great victory.
3. To encourage anti-German hatred – the government spread propaganda stories of atrocities committed by German soldiers. As the Germans advanced through Belgium during the first phase of the war, British newspapers carried reports of babies being killed by bayonet and women being attacked and raped.
4. To shame people if they had not signed up – for example, women handed out white feathers (a symbol of cowardice) to young men not in uniform.

▶ SOURCE 3 *Recruitment posters from the First World War.*

Why is this word used to describe the British soldiers?

Why is this word underlined?

Why are the soldiers marching towards this image?

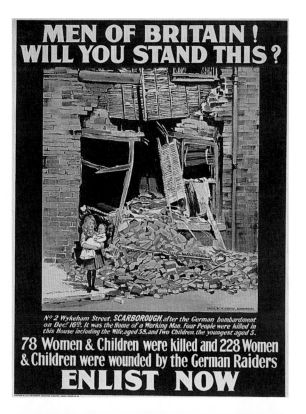

ACTIVITY

1 Look carefully at Sources 3–7. What is the main aim of each source? Make sure you can explain how the source achieves this aim. Think about the visual image and the words on the poster.
2 What can you learn from these government propaganda posters about why men signed up to fight? What appears to be the main reason?
3 Can you think of other reasons why men may have signed up to fight? Think back to the conflicts you have already studied in Years 7 and 8. What motivated people to fight in those wars?

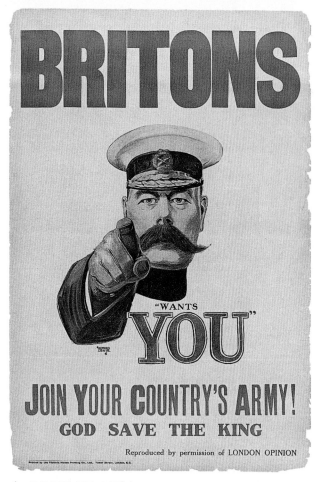

Daddy, what did *YOU* do in the Great War?

▲ SOURCE 5 *'Daddy, what did you do in the Great War?'*

▲ SOURCE 4 *This poster features Lord Kitchener. It became one of the most famous posters of the war.*

YOUR COUNTRY'S CALL

Isn't this worth fighting for?
ENLIST NOW

▲ SOURCE 6 *'Your country's call – Isn't this worth fighting for?'*

REMEMBER BELGIUM

ENLIST TO·DAY

◀ SOURCE 7 *'Remember Belgium.'*

Men signed up to fight in the First World War for a variety of reasons. Some men signed up for an adventure and to escape boring, low-paid jobs. Many thought that the war would be over quickly and that Britain would be victorious. They saw a chance of glory and an opportunity to prove themselves.

For most soldiers the main reason they signed up was **patriotism**. Most soldiers felt that they were fighting for their home and country. Schools stressed to children the importance of loyalty to their country and the willingness to defend their nation and their family. To die fighting for your country was seen as an honourable and glorious thing to do.

However, perhaps the really important question is not 'Why did men sign up?' but 'Why did they carry on fighting?'. It is remarkable that there were very few deserters from the British army, especially considering the large numbers who signed up. In 1917 there was a major mutiny amongst French soldiers and large numbers refused to fight on. However, this did not happen in the British army. Can you explain **what motivated British soldiers to continue fighting?**

What motivated British soldiers to continue fighting in the trenches?

SOURCE 8 *An extract from a letter written by Laurie Rowlands, 15th Battalion, Durham Light Infantry. This letter was written in February 1918.*

Not a single man has an ounce of what we call patriotism left in him. No one cares a rap whether Germany has Alsace, Belgium or France too for that matter. All that every man desires now is to get done with it and go home.

Clearly this is just one account of life in the trenches but many other sources also seem to indicate that, whilst patriotism may have motivated some soldiers to carry on fighting, it was not the main motivation for the majority of soldiers. Your task is to find out what was.

ACTIVITY

Look at the seven explanations given below.

1 Develop a hypothesis – rank the explanations in order of importance.

2 Test your hypothesis – Use the Evidence Files below and source material on pages 63–67 to develop a better understanding of why men continued to fight in the trenches.

3 Develop a new hypothesis. Make sure you use the advice on page 62 to help you construct a detailed explanation that answers this Big Question:
   What motivated British soldiers to continue fighting in the trenches?

4 Compare what motivated men to carry on fighting in the trenches with what motivated people in previous conflicts you have studied (in Years 7 and 8). What similarities and differences can you find?

5 What about today? Do you think the factors that motivated soldiers to fight in the First World War are still important factors that motivate people to fight in conflicts today?

EXPLANATION 1
British soldiers were well cared for. The army did as much as they could to keep morale high. A rotation system made sure that soldiers did not spend too long at the front line. The army tried to ensure that soldiers were well fed and that they received good medical care.

EXPLANATION 2
Trench conditions were not as bad as they have been presented in poems, films and novels. Trenches were carefully designed and kept as hygienic as possible.

EXPLANATION 3
Army discipline – men continued to fight because they were afraid of being punished if they did not follow orders.

EXPLANATION 4
Comradeship – men continued to fight because they did not want to let their friends down.

EXPLANATION 5
British soldiers were not let down by their commanding officers. The tactics and decisions taken by generals and commanding officers were not as bad as some accounts of the war make out. The British commanders remained popular with the soldiers.

EXPLANATION 6
The joy of war – soldiers carried on fighting because they enjoyed it.

EXPLANATION 7
Different times/different attitudes – soldiers were brought up in a different Britain from the one that exists today. Their attitudes were very different to those that exist among people in Britain today. People at the time were used to hardship.

DOING HISTORY: Causation – building substantiated explanations

In Years 7 and 8 you may have used a **Hamburger Paragraph** to help you explain why things happen in history.

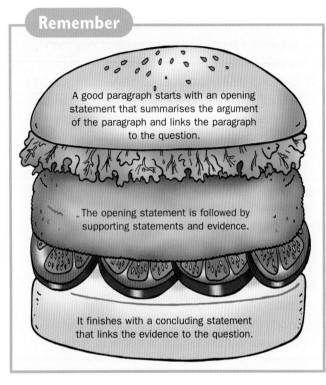

Remember

A good paragraph starts with an opening statement that summarises the argument of the paragraph and links the paragraph to the question.

The opening statement is followed by supporting statements and evidence.

It finishes with a concluding statement that links the evidence to the question.

You can use this approach to help you answer the Big Question of this enquiry:

What motivated British soldiers to continue fighting in the trenches?

STAGE **1** ▶ **Planning your answer**

- Your answer to this question should start with an introduction.
- This should be followed by a series of hamburger paragraphs that explore the main reasons why men fought in the trenches. Each paragraph should cover **one** of the explanations listed on page 61. Make sure you give a range of explanations as to why men fought in the war. Remember – in history most events have a number of causes.
- Your answer should finish with an overall conclusion. Give your opinion. What was the *main* factor that motivated soldiers to fight? Remember – all causes are not equally important.

STAGE **2** ▶ **Writing each paragraph**

(a) Signposting
Starting each paragraph should be straightforward. Make sure that you make it clear which factor you will be writing about. Think of your opening statement as a signpost for the rest of the paragraph.

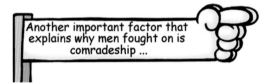

Another important factor that explains why men fought on is comradeship ...

(b) Making the middle section even tastier!
You can make the middle section of your hamburger paragraph stronger by adding: *quotes from source material* and *specific examples* to support your opening argument and its supporting statements. This is called building a *substantiated explanation*. An example is given below.

One of the key factors that motivated soldiers to fight was that they were well cared for.
(opening statement)

The army aimed to keep morale as high as possible. A rotation system made sure that soldiers did not spend too long in the front line.
(supporting statement)

For example, a battalion spent about ten days a month in the trenches. Most soldiers spent more than 60 per cent of their time behind the front lines.
(specific supporting example)

In addition, the army tried to ensure that soldiers were well fed and that they received supplies of everything they needed.
(supporting statement)

An extract from a letter, written in 1916 by Private Bowles supports this. He states that at times soldiers 'lived like lords. Eggs and bacon for breakfast, Welsh rarebit and tea for supper, tinned fruit and cream for tea.'
(supporting source material)

British soldiers did not spend four years of the war in the firing line, or even at the front. Men were regularly **rotated** from the firing line to the support and reserve lines and then back to billets (usually well behind the battle area). The average British soldier would see dreadful things – but not every day.

This system of rotation was very important for morale. The firing line was an unpleasant place to be but the soldier knew that in a few days he would be back in a billet eating hot food and out of immediate danger.

On average, a battalion could expect to spend ten days a month in the trenches. For many soldiers more than 60 per cent of their time was spent behind the lines. Even when a battalion was 'in the line', half of the battalion was usually placed in the reserve trenches. It was unusual to find any battalion spending more than four or five days a month continuously in the firing line.

SOURCE 9 *An extract from a letter by Private J. Bowles, 2nd/16th Battalion Queens Westminster Rifles, written in 1916.*

Last Saturday I was sent to Maroeuil on guard, and I am writing this in the sentry box. We expect to be relieved tonight but I don't care if we are not because this isn't a bad 'stunt' and I must say I have enjoyed myself immensely. I was off duty at 6 p.m. We cooked our own grub and lived like lords. Eggs and bacon for breakfast, Welsh rarebit and tea for supper, tinned fruit and cream for tea.

▲ SOURCE 10 *A cartoon by Captain Bruce Bairnsfather, of the Royal Warwickshire Regiment, who served on the Western Front. The caption was 'The spirit of our troops is excellent'.*

British commanders were fully aware that men who were hungry or not provided with healthy food would not fight effectively. A balanced diet was provided to soldiers. The British army aimed to give its soldiers at the front a daily intake of over 4000 calories (today it is considered that an active adult male needs between 3000 and 3,500 calories a day).

Soldiers rarely went hungry and sick rates were low. Where possible, fresh meat and bread were issued but for many men on the front line meals consisted of corned beef and biscuits. The tea issued was enough to provide each man with six pints of army tea a day. Tobacco was widely available – there were frequent issues of cigarettes and pipe tobacco.

It should be remembered that this diet was often a far better diet than most soldiers were used to at home. There are reports of soldiers gaining 2.5 cm in height and 6 kg in weight within a month of joining the army.

SOURCE 11 *An extract from* Goodbye to all that, *the memoirs of Robert Graves, published in 1929. Graves served in France with the Royal Welsh Fusiliers.*

From the morning of September 24th to the night of October 3rd, I had eight hours' sleep. I kept myself awake and alive by drinking about a bottle of whisky a day. We had no blankets, greycoats, or waterproof sheets, nor any time or material to build new shelters. The rain poured down. Every night we went out to fetch in the dead of other battalions. After the first day or two the corpses swelled and stank. I vomited more than once whilst supervising the carrying.

Interviews with survivors and the memoirs of some soldiers who fought in the war indicate that some men carried on fighting because they actually enjoyed the whole experience. For some soldiers the sense of danger made the war very exciting. They liked the sense of adventure. Other soldiers enjoyed the challenge – they saw war as the ultimate test.

SOURCE 12 *An extract from the diary of Captain Julian Grenfell, First Royal Dragoons, October 1914.*

> Four of us were talking and laughing in the road when a dozen bullets came with a whistle. We all dived for the nearest door which happened to be a lav, and fell over each other yelling with laughter ... I adore war. It's just like a big picnic, without the objectlessness of a picnic. I've never been so well or so happy.

SOURCE 13 *An extract from* Passchendaele and the Somme, *the memoirs of Hugh Quigley, published in 1928.*

Our division had the task of attacking Passchendaele. None of us knew where to go when the barrage began, whether half left or half right. A vague memory of following the shell bursts as long as the smoke was black and halting when it came to white came to me. The whole affair appeared rather good fun. You know how excited one becomes in the midst of danger. I looked at the barrage as something provided for our entertainment. I never enjoyed anything so much in my life – flames, smoke, SOSs, lights, drumming of guns, swishing of bullets – all appeared stage props to set off a majestic scene.

Firm friendships were built by men who fought alongside each other. There was a real sense of 'being in it together'. Soldiers shared the same experiences and helped each other ease the fear and insecurity of life in the trenches.

A shared sense of humour made the suffering more bearable. Soldiers gave comic names to the things around them. A cemetery became a 'rest camp'; going over the top became 'jumping the bags'. Many soldiers were able to laugh not only at themselves and at others, but also at the horrors of war itself.

In the early years of the war **Pals Battalions** were formed in which friends from the same area joined together and served together. Men often served alongside their friends, their neighbours and their workmates. This increased their desire to 'stick it out'. It meant that men had shared interests and that they were determined not to let down their friends or those they could be working with when the war was over. The men had pride in their local area and were determined that their battalion would be better than those from other areas.

▶ **SOURCE 15** *An official photograph. The caption reads 'Bringing in the wounded. This man is actually under heavy fire. He brought in 20 wounded in this manner.'*

SOURCE 14 *An extract from a letter written to home by Private Mudd.*

> Out here dear we're all pals. We share each other's troubles and get each other out of danger. You wouldn't believe the kindness between men out here. It's a lovely thing is friendship out here.

EVIDENCE FILE: Death Rates in the First World War

Four British Lieutenant Generals, twelve Major Generals and 81 Brigadier Generals died or were killed during the war. A further 146 were wounded or taken prisoner. One in every seven British army officers in the Great War was killed, compared to one in every eight of other ranks. This suggests that officers did not hide away in safety well away from the front line.

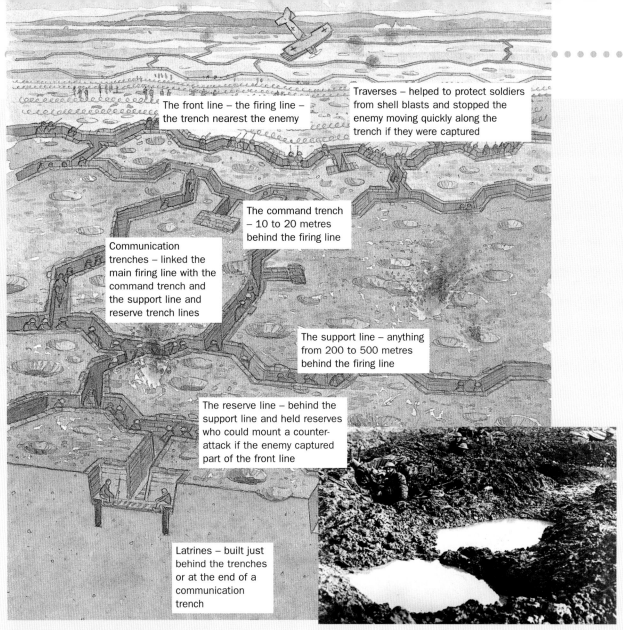

The front line – the firing line – the trench nearest the enemy

Traverses – helped to protect soldiers from shell blasts and stopped the enemy moving quickly along the trench if they were captured

The command trench – 10 to 20 metres behind the firing line

Communication trenches – linked the main firing line with the command trench and the support line and reserve trench lines

The support line – anything from 200 to 500 metres behind the firing line

The reserve line – behind the support line and held reserves who could mount a counter-attack if the enemy captured part of the front line

Latrines – built just behind the trenches or at the end of a communication trench

Parapet – A bank of earth thrown up in front of the trench itself to allow a man to fire from the trench with a rest for his elbows and as much protection from incoming fire as possible. Parapets were required to stop a German rifle bullet. They were therefore four to five feet thick.

Parados – Was the equivalent of the parapet but behind the trench. It was designed to stop bullets carrying on to the next line of trenches and to shield men from the blast of a shell exploding behind them.

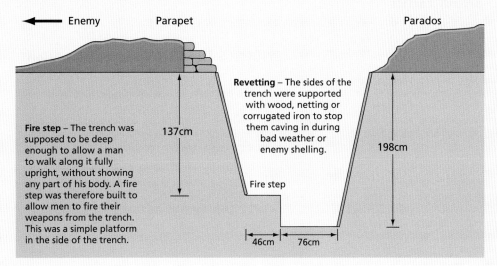

Enemy   Parapet   Parados

Fire step – The trench was supposed to be deep enough to allow a man to walk along it fully upright, without showing any part of his body. A fire step was therefore built to allow men to fire their weapons from the trench. This was a simple platform in the side of the trench.

137cm

Revetting – The sides of the trench were supported with wood, netting or corrugated iron to stop them caving in during bad weather or enemy shelling.

Fire step

198cm

46cm   76cm

In the early stages of the First World War, soldiers dug trenches where and when they could. They used drainage ditches, banks, hedges and dips in the ground. Once the conflict settled down into siege warfare the trenches were improved with bunkers, dugouts, drains and fire steps. The diagram on the left shows the ideal design for a British trench. Not all met this standard – as the photograph above shows.

EVIDENCE FILE: Medical Care

Each battalion (usually made up of 700–1000 men) had one Regimental Medical Officer (who was a qualified doctor), with a team of medical orderlies and stretcher-bearers.

A Regimental Aid Post (RAP) was usually set up in the reserve line. If the British were about to attack it was set up closer to the front line. A lightly wounded soldier could be attended to quickly and sent back to his company. If a soldier was more seriously wounded he would be treated at the RAP then sent to the Advanced Dressing Station, positioned further away from the front line. Medical care and survival rates improved dramatically as the war went on.

EVIDENCE FILE: Attitudes of the Generals and Commanding Officers

- Generals had to be close enough to the fighting to know what was going on. Generals regularly visited the front lines. Battalions in the line would see their brigade commander at least once a week. Brigade and divisional commanders were somewhere in the front lines at least once a day.

- Commanders such as Field Marshal Sir Douglas Haig often worked for eighteen hours a day. He also remained popular with many of the soldiers. Haig played an important role in planning the series of victories that finally broke the German army in 1918.

EVIDENCE FILE: British Tactics

- The Battle of the Somme (1916) is often presented as a 'pointless' attack. However, in 1916, it was crucial that the British helped to relieve pressure on French forces under attack at Verdun. The Somme sector was originally held by six German divisions. The Germans were forced to employ 69 divisions in this area during the battle. If these divisions had been free to attack at Verdun the French may well have been defeated and knocked out of the war.

- British tactics did improve during the war. Some historians argue that the autumn of 1918 saw the greatest series of victories in the British army's entire history. By August 1918, Field Marshal Sir Douglas Haig's forces were using tanks, aircraft, motorised machine gun units, wireless and aircraft effectively. Nearly 200,000 German prisoners were captured.

EVIDENCE FILE: A Different Generation

Soldiers were brought up in a different Britain from the one that exists today. Many of the soldiers who fought in the war would have been used to seeing death; used to seeing parents and relatives die at a relatively young age from diseases that today are preventable.

Generally speaking, people at the time were tougher because they came from a harsher environment. The things that they saw were not always as much of a shock as we may think. This was a generation that was used to living through hardship.

- The army had high standards of cleanliness and hygiene and these were strictly enforced. Rats were a problem in the early days of the war so a great effort was made to remove rubbish and scraps of food.

- In order to tackle the problem of lice, men had their uniforms fumigated, washed and ironed when they came out of the line.

- Another problem for soldiers was that of trench foot. The winter of 1914–1915 was exceptionally cold and wet. Trenches, especially in Flanders, often became flooded. This led to large numbers of men suffering from trench foot.

Trench foot was caused by a lack of circulation in the feet and the legs. If untreated it led to gangrene and amputation. However, the army introduced a number of measures to prevent soldiers suffering from trench foot. Soldiers were provided with thigh-high rubber waders and whale oil, which was rubbed into the feet before entering the trenches. They were encouraged to change their socks regularly and a greater effort was made to drain trenches effectively (mechanical pumps were provided later in the war). By the middle of 1915 trench foot had been almost totally eliminated.

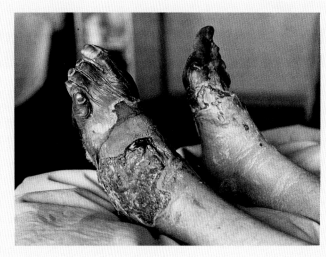

When they were not on front line duty soldiers were sent back to billets. These were usually quite a distance from the front line and were generally civilian houses in villages. However, there were times when men were put up in stables, tents or huts erected by the Royal Engineers. Here men would recover from the fighting, undergo training, eat freshly prepared food, have hot baths or showers and get new clean clothing.

Sometimes the billets were shelled but they were usually relatively safe and comfortable. If a battalion was not in reserve or on stand-by for a move, soldiers were allowed to visit nearby villages and towns. Football matches and concerts were organised for troops.

EVIDENCE FILE: Army Discipline

Many people believe that the military justice system was cruel and that large numbers of men were quickly sent to their death, without any sympathy for the reasons for their behaviour. However, in all cases the accused was offered the services of a defending officer. Some soldiers chose to defend themselves.

- Five million men served in the British army; 3,080 death sentences were passed during the war. Of these 3,080 men, 346 were executed. Nearly 90 per cent had their death

sentences suspended, or changed to imprisonment or field punishment.

- Charges of cowardice were brought at 551 trials. Eighteen soldiers were executed for cowardice.

- Four hundred and forty-nine men were sentenced to death for sleeping at their post between 1914 and 1918 but in only two cases were the sentences carried out.

A quick history of the Second World War

When and why did the Second World War turn against Hitler and his allies?

In late 1939 a very small British army went to France and took up the positions it had held in 1914 – on the left of the French army and close to the Channel coast. Both the British and French armies expected to fight a war in trenches much as they had in the First World War. They were confident, and outnumbered the Germans in men, aircraft and tanks. Nothing of significance happened over the winter of 1939–1940. Each side dropped leaflets urging the other to surrender.

Then on 10 May 1940 all hell broke loose. The Germans had no intention of fighting a re-run of the First World War and attacked using revolutionary new tactics to force France to surrender and the British army to return home. This was the start of a disastrous few years for the countries fighting against Hitler and his Italian and Japanese allies.

Yet by May 1945 Germany lay in ruins. The Soviet, US and British armies stood triumphant on her territory and received her unconditional surrender. Hitler was dead along with three and a half million other Germans.

How and when did the tide of war turn? Was there a pivotal moment that sealed the fate of Hitler and his allies or did the balance gradually move? Your task is to try and identify when and why the balance shifted against Hitler and his allies.

> **ACTIVITY**
>
> **Step 1**
> Gain a quick overview of the war. Read the Key Events cards on pages 68–72. Can you spot any possible turning points in the war?

Significant battles and events of the Second World War

Occupation of Norway and Denmark

April 1940

The British and French planned to respond to the attack on Poland by cutting off Germany from her vital supplies of iron ore by placing mines (floating bombs) in Scandinavian waters. Hitler ordered German troops into action and Denmark and Norway were immediately invaded. The British and French landed troops in Norway but these were defeated very rapidly and were evacuated by the Royal Navy. Germany had secured the vital resources of iron ore and timber and was in complete control of both Norway's and Denmark's wealth and military bases.

May 1940

Blitzkrieg

The British and French were taken completely by surprise when the German armies adopted a bold new plan devised by General Erich von Manstein for the invasion of France. Instead of fighting in long, extended lines as in the First World War, Manstein concentrated all of Germany's tanks in powerful Panzer or armoured divisions. When supported by terrifying dive bombing aircraft these were capable of punching a hole through the enemy's lines and rushing onwards into the undefended areas behind the enemy army.

In May 1940, German tanks smashed through the Ardennes forest, crossed the River Meuse and drove on to the sea. The French armies in the north were split, trapped and demoralised. The British lost faith in their French allies and prepared to evacuate France through the one port remaining in their control – Dunkirk. The Germans felt invincible. In weeks they had done what the Kaiser's armies in the First World War had not been able to do in years – smash through the enemy's lines at minimal cost. This was known as Blitzkrieg or 'lightning war'.

Dunkirk

May – June 1940

Between 27 May and 4 June 1940, 338,000 British and French troops were evacuated to Britain from the beaches of Dunkirk in France. In order to bring the soldiers off the beaches the British appealed for owners of small boats to sail to France. These were then used to ferry troops from the sand out to the waiting large ships of the Royal Navy. Without this evacuation Britain could not have continued the war. But the British soldiers were forced to leave behind almost all of their equipment. France surrendered on 25 June. German forces were now only 22 miles from Britain. Dunkirk was a defeat and a humiliation for Britain and France.

July–September 1940

The Battle of Britain

Goering, Reichsmarschall of Hitler's air force, boasted that he could bomb Britain into surrender after the Dunkirk evacuation. He turned his planes on Britain – at first bombing in daylight. However, Goering had underestimated the British RAF. Fighting over their own territory, the RAF's modern fighter planes – flown by pilots of many nations – were directed by radar against the German bomber formations. The RAF had no problem with fuel supply. In contrast, German fighters could only stay over London for ten minutes before their fuel became dangerously low.

Even so Goering nearly won. His attacks on British fighter airfields seriously damaged the RAF's ability to fight on. It was only Hitler's order to focus the bombing attacks on London that perhaps saved Britain. By the end of 1940, 13,596 Londoners had died as a result of air attacks but the RAF was able to fight on. On 15 September 1940, 56 German planes were shot down and Goering had to abandon daylight bombing. Germany had tried to force a British surrender and had failed. Churchill said of the British fighter pilots: 'Never in the field of human conflict was so much owed by so many to so few.'

Lend Lease

In February 1941 President Roosevelt of the USA, despite the fact that his country was officially neutral, managed to get the US congress to agree to supply weapons, industrial equipment and supplies to Britain on a credit agreement known as Lend Lease. This meant that Britain would be supplied by US factories immediately but would only have to pay after the war was won.

Under Lend Lease, Britain (and later the Soviet Union) was able to gain access to over 50 *billion* dollars' worth of goods. This bought 17 million rifles, 315,000 cannons, 87,000 tanks, 2,434,000 motor vehicles and 296,000 planes. After Lend Lease, Britain was never short of equipment as the USA was the most dominant industrial power in the world.

'Operation Barbarossa': Hitler's invasion of the Soviet Union

Hitler had signed a pact of friendship with the communist Soviet Union in August 1939 – largely to allow himself a free hand in attacking Poland. Anybody studying Hitler's previous speeches would have been amazed by this pact of friendship. Hitler had always detested communism, which he saw as a Jewish idea.

By 1941 Hitler felt powerful enough to move against communism. Without warning, in June 1941, a German force of three million men invaded Russia. Progress was rapid as the surprised and unprepared Soviets retreated in chaos. By the winter of 1941 German forces had taken a million prisoners and were at the gates of Moscow. The bitter Russian winter halted the Germans but it seemed that once the thaw came nothing could prevent Russia's collapse. Already, Germany had captured huge amounts of rich agricultural land and had destroyed much of Russia's industry.

SOMEONE IS TAKING SOMEONE FOR A WALK

Greece, Yugoslavia and North Africa invaded

Germany and Italy invaded Yugoslavia and later attacked Greece. The Greek army and the British and Empire troops were sent in as support but they were defeated. Once again vast amounts of equipment was lost as British troops were evacuated by sea.

In North Africa German troops under the famous General Rommel had landed and were advancing rapidly towards Egypt, which was

controlled by the British. If they were successful, the Germans would gain control of vast oil reserves and (by capturing the Suez Canal) could cut off Britain from its Eastern empire and India. In June 1942 the British fortress of Tobruk fell to the Germans. The road to Egypt was wide open and German forces seemed unstoppable.

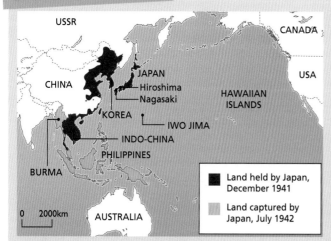

■	Land held by Japan, December 1941
▨	Land captured by Japan, July 1942

Pearl Harbor

During the first three decades of the twentieth century, Japan emerged as a growing industrial power, looking to expand and gain control of East Asia. Since 1931, Japan had been taking advantage of China's weakness and had been fighting a brutal war for territory with that country. In 1941 France and the Netherlands were occupied by Nazi Germany, and Britain was fighting for its very survival. Japan took advantage of this by occupying French Indo-China (later to be called Vietnam).

The USA responded by refusing to supply Japan with oil. On 27 September 1941 Japan signed an alliance with Nazi Germany and Fascist Italy. On 7 December 1941, whilst talks with the USA were still in progress, Japan attacked, without warning, the US naval base at Pearl Harbor. It was a peacetime Sunday morning and the US fleet was far from on full alert. Four battleships were sunk and 28 ships were damaged with the loss of 2,350 dead. The USA responded by declaring war on Japan.

The US public were still far from convinced they should fight Germany as well as Japan. Luckily for Britain, Adolf Hitler solved the problem by declaring war on the USA in support of his Japanese ally. He was now at war with the world's largest empire (Britain's); its largest country (the Soviet Union); and its richest country (USA).

At first the war went well for the Japanese. By early 1942 the Japanese had taken over much of the Pacific with its rich resources and were on the verge of invading India and Australia. US and British forces were in retreat everywhere.

El Alamein

By a combination of good equipment, fighting skill and dedication, General Rommel had come very close to defeating the British and Empire troops in North Africa. By the autumn of 1942 Rommel had been stopped 150 miles west of Cairo as his men became exhausted and his equipment ran short or wore out. The Royal Navy in the Mediterranean had cut off much of Rommel's supplies.

In contrast to Rommel's weakness, the British Army's strength was increasing as vast quantities of US tanks and other equipment were arriving through Lend Lease. Also, a new and confident commander, General Montgomery, had been appointed commander of the British and Empire troops of the 8th Army – by now twice as strong in men and three times as strong in tanks as Rommel's army.

A brilliantly planned attack through minefields dislodged Rommel's men and sent them into retreat. Finally, the Germans were trapped between the British and Empire troops advancing from El Alamein and a US army advancing from Tunisia. 275,000 German troops surrendered, but Rommel escaped back to Germany. Now both the British route to India and the oil supplies of the Middle East were safe from German control.

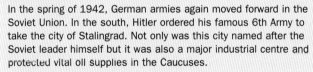

The Battle of the Atlantic

Despite being poorly prepared with only 20 U-boats and crews at the start of the war, the Germans quickly realised that Britain's sea supply lines and trade routes were very vulnerable to attack. The U-boat fleet was expanded quickly and organised to attack convoys of ships going to and from Britain. The Germans had the use of bases on the French Atlantic coast.

Results at first were spectacular as the U-boats learned to avoid British detection devices by attacking on the surface. A U-boat's low profile was very hard to pick out in the stormy grey Atlantic Ocean. In April 1941 alone, over 700,000 tonnes of shipping and cargoes were lost. This represented a loss of more than 70 ships carrying vital supplies. It seemed as if Britain's economy would collapse and she would be starved into surrender. Churchill said after the war that: 'The only thing that ever really frightened me during the war was the U-boat peril.'

By autumn 1941 things began to improve. Large numbers of US warships joined British ships on convoy protection duty. Gradually the use of radar helped ships and newly developed long-range aircraft to spot U-boats more easily. By the end of 1943 the U-boats were effectively defeated. Approximately 90 per cent of men who served in U-boats were killed in action.

Stalingrad

In the spring of 1942, German armies again moved forward in the Soviet Union. In the south, Hitler ordered his famous 6th Army to take the city of Stalingrad. Not only was this city named after the Soviet leader himself but it was also a major industrial centre and protected vital oil supplies in the Caucuses.

A bitter hand-to-hand struggle ensued in what rapidly became a ruined city. In the end, the German army found itself surrounded and cut off from help just as winter set in. After a terrible siege of three months, over 90,000 German soldiers surrendered. This was no ordinary defeat: it was a catastrophe. More German equipment was lost in this one battle than was possessed by the entire British army. From this point on there was never less than 65 per cent of the whole German army fighting the Russians. The British and Americans were facing the other 35 per cent.

The Battle of Kursk

Furious because of the defeat at Stalingrad and in an attempt to capture the city of Kursk, Hitler threw his latest generation of tanks into a desperate attack against the Soviets. The Soviets had been warned by British code breakers that an attack was imminent and had found out the exact date of the attack from German prisoners. Hitler insisted on mounting the attack against the advice of his generals and launched 2,700 tanks at the Russians – who countered with over 3000 (albeit smaller) tanks of their own.

This remains the largest tank battle of all time. Many of the new German tanks broke down and many more were smashed by the Soviet defence lines. The attack failed totally. Germany lost so many men and tanks that it was never again in a position to mount a major attack in the east. After Kursk, the Germans were in steady retreat towards Germany. By the end of 1943 Soviet troops had crossed the Polish border.

The Burma Campaign

By June 1942 the Japanese had seized the whole of Burma and had begun to advance towards India. They seemed invincible in this type of jungle warfare.

Fighting took place in dreadful conditions. Malaria and other diseases were as much of a hazard to life as wounds caused in battle. However, by coordinated attacks and inspired leadership, combined operations between British and Indian troops, along with US, Chinese and some Dutch forces, began to drive the Japanese back. The Japanese lost approximately 144,000 men defending Burma.

6 June 1944

D-Day

Stalin – the Soviet leader – had been pressing for the British and Americans to invade German-occupied France. As the Soviets advanced in the east and the British and Americans in the west, this would squash the German armies from both sides and would take considerable pressure off the hard-pressed Soviet armies.

Invasion of France was no easy matter. By 1944, the coast was heavily defended and a successful invasion would require transporting large numbers of troops across an unpredictable English Channel and landing them in sufficient strength to stand up to German counter attacks. After careful planning lasting several years, on 6 June 1944, 4000 Allied ships landed 156,000 British, American, Canadian and French soldiers on the coast of France. Resistance was tough but by August they had crushed the German armies who began retreating towards Germany. It seemed possible that the war would be over by Christmas 1944.

December 1944–May 1945

The Battle of the Bulge

As a last gamble in the west, Hitler gathered what remained of his tank forces and ordered an attack on the British and Americans who were advancing towards Germany. Only a heroic defence in the snow by American parachute troops, plus a German shortage of fuel, brought the Germans to a halt. Once the weather cleared, the German tanks were smashed by Allied rocket-firing aircraft. 19,000 US troops died, but the Germans had not broken through and had lost most of their remaining tanks and effective troops.

The Battle for Berlin

The British and Americans agreed to let the Soviets attack Berlin. Berlin was already badly damaged by massed Allied air raids, but in the fighting it was reduced to rubble. Over 90 per cent of the city was destroyed and 100,000 people died. Adolf Hitler had remained in Berlin and, after marrying his long-term mistress, Eva Braun, he committed suicide on 30 April.

On 1 May 1945 the Soviet red flag was raised above the German Parliament building, the Reichstag. Fighting stopped in the city on 2 May. German forces across the whole of Europe surrendered unconditionally and all fighting had stopped by 8 May 1945.

Hiroshima and Nagasaki

From 1943 onwards, the US forces gradually forced the Japanese back across the Pacific. Island after island was recaptured but at enormous cost to the invaders. By August 1945 the US was faced with the daunting prospect of mounting an invasion of Japan. Japan was completely exhausted by the war but surrender did not look likely and sections of the military seemed determined to fight to the death.

President Truman took the decision to drop the atomic bomb on the hitherto undamaged city of Hiroshima. Despite the destruction of the city and the immediate loss of 70,000 lives, Japanese surrender was still not forthcoming. A second bomb was dropped on Nagasaki three days later, with similar casualties and destruction. Finally Japan surrendered on 15 August 1945.

6 and 9 August 1945

When did the Second World War turn against Hitler and his allies?

Step 2

Now you have an overview of the war it is time to try and work out when the Second World War turned against Hitler and his allies.

Work in threes.

- Take a broad flat ruler. Tape two pencils together, one above the other, and then tape them to the centre of the ruler at 90 degrees. These pencils will act as the balance point. One side of the ruler represents battles won by the Axis Powers (Germany, Japan and Italy). The other side represents battles won by the Allies.

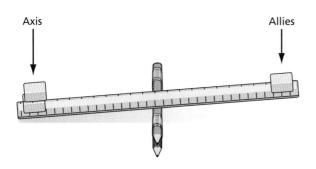

- After debate and discussion your group will award each battle a number of counters (or sweets such as Polos) *up to a maximum of three* according to your judgement. The more important the battle's effect the more counters you will award. You are looking for each battle's *contribution to its own side's progress in the war as a whole.*
- Counters awarded will be placed on the end of the ruler allocated to the side that won that particular battle. For example, if the Allies win a battle and you award that battle three counters, those three counters placed on the Allied end of the ruler.

Pay attention to three broad factors when judging a battle's significance (or weight) in determining its side's progress in the war.

Do not feel that one counter needs equate directly to one of these factors. If a battle has huge military significance, for example, you could award all three counters for that alone if you wished.

1 Military importance

How much did this victory boost its side's chances on the actual battlefield in that particular theatre of war? How far did it damage the enemy armed forces in terms of casualties, loss of equipment or loss of an advantageous position?

2 Economic importance

How much did this victory boost a side's access to vital resources, trade or supportive allies?

3 Effect on morale

How far did this victory boost the confidence of both its fighting forces and civilian populations?

Use pages 68–72 as a starting point. If you really feel effects were split or victory is debatable you can award counters to both sides – but this will not be common. For the most part the counters for a battle will go to the side that won that actual battle.

Germany, Italy and Japan lost the war and, at some point, your balance will tip against them even though at first the ruler will seem heavily weighted on their side. Make a note of when and why the balance tips.

Does it stay tipped or does another battle bring it back?

When it seems clear that the balance has finally swung in the Allies' favour look at which battles have done this. Is any one battle responsible?

Work together try to answer the Big Question:

When and why did the Second World War turn against Hitler and his allies?

Your explanation must be less than 200 words.

DOING HISTORY: Interpretations

Why does the way that the Second World War is presented still matter?

The Second World War may have ended many years ago but it can still cause arguments. You have already seen how different people tell different stories of the past by including some events or evidence and leaving out or downplaying others. Interpretations are determined by the attitudes and beliefs of the person creating the interpretation. So the attitudes and beliefs of the country someone comes from can be a reason why interpretations differ.

DISCUSS

Look at the three case studies below and opposite. Why do you think interpretations of the Second World War vary so much from country to country?

Case Study 1: Arguments over the key turning points of the war and who played the key role in defeating Germany and her allies

When it comes to debates about which countries played the key role in defeating Germany and her allies, arguments can become heated.

Winston Churchill once said: *'History will be kind to me because I intend to write it.'* There was some truth in this statement. Soon after the end of the Second World War, Churchill published his own history of the conflict. It had a major influence on how the story of the conflict was portrayed in the Western world. In his history, Britain played a crucial role and El Alamein was seen as one of the key battles.

Many Americans see D-Day, rather than El Alamein, as the key turning point of the war. They also see their role as being crucial, both in terms of the defeat of Japan and Germany.

Quite clearly D-Day was a decisive turning point of the war. Its success meant that Hitler's Germany was fighting a land war on two fronts. Before then he could always support his forces in the east by drafting replacements from the relatively unused occupation army in Western Europe. After D-Day he was fighting a desperate battle for survival in both east and west. It gave the Russians much needed relief. America played the key role in the west. The British army deployed 28 army divisions compared to the American army's 99 divisions.

Many Russians would argue that their army played the key role in Germany's defeat; the efforts of America and Britain were of secondary importance. They would argue that the Americans, for example, arrived too late and in too few numbers to play the key role.

However, they may choose to overlook the fact that, until the German attack on the Soviet Union in June 1941, there was a Nazi–Soviet pact that allowed both countries to take over territory.

D-Day was spectacular but of secondary importance in the European war. Its significance has been overstated by British and American historians trying to underplay Russia's massive contribution to the defeat of Hitler's Germany. During the conflict there was never less than two-thirds of the German army fighting the Russians. The British and Americans between them took on the other one-third – and then only after the Russians had destroyed German morale! The Battle of Stalingrad was the most truly significant battle in changing the balance of the war. A German army of 250,000 men was destroyed and more equipment was captured than was possessed by the whole British army! About 156,000 troops were involved in the D-Day invasion and by then the German army was well on the way to total defeat. It accelerated Germany's defeat but did not cause it. Remember, 75–80 per cent of all German losses were inflicted on the Eastern front.

Case Study 2: Disagreements over when the war started

Countries even argue about the dating of the war. People in Britain and France tend to date the war from September 1939. For the Russians, the 'real war' began in June 1941; for the Americans, December 1941.

Some Japanese date the Second World War from 1931, when their troops occupied Manchuria, a border province of China. By 1937, the conflict between Japan and China had spread to all of eastern China. It is estimated that in this war two million soldiers from China were killed and 1.7 million wounded. In addition, around 15 million Chinese civilians also died between 1937 and 1945, killed mainly by starvation and exposure rather than by direct military action.

Case Study 3: Different countries – different interpretations

In 2004, the BBC worked with US, French and German broadcasters to produce a drama-documentary on D-Day and the Allied invasion of Normandy. But audiences in different countries saw different versions of the film. Each country chose to edit the film to suit their national audiences.

THE TIMES 17 MARCH 2004
BBC Film Sets Record Straight on British Role in D-Day

As can be seen by the headline, the BBC felt that it was important to show that British, Canadian and Commonwealth troops made up nearly 40 per cent of the Allied invasion force. In the past, many Hollywood films had given the impression that it was an almost exclusively American invasion force.

The French version emphasised the role played by resistance fighters. A key part of the film shown in France was the execution by the Germans of 80 resistance fighters at a prison in Caen on D-Day itself.

The Germans concentrated more on the decisions taken by Field Marshal Rommel and the experiences and fighting qualities of their veterans.

How would you tell the story?

ACTIVITY

Planning your own D-Day programme

The struggle for superiority in the early days of the Allied invasion of Normandy is shown powerfully in the accounts of some of the men who fought there (pages 76–77, Sources 16–26). Remember, though, that on both sides hundreds of thousands of individuals were involved from many different nations. Your task is to plan the conclusion to the programme.

What does the evidence tell us about both armies?

Step 1

From the sources given on pages 76–77 look for the following in both armies, Allied and German:

Code	Evidence of
C	Courage
F	Fear
S	Fighting skill
I	Inexperience or poor tactics
E	Effective equipment

Every time you identify one of the qualities from the table, put its code letter and a few words of explanation in a grid such as the one below. Sometimes an act will merit two or more code letters, for example:

German army	Allied army
F, S and **C** – **Source 26**: The attack by Michael Wittmann on the British tanks at Villers-Bocage	**C** – **Source 24**: Sergeant Major Hollis' capture of the pillbox and 25 prisoners **I** – The US advance down a road instead of across fields

Step 2

Now count the numbers of each letter shown for each side. For example do the Allies have most Cs? Discuss what this tells us about the strengths and weaknesses of each side.

Step 3

What conclusions do you draw?

Plan the final part of the documentary programme. Keep it short. In reality you may only have 50 words to leave viewers with a clear impression of the big story.

The evidence

All sources are from *D-Day and the Battle for Normandy 1944* by Max Hastings, published in 1984.

All sources are from *D-Day and the Battle for Normandy 1944* by Max Hastings, published in 1984.

SOURCE 16

Between June and November 1944, a staggering 26 per cent of American soldiers in combat divisions were treated for some form of a battle fatigue (mental stress caused by combat).

SOURCE 17

Each day Sergeant Helmut Gunther, of 17th Panzer-Grenadiers (German) watched his company whittled away without hope of replacement. All these old friends and many more were gone. 'I used to think "What a poor pig I am fighting with my back to the wall". ' Yet Gunther's self-pity was mixed with astonishment that the survivors stood the strain and the losses so well, and fought on. He was astounded the Americans did not break through their line in early July. His own company was reduced to 20 men out of 120, yet when he sought permission to withdraw 40 metres it was refused.

SOURCE 18

The 12th battalion, Parachute Regiment (British), in a brilliant sacrificial battle, gained Breville at a cost of 141 men out of 160 who advanced. The German defenders were reduced from 564 men to 146 before withdrawing.

SOURCE 19

A lone American soldier rounded the corner of the road, helmet tilted back. Behind him Schinker (a German soldier) could see long files of enemy infantrymen. Schinker marvelled, because if the enemy had advanced across fields instead of along the road 'they could have walked into the village we were defending'. Instead 'it was as if they were out for a Sunday stroll'. Jupp asked, 'Do I start now?' and settled over the butt of his MG42. The hail of German fire scythed through the files of approaching men. It stopped quite simply, when the two guns had fired all of their ammunition. In the silence that followed the defenders could hear wounded Americans screaming for help.

SOURCE 20

When Corporal John Kelly (American soldier) found his platoon pinned down by machine-gun fire from a German pillbox he crawled forward to place a charge beneath its firing slit. He returned to his own men to find that the charge had failed to detonate so he went back with another one. This blew the barrels off the German guns allowing Kelly to climb the slope a third time to throw grenades in through the rear door.

SOURCE 21   *Interview with British tank commander.*

What tank do the Germans have most of?
Panthers. The Panther can slice through our tanks like a knife through butter.
How does one of our (British) tanks get a Panther?
It creeps up on it. When it reaches close quarters the British gunner tries to bounce a shot off the bottom of the Panther's turret. If he's lucky it then goes through the thin armour above the Panther driver's head.
Has anybody ever done it?
Yes, Davis in C squadron. He's back at headquarters now trying to recover his nerve.

SOURCE 22

For the German soldier in the first few weeks of the Normandy battle, actions usually took the form of: a rush to the threatened sector; a fierce and expert defence against clumsy Allied tactics; growing casualties as the enemy's massed firepower was brought to bear; and at last a retreat of a few hundred yards to the next line to be equally doggedly defended.

There was nothing cowardly about the performance of the British army in Normandy. But it proved too much to ask a citizen army in the fifth year of war, with the certainty of victory in the distance, to display the same sacrificial courage as some of Hitler's troops, faced with the collapse of everything that in the perversion of Nazism they held dear. Brigadier Williams said, 'We were always very aware of the belief held by our men: "Let metal do it rather than flesh. Waste all the ammunition you like but not our lives." '

SOURCE 23 *Report from a commanding officer of a British regiment.*

Three days running, one of my majors has been killed or seriously wounded because I have ordered him to, in effect, stop the men running under attack from mortar bombs.

SOURCE 24 *Interview with British Sergeant Major Hollis V.C.*

And Major Lofthouse said to me, 'There is a pillbox there, Sergeant Major.' Well when he said that, I saw it. It was very well camouflaged and I saw these guns moving around in the slits. So I got my sten gun and I rushed at it just spraying it hosepipe fashion. They fired back at me and they missed. I don't know whether they were more panic-stricken than me but they must have been, and I got on top of it and I threw a grenade through the slit and it must have sickened them. I went round the back and went inside and there were two dead, quite a lot of prisoners (25). They were quite willing to forget about the war.

SOURCE 25 *A letter home from a German soldier that was never posted.*

My Irmi love,
… It doesn't look very good; that would be saying too much, but nevertheless there is no reason to paint too black a picture. You know the high spirits with which I face things which allow me to stroll through difficult situations with some optimism and a lot of luck. Above all there are so many good and elite divisions in our encirclement that we must get through somehow. The most difficult thing has been and remains the enemy air force … it is there at dawn, all day, at night, dominating the roads.

DISCUSS

1 Imagine that TV companies in the United States, Britain and Russia are making a documentary series on the whole Second World War. Which events would each of the TV companies choose to concentrate on? Choose three key events from pages 68–72.
2 If you were producing the documentary series what events would you focus on?
3 Do think that the way that the Second World War is presented will still matter to people and cause arguments in 100 years' time?

SOURCE 26 *Account of the power of the German 'Tiger' tank in the skilled hands of Michael Wittmann.*

In all, attacking alone in his huge 'Tiger' tank, Hauptsturmfuhrer Michael Wittmann (of the German Waffen SS) destroyed some 12 British tanks in his attack of 13 June at the village of Villers-Bocage. He had more or less single-handedly prevented the advance of the British 7th Armoured Division.

Wittmann himself was killed in his Tiger tank almost two months later in an ambush by a number of British tanks.

Why did civilians in the Second World War find themselves at greater risk of death than ever before?

The First World War was mainly fought between soldiers on the ground. Only 5 per cent of deaths in the First World War were civilian deaths, and casualties from air attacks were rare. During the Second World War the way that wars were fought changed. Civilians became 'military' targets. More civilians died than soldiers. In Britain, Germany and Japan, civilians living in their own homes found themselves at greater risk than ever before as both sides launched bombing campaigns on enemy towns and cities. In this enquiry you will compare the experiences of civilians who came under attack from the air and debate whether these attacks were justified.

DISCUSS

Look at the lists of names below.
- Do you notice anything unusual that gives you a clue as to how these people died?
- Can you form a hypothesis about the kind of building they might have died in?
- What do you think is likely to have happened to these children?
- Why might the date of death be surprising?

In the middle of East London's Docklands stands the small green square of Poplar Park. At the centre of this beautifully kept park is a stone war memorial showing an angel above a square column of names. It looks like countless other memorials to the dead sailors, soldiers and airmen of the First and Second World Wars.

But this memorial is different. It shows no weapons or military equipment, yet closer inspection reveals that it does indeed commemorate eighteen dead people from the First World War. All died at least 250 miles from any battlefield on the same day: Wednesday 13 June 1917. However, they did die from enemy action and they died together.

GRACE JONES
AGED FIVE YEARS
ROSE MARTIN
AGED TEN YEARS
GEORGE MORRIS
AGED SIX YEARS
EDWIN C.W.POWELL
AGED TWELVE YEARS
ROBERT STIMSON
AGED FIVE YEARS
ELIZABETH TAYLOR
AGED FIVE YEARS
ROSE TUFFIN
AGED FIVE YEARS
FRANK WINGFIELD
AGED FIVE YEARS
FLORENCE L.WOODS
AGED FIVE YEARS

IN MEMORY OF
18 CHILDREN
WHO WERE KILLED

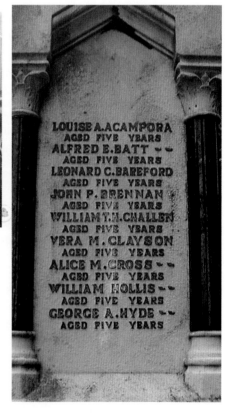

LOUISE A.ACAMPORA
AGED FIVE YEARS
ALFRED E.BATT
AGED FIVE YEARS
LEONARD C.BAREFORD
AGED FIVE YEARS
JOHN P.BRENNAN
AGED FIVE YEARS
WILLIAM T.H.CHALLEN
AGED FIVE YEARS
VERA M.CLAYSON
AGED FIVE YEARS
ALICE M.CROSS
AGED FIVE YEARS
WILLIAM HOLLIS
AGED FIVE YEARS
GEORGE A.HYDE
AGED FIVE YEARS

The story behind the memorial

During the First World War, British civilians found themselves under direct attack from the air as the German navy flew huge hydrogen airships, called Zeppelins, to bomb England by night. However, bomb loads were too light and accuracy too poor for these slow, lumbering craft to cause any serious threat to Britain's war effort. In 1915, one of the first raids had hit a house in Sheringham on the Norfolk coast with no more effect than blowing up its cooker! Later raids did cause loss of life but by 1917 increasingly efficient British aircraft and ground-based guns had made further airship raids impossible. It was not uncommon for parents to take young children outside during the last Zeppelin raids to watch as searchlights lit up the great crafts as they flew overhead.

Towards the end of the war a more serious threat to British civilians emerged. The Germans developed a fleet of aeroplanes capable of travelling at high speed to and from London whilst carrying a relatively large load (roughly 2000 kg) of high-explosive bombs. These aeroplanes – known as 'Gotha' bombers – were the first to be designed purely for long-range bombing over the enemy heartland.

On Wednesday 13 June 1917 at 11.40 a.m. onlookers in London's East End were able to see a dozen or so big aeroplanes 'scintillating like so many huge silver dragonflies in the sky'. The bombers were attacking the nearby London Docks but that morning one of their bombs found a very different target: it hit Upper North Street School in Poplar. The bomb travelled down through the roof and two floors before exploding in the infants' class in

the school's basement. The caretaker had raised the alarm on first hearing the planes but, in the absence of proper shelters, the children and their teachers had been able to do nothing more than hide under the desks – a woefully inadequate response. Sixteen five-year-olds died that day. Among them was the caretaker's child.

The newspapers led a huge propaganda outcry against what was portrayed as 'German barbarism'. £1,400 – a great deal of money in those days – was raised in a tide of public sympathy. The memorial was built that still stands in Poplar Park. But very soon the British had developed and used their own heavy bombers. The way that wars were fought was about to change.

A new era?

Ten years after the bombing of Upper North Street School the head of the new British Royal Air Force spoke in chilling and remarkably accurate terms about air attack.

SOURCE 27 *Sir Hugh Trenchard, 1927 (adapted from a quotation in* Dresden *by Frederick Taylor).*

This new form of warfare will extend to the whole community the horrors and suffering up until now largely confined to the battlefield. But there is not the slightest doubt that in the next war both sides will send their aircraft without scruple to bomb those objectives which they consider the most suitable.

DISCUSS

- Is it legitimate to risk civilian deaths when attacking by air a vital industrial or military target?
- Why might one country deliberately target civilians in an enemy town or city?

The civilians' story: Air attack during the Second World War

To study the terrible development of air attack against civilians in the Second World War, we will look at the experiences of civilians in three hard-hit cities: London, Dresden and Hiroshima. These were not the only cities that suffered greatly from air attack but each is especially significant in some way.

In Britain many towns and cities suffered greatly from enemy bombing. During the Second World War, 60,595 people were killed in air raids in Britain. Nearly half of those killed lived in London.

Virtually every major German city was hit by air attack. Berlin, for example, was bombed 363 times and saw at least 50,000 of its citizens killed. However, the experience of the citizens of Dresden as they underwent a terrible firestorm on the night of 13–14 February 1945 is seen as particularly horrific and controversial. Approximately 25,000 died in one night in the city.

Japanese cities were also heavily bombed. More people died in Tokyo on a night of US firebombing than were killed by atomic attack in the city of Hiroshima. However, Hiroshima marked the first use of atomic warfare and moved the world into a nuclear era where, for the first time, total destruction of civilisation became possible.

Case Study 1: London – a lost childhood?

On Thursday 5 September 1940, a little girl, Alma McGregor, and her brother went to East Ham Public Library in London. She borrowed *The Green Fairy Book* – a compendium of children's magic stories. Today that book remains in Alma's house. It has never been returned and technically she owes nearly 70 years of library fines!

Alma was nine years old in 1940. Even though the war had been going on for over a year, so far her life had been largely untouched by it. Her mother – recently widowed through her husband's sudden illness in 1939 – had refused to allow Alma to be evacuated to the countryside. True, a corrugated iron Anderson shelter had been installed in the garden of her family's house in Meath Road, London, E15. At times, she and the rest of the family had even taken shelter in it as fighter aircraft fought high in the London sky but, so far, London had not been the target of the Luftwaffe's enormous bombing fleet and the trips to the shelter had seemed like a game.

At 5 p.m. on Saturday 7 September the game ended. Air-raid sirens sounded over East London. Londoners, including Alma's family, went to their shelters fairly confident that no bombs would drop. But this time 300 Luftwaffe bombers and escorting Messerschmitt fighters were following the River Thames intent on bombing the London Docks – the largest port in the world and vital for Britain's war effort. Meath Road was less than two miles from those docks and one mile from the railway junction and locomotive works in Stratford, E15.

Soon bombs began to fall and the war at last seemed real – and terrifying. Alma remembers an evening of thumps as bombs fell, and sharp cracks as the British guns fired back. Later she saw the shadow of a plane passing over the shelter as she looked out of the door. She remembers no crash.

In less than two hours the raid was over and both Alma's shelter and house were untouched. Strange, then, when a knock at the door at about 7 p.m. revealed the local Police Officer and Air Raid warden. Alma's family were ordered to leave the house as quickly as possible. She wasn't even allowed to take the family dog with her. The warden insisted that silence be maintained and that everybody should tread as lightly as possible.

Frightened, the McGregor family obeyed his orders without question – for outside the house, visible in a hole by the lamppost was the cylindrical shape of an unexploded bomb. A bomb quite capable of killing the whole family instantly, demolishing several houses and blowing windows out along the whole street. A little girl who two days before had been enjoying fairy stories was now in real danger of being blown to pieces. The kind of danger once experienced only in combat by soldiers, sailors and airmen.

In fact, Alma's family had not had just one lucky escape that night – but two. In the middle of the raid high above East London, after being attacked by a British fighter plane from 242 Squadron RAF, Lieutenant Gunther Genske of the German Luftwaffe had parachuted out of his burning Messerschmitt Bf109E. Genske floated safely to earth, landing eight miles away – but his plane crashed violently in a fury of exploding ammunition, ploughing into an Anderson shelter and killing its occupants. The crash was about 50 metres from where Alma was sheltering.

Shaken by the experience of the unexploded bomb, and aware of the plane crash so nearby, Alma's mother took her family away from London's East End to the relative safety of Barnet on the outskirts of North London, well away from the Docks. The library book remained unreturned in their haste to leave.

DISCUSS

Which of Alma's experiences might you have found most frightening: the sirens; the noise of bombs and guns; the shadow across the shelter; or the evening evacuation around an unexploded bomb?

How well protected were the poor in British cities?

The British government was well aware of the potential of air attack to cause huge casualties. Aeroplanes had become far larger than those in the First World War and could carry large bomb loads over very long distances. Consequently, the government made sure that everybody in Britain had access to some form of shelter. No shelter could protect against a direct hit but they could give protection to some degree from blasts and flying metal fragments called shrapnel. Three types of shelter were available but these were often supplemented by people sheltering in underground train tunnels.

The Anderson Shelter

- This was a highly effective bolt-together corrugated steel shelter. When covered in earth these shelters were capable of protecting occupants from bombs landing within a few yards of the shelter. The combination of an earth cover and corrugated steel construction made it particularly strong.
- But ... these shelters needed a relatively large garden.

The Morrison Shelter

- This type of shelter did not need a garden! This indoor shelter was essentially a super strong table made of steel. It was capable of sheltering a whole family.
- But ... if a house was hit, people could easily become trapped inside.

The Brick-Built Street Shelter

- This was built of one and a half thicknesses of brick and topped by a reinforced concrete roof. These shelters typically seated 50 people. They were usually built in areas where people tended to live in large blocks of flats.
- But ... rumours spread that a near miss could lead to the people inside being crushed by the concrete roof.

The Tube Station

- London's underground ('tube') stations were used extensively as shelters. Initially the government tried to prevent this but eventually had to bow to public opinion. Londoners simply wouldn't take no for an answer!
- But ... not all tube stations were very far below the surface.

The most common shelter in the poorest parts of Britain's cities was the brick-built street shelter. This was because most people in those areas lived in tenement blocks and could not therefore use the other types of shelter. Many well-off people in the suburbs had paid for their own concrete shelters and many in wealthy city areas took advantage of the massively strong shelters in the basements of luxury hotels.

Brick-built street shelters had been designed and built in great haste and as the bombing wore on rumours began to spread that they were unsafe. The famous US journalist Ed Murrow, broadcasting from London in 1940, hinted strongly about the issue.

SOURCE 28 *From a radio broadcast on 10 September 1940.*

This is London and the raid which started about seven hours ago is still in progress. Larry Le Sueur and I have spent the last three hours driving about the streets of London and visiting air-raid shelters. We found that, like everything else in this world, the kind of protection you get from the bombs on London tonight depends on how much money you have.

DISCUSS

How well protected do you think the poor were in Britain's cities?

ACTIVITY

1 Look at the evidence that follows. To what extent did the German bombing campaign achieve its aims?

2 Which of the two documents above do you think is the strongest evidence that the morale of British civilians was not being destroyed by the bombing?

Did the German bombing campaign achieve its aims?

The German military had two main reasons for bombing British cities:

1. To destroy or severely disrupt war industries.
2. To demoralise or kill civilian workers.

Britain's docks, transport system, commerce and industry didn't stop operating during the Blitz. Every death was a tragedy but Britain was always able to provide workers for her industry and agriculture. Civilian morale remained high – as this extract shows.

DOCUMENT A *Extracts from* Reports on Morale, *Ministry of Home Security, 19 September 1940. This document was highly confidential.*

Out of some fifty confidential reports from Chief Constables concerning the morale of this country it is notable that in no single instance is there any suggestion of the least faltering in the public courage.

DOCUMENT B *Ed Murrow was a neutral foreign observer and admired the British spirit in the midst of the bombing. From a broadcast on 18 August 1940.*

It's about the people I'd like to talk, the little people who live in those little houses, who have no uniforms and get no decorations for bravery. These men whose only uniform was a tin hat were digging unexploded bombs out of the ground this afternoon. There were two women who gossiped across the narrow strip of tired brown grass that separated their two houses. They didn't open their kitchen windows in order to talk. The glass had been blown out. These people were calm and courageous. About an hour after the all-clear had sounded people were sitting in deck chairs on their lawns reading the Sunday papers. To me these people were incredibly brave and calm.

Case Study 2: Dresden – another lost childhood?

The intensive Luftwaffe bombing of Britain ended in June 1941 as Hitler turned his forces east to attack the Soviet Union. Raids did continue throughout the war but never again would the British be driven to their shelters night after night. The British had withstood modern air attack – soon it would be Germany's turn to endure the same ordeal.

Pre-war Dresden (see photo, right) was known as 'Florence on the Elbe' because of its great beauty, reputation for culture and for the number of art treasures housed in the city.

At 10 p.m. on Tuesday 13 February 1945, the first British marker flares drifted down towards this beautiful city that had been almost untouched by bombing. Unbeknown to Dresdeners who, like young Alma McGregor in London, had sheltered so often before for false alarms, this time the danger was real. Droning through the night were almost 800 RAF heavy bombers. In their bomb bays was a deadly concentration of high-explosive and fire-causing incendiary bombs. Each Lancaster bomber carried roughly 1.5 tonnes of high explosive bombs and 2.25 tonnes of incendiaries.

These bombs were capable of causing a deadly 'firestorm' creating temperatures of over 1000°C. Such a firestorm would suck the oxygen from the air at ground level and any civilians who survived incineration would almost certainly die of suffocation. The RAF aircrews had little option but to trust the orders they had been given. They were told that such raids would hasten the end of the war. Nonetheless, many were troubled – or would be troubled in the future – by what they were about to do and by what they had done.

Dresden had very few air-raid shelters. Most people sheltered in cellars underneath their houses. By the time the British bombers headed home at 1.42 a.m. on 14 February most of central Dresden was in the grip of a terrible firestorm.

▲ *The Frauenkirche in Dresden.*

SOURCE 29 *Margaret Freyer, '*The Bombing of Dresden', *quoted in* Eyewitness to History *by John Carey.*

We saw the burning street, the falling ruins and the terrible firestorm. My mother covered us with wet blankets and coats she found in a water tub. We saw terrible things: cremated adults shrunk to the size of small children, pieces of arms and legs, dead people, whole families burnt to death, burning people ran to and from, burnt coaches filled with civilian refugees, dead rescuers and soldiers, many were calling and looking for their children and families, and fire everywhere, everywhere fire, and all the time the hot wind of the firestorm threw people back into the burning houses they were trying to escape from.

SOURCE 30 The Firebombing of Dresden: an eyewitness account *by Lothar Metzer, recorded May 1999 in Berlin.*

The firestorm [was] incredible, there [were] calls for help and screams from somewhere but all around [was] one single inferno ... suddenly, I saw people again, right in front of me. They scream[ed] and gesticulate[d] with their hands, and then – to my utter horror and amazement – I [saw] how one after the other they simply seemed to let themselves drop to the ground. Today I know that these unfortunate people were the victims of lack of oxygen. They fainted and then burnt to cinders.

Beneath the bombs was thirteen-year-old German schoolgirl, Nora Lang. Nora had just been playing a game with decorated masks to celebrate Shrove Tuesday when the sirens went. Nora's family had no proper shelter, merely the cellar of her family's apartment block home. She sheltered there with her parents, five-year-old brother and about ten other occupants of the building. They crouched terrified in the basement as incendiaries punched holes in the roof of the building above. As the first wave of British bombers passed there was a lull as fires blazed. Nora's parents decided to take their chance to head out of the city centre before the fires really took hold. The raid seemed over. But it was not.

▲ Nora (centre) with her family.

Nora and her tiny brother stood in the open as her parents rummaged in their apartment trying to save the family's possessions. As the fires took hold, Nora was bundled away by a well-intentioned woman whilst her parents were still inside. Terrified, the two children made their way through the beginnings of the firestorm. All the way Nora clutched the heavy suitcase her mother had entrusted to her and dragged her five-year-old brother behind her.

Unbelievably bombs began to fall again as the second wave of British bombers arrived over Dresden. Rescue crews and desperate civilians were caught in the open. Conditions were so bad that Nora's group decided to find another cellar in which to hide until the morning. The building above collapsed so Nora and her brother clambered through a hole into the next cellar. Many old and sick people were unable to follow and later died where they sat. As Nora and her brother emerged into the open she had difficulty breathing as the oxygen was sucked from the narrow street by the raging fires. Finally and luckily, they stumbled into a wider street where the breeze from the River Elbe made the air breathable.

> We tried to make progress along the Durerstrasse. But this was scarcely possible, because there was fire everywhere. We had to walk along the middle of the street, to avoid being hit by flying roof tiles or burned out window frames, or all the stuff that was flying around. It was like a hurricane made of fire.

It was still not over. At midday on 14 February, American bombers arrived. Although aiming specifically at factories and railway installations and using fewer firebombs than the British, they still hit the homes of many civilians. They also managed to destroy the suitcase that Nora had dragged through the streets of Dresden with such effort! Nonetheless, Nora and her brother met their parents again at their grandparents' property on the edge of the city. They had survived. Thousands had not.

> … that we didn't die was pure luck. Some houses were still standing. And there was a truck trailer there. We crept under it and just lay down. We were so exhausted. And … it was so cruel … there was this man there who had gone mad. He just stood there and bawled into the night, over and over again: Carl! Carl! My brother was five years old at the time so he can't remember much of what happened except for that man's voice.

ACTIVITY

Compare Nora Lang's experiences in Dresden with those of Alma McGregor in London. Make a note of similarities and differences.

Why did the British plan and carry out attacks on civilian areas of German cities?

It is estimated that over half a million German civilians were killed in Allied bombing raids.

> **SOURCE 31** *Winston Churchill speaking on 14 July 1941.*
>
> If tonight our people were asked to cast their vote whether a convention should be entered into to stop the bombing of cities, the overwhelming majority would cry, 'No, we will mete out to them the measure, and more than the measure, that they have meted out to us.'

> **SOURCE 32** *Paper distributed by British Air Staff on 23 September 1941.*
>
> The ultimate aim of an attack on a town area is to break the morale (confidence and determination to continue the war) of the population. To ensure this we must achieve two things: first we must make the town physically uninhabitable and second we must make the people conscious of constant personal danger. The immediate aim therefore is to produce i) Destruction ii) Fear of death.

DISCUSS

1 Look at Sources 31 and 32 (left). Why did the British bomb German cities?
2 How similar are they to the reasons the German military had for targeting British cities? (See page 83.)

Can the bombing of Dresden be justified?

By the end of the raids at least 25,000 civilian men, women and children had suffered appalling deaths in Dresden. Even Winston Churchill was shocked by the effects of the bombing in Dresden (see photo, right).

> **SOURCE 33** *Winston Churchill, 28 March 1945.*
>
> It seems to me that the moment has come when the question of bombing German cities simply for the sake of increasing the terror, though under other pretexts, should be reviewed. Otherwise we shall come into control of an utterly ruined land.

> **SOURCE 34** *Sir Arthur Harris, Head of RAF Bomber Command, replying to Churchill.*
>
> The feeling, such as there is, over Dresden, could easily be explained by any psychiatrist. It is connected with [the city's public image of] German bands and china Dresden shepherdesses. Actually, Dresden was a mass of munitions works, an intact government centre, and a key transportation point to the east. It is now none of these things.

ACTIVITY

Using Nora's and Alma's stories, Sources 30–34, and the Evidence Cards on page 87, prepare for a class debate on the question:
Should Dresden have been bombed?

Once you have had a chance to consider all the information decide if you will argue for the 'Dresden *was not* a war crime' side or the 'Dresden *was* a war crime' side.

1 Dresden's rail yards were well away from the centre of the city.

2 Dresden was a very important rail centre for moving troops, concentration camp prisoners and materials of war.

3 Most factories were in the outskirts of the city, well away from the historic centre actually bombed.

4 Many industrial workers lived in the very centre of the city.

5 Dresden contained factories that produced shells, lenses for submarine periscopes, aircraft radios, fuses for anti-aircraft shells and engines for fighter aircraft.

6 Dresden was a city of great beauty.

7 Dresden held many priceless art treasures.

8 By February 1945, Germany had no realistic prospect of winning the war.

9 German troops were still fighting bitterly in defence of their country.

10 The Russians were advancing swiftly into Germany.

11 In 1934, Germany withdrew from the Geneva Disarmament Conference, refusing to support a British proposal that aerial bombing be banned.

12 The Russians were asking for help from Britain and the USA.

13 Day bombing of precise targets had been tried and had resulted in huge casualties among air crews.

14 The war factories of Dresden employed around 10,000 people.

15 Dresden was very close to the Russian front line.

16 The Nazis had designated Dresden as a defence zone meaning it would be defended street by street if necessary.

17 The number of casualties were a direct result of the Nazi failure to provide air-raid shelters.

18 The British deliberately tried to start a firestorm.

19 So many bodies were left in Dresden that over 7000 had to be cremated on the market square.

20 So many people died in the basements of collapsed houses that the Germans called recovery workers 'corpse miners'.

21 The gap between the British raids lured many German rescue services back out into the open.

22 Britain had never sought war.

23 German bombers had devastated many cities in Europe such as Rotterdam and Warsaw.

24 In November and December 1940 the centre of Coventry and the City of London had very nearly been engulfed by firestorms as the Luftwaffe dropped incendiaries. Only the small bomb loads prevented this.

Case Study 3: Hiroshima – did science accelerate the end of the war?

Background – the war in the Pacific

At first the Japanese conquered a lot of territory in the Pacific but by 1944 the massive industrial power of the USA began to tell. One by one the islands and territories the Japanese had conquered were recaptured by US marines and soldiers. The cost in human life was heavy since the Japanese soldiers had been taught that surrender meant dishonour.

By August 1945, the Japanese had been forced back and were preparing to defend their homeland against US invasion. This battle looked likely to cause vast numbers of US and Japanese casualties since the recent battle in July for the most distant Japanese home island of Okinawa had led to at least 12,000 US dead and 37,000 wounded. Approximately 60,000 Japanese had died.

The appliance of science and the first atomic bomb

Since the late 1930s the possibility of creating a weapon based on atomic energy had become clear. President Roosevelt established 'The Manhattan Project' aimed at developing atomic power for the USA before any other country. By July 1945 the USA had perfected the atomic bomb and had tested it in secret in the New Mexico desert.

The new US President, Harry S. Truman, knew full well that he had a bomb that could destroy a sizeable city. The atom bomb was the equivalent of 13,000 tonnes of high-explosive bombs. As a point of comparison, a large lorry on today's roads weighs about 30 tonnes. During the Dresden raid 800 bombers had dropped a total of just over 4000 tonnes of high-explosive bombs and this was considered a very heavy raid.

Was it necessary to use the atomic bomb?

President Truman took the decision to use the bomb. In fact he used it twice, once on Hiroshima and again on Nagasaki because the Japanese did not surrender immediately after Hiroshima. The Japanese finally surrendered on 15 August 1945 – six days after the second bomb. Truman later claimed dropping the bomb was a relatively easy decision to make and he was convinced that it had played the biggest part in ending the war.

> The bomb was no 'great decision'. It was used in the war and for your information there were more people killed by firebombs in Tokyo than dropping the atomic bombs accounted for. It was merely another powerful weapon in the arsenal [weapon store] of righteousness. The dropping of the bombs stopped the war and saved millions of lives.

Even the pilot who dropped the bomb, Colonel Paul Tibbets, seemed untroubled by its use, convinced that it was the right thing to do (see Source 35).

SOURCE 35 *Colonel Paul Tibbets – speaking in 1972.*

I was just relieved it worked. On the way back I put the plane on autopilot and went back to get some sleep.

SOURCE 36 *Marquis Kido, Japanese Lord Privy Seal. Extracts from interviews for* The World at War, *Thames TV.*

In a way it could be said that the atomic bombings, and Russia's sudden attack on Japan, helped to bring about the end of the war. If these things had not happened, Japan probably could not have stopped fighting.

The younger officers in the army ... the extremists – thought we should fight to the bitter end – until every man had been killed; but the War Minister, General Anami, didn't agree. He thought if we fought on until the Americans invaded the mainland, then hit their forces hard on the beaches, we could then negotiate peace on terms more favourable to Japan.

SOURCE 37 *General Curtis le May (Commander of US 9th Army Air Force) speaking in 1972. Extracts from interviews for* The World at War, *Thames TV.*

It was a hopeless situation for them. The B29s were flying over Japan at will and they couldn't do anything about it. We could destroy any target at will ... with this hopeless sight they didn't have the will to continue. As a matter of fact, they'd been trying to get out of the war for about three months before they actually did.

I believe President Truman made the proper decision to use the bomb because it probably hastened the negotiations – and even if we just saved one day to me it would be worthwhile. You just had to do it.

SOURCE 38 *Toshikazu Kase – Japanese Foreign Minister 1945, speaking in 1972. Interviewed for* The World at War, *Thames TV.*

I thought it was absolutely unnecessary. Because by the time the bomb was dropped on Hiroshima we were conducting negotiations with the Soviet government. We were completely exhausted. The navy and the army too were slowly becoming more amenable to the idea of peace.

SOURCE 39 *Averill Harriman, US Ambassador to Moscow 1945. Interviewed for* The World at War, *Thames TV.*

Truman made the decision on the basis of necessity and I think an impartial analysis, particularly from the Japanese themselves, shows more evidence is coming out that they would have fought on fanatically. You know they did fight on fanatically in some of the islands. The Emperor wouldn't have had the courage to call it off, wouldn't have had the support to call it off, without the bomb.

ACTIVITY

1 What do you think? Was it necessary to use the atomic bomb to end the war? Use Sources 35–43 (pages 89–90) and Michihiko Hachiya's story (pages 90–91) to help you to make up your mind.

2 Write a speech in which you either defend or attack President Truman's decision to use the atomic bomb. Make sure that you use source material to support your arguments.

SOURCE 40   *Yoshio Kodama, right-wing activist speaking in 1972. Interviewed for* The World at War, *Thames TV.*

You must remember that Japan's honour was at stake. The pride of the Japanese at that time, who thought that the only honourable way out of the war was not to surrender but to fight to the last man.

SOURCE 42   *Robert Oppenheimer, director of the project that developed the atomic bomb, being questioned by the American Senate in 1954.*

Q: Wasn't there a particular effort to produce a bomb before the Potsdam Conference (a meeting of the Allies in July 1945)?
A: It was the intention of the President to say something about this to the Russians. The President said no more than that we had a new weapon that we planned to use in Japan, and it was very powerful. We were under incredible pressure to get it done before the conference. *[The implication here is that the bomb was dropped to impress the Russians with US power, in case they were tempted to use their army against the West after the war against Germany and Japan had ended.]*

SOURCE 41   *From an interview with James Byrnes, American Secretary of State, 1965.*

We were talking about the people who hadn't hesitated at Pearl Harbor to make a sneak attack, destroying not only ships but also the lives of many American sailors.

Michihiko Hachiya's story – What was it like to be on the receiving end of an atomic attack?

Michihiko Hachiya was a doctor at the Hiroshima Communications Hospital. In addition to his duties as a doctor, he was a night-time air-raid warden. Although Hiroshima had not been bombed yet, its citizens were aware that the possibility existed. Although they had never heard of an atomic bomb the possibility of ordinary bombs was bad enough.

At 8.15 a.m. on 6 August 1945, as Michihiko rested on his living room floor recovering from an exhausting night on duty as a warden, three planes were droning towards Hiroshima at enormous height. The lead plane, named 'Enola Gay' (after its pilot's mother), carried the atomic bomb nicknamed 'Little Boy'. The bomb was released and Enola Gay banked swiftly to avoid the effects of the explosion. The pilot looked back at Hiroshima and described it as looking like a 'barrel of rolling, boiling tar'. Within two minutes the shock wave and mushroom cloud had climbed to 10,000 metres, shaking the plane like an invisible hand.

▼ SOURCE 43   *The Hiroshima A-Bomb detonates, 6 August 1945.*

Underneath the bomb, one mile from the centre of the explosion, were Michihiko and his wife …

> Suddenly, a strong flash of light startled me – and then another. So well does one recall little things that I remember vividly how a stone lantern in the garden became brilliantly lit and I debated whether this light was caused by a magnesium flare or sparks from a passing trolley. Garden shadows disappeared. The view where a moment before had been so bright and sunny was now dark and hazy. Through swirling dust I could barely discern a wooden column that had supported one corner of my house. It was leaning crazily and the roof sagged dangerously.

Michihiko was injured – strangely all of his clothes had been torn from his body by the combination of heat and blast. He staggered to his feet …

> Moving instinctively, I tried to escape, but rubble and fallen timbers barred the way. By picking my way cautiously I managed to reach the outside hallway and stepped down into my garden. A profound weakness overcame me, so I stopped to regain my strength. All over the right side of my body I was cut and bleeding. A large splinter was protruding from a mangled wound in my thigh, and something warm trickled into my mouth. My cheek was torn, I discovered as I felt it gingerly, with my lower lip laid wide open. Embedded in my neck was a sizeable fragment of glass, which I matter-of-factly dislodged, and with the detachment of one stunned and shocked I studied it and my blood-stained hand.

Michihiko and his wife Yaeko-san staggered from the ruins of their house. They began to walk to the hospital, which was only 100 metres away. This was too much for Michihiko who ordered his wife to go on alone. She agreed but promised to bring help.

> Yaeko-san looked into my face for a moment, and then, without saying a word, turned away and began running towards the hospital. Once, she looked back and waved and in a moment she was swallowed up in the gloom. It was quite dark now, and with my wife gone, a feeling of dreadful loneliness overcame me. Could I go on? I tried. It was all a nightmare – my wounds, the darkness, the road ahead. My movements were ever so slow; only my mind was running at top speed.

At last he found the hospital …

> Through the dim light I could make out ahead of me the hazy outlines of the Communications Bureau's big concrete building, and beyond it the hospital. My spirits rose because I knew that now someone would find me; and if I should die, at least my body would be found. I paused to rest. Gradually things around me came into focus. There were the shadowy forms of people, some of whom looked like walking ghosts. Others moved as though in pain, like scarecrows, their arms held out from their bodies with forearms and hands dangling. These people puzzled me until I suddenly realised that they had been burned and were holding their arms out to prevent the painful friction of raw surfaces rubbing together.

Michihiko's weakness had almost certainly been caused by radiation, a by-product of the bomb: apparently unforeseen by the Americans. The radiation alone killed an estimate of 30,000 people. The explosion itself killed at least 66,000 people by its immediate effect or by awful burns. Probably some injuries suffered in Dresden and London were as bad, but remember this dreadful death toll and suffering had been inflicted by one plane's bomb load. At this time there was no defence against the B-29 Superfortress with its atomic load.

▲ Michihiko (left) with his family.

At a distance of one mile from the centre of the explosion there was a 70 per cent chance of surviving the heat flash and blast. Anybody within 300 metres had only a 7 per cent chance of survival. Many close to the centre of the flash disappeared entirely leaving only a shadow on pieces of surviving wall as their body had delayed the heat for a millisecond.

The world had entered a new age of destruction. An age that is still not over.

A quick history of the Cold War

The world holds its breath for 40 years: Why did civilians live in fear after Hiroshima?

As you have seen, nuclear bombs played a key role in ending the Second World War. They also helped to shape the way the world developed after the war. As a result of what happened in Hiroshima the world changed forever.

During the Second World War, the Allies (Britain, the Soviet Union and the United States) had helped each other in the common cause of defeating Nazi Germany but after the war they soon began to fall out. A rivalry began to emerge over the best way to run the countries of Europe after the war. The Soviet Union operated a strictly controlled communist system of politics and economics and the other Allies were capitalists. Their attitudes were deeply divided.

We believe that in the very long term all people should be equal within a country and should own an equal share of all that country's wealth. This is communism and it will lead to rich people losing wealth and property to the poor. Under communism every field of business, manufacture or trade will be controlled by the government on behalf of the people.

We believe that all people should be free to own businesses and make money for themselves. Only by this natural process of people competing against each other can technology truly advance and money be made. This technological advance and created wealth will, in the long term, improve the lives of everybody in Europe and the world.

This division formed the basis of a conflict known as the 'Cold War': a conflict that brought the world close to nuclear destruction on several occasions between 1945 and 1989. By 1949, the Soviet Union had developed its own nuclear weapons. During the next 40 years both sides developed nuclear forces capable of destroying the whole planet. In 1952, the USA tested the first **hydrogen bomb**, destroying the Pacific island of Elugelab. The new bomb released a thousand times more destructive energy than the atomic bomb. The Soviet Union developed its own H-bomb in 1953. In 1957 the Soviet Union launched the first satellite into orbit (Sputnik 1) which meant that intercontinental rockets could be developed that brought the whole world within range of a nuclear attack. Over time other countries developed their own nuclear weapons, raising public fears of nuclear annihilation and placing a heavy burden on many economies.

A divided world

After the 1945 Potsdam Agreement between the Allies, Europe became divided. Many countries in the East came under the indirect control of the Soviet Union and were pushed into adopting a communist system of government. Countries in Western Europe became heavily influenced by the USA and tried to rebuild under a capitalist, free market system. In other parts of the world the US and the Soviet Union tried to increase their influence.

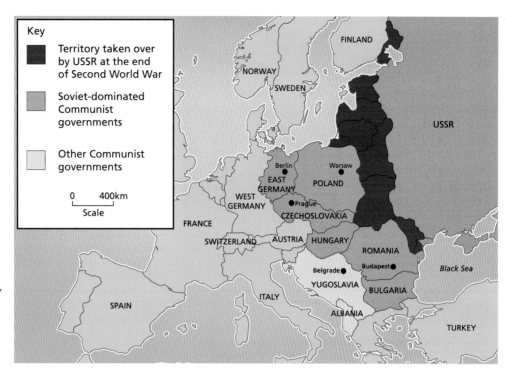

Key

■ Territory taken over by USSR at the end of Second World War

▨ Soviet-dominated Communist governments

□ Other Communist governments

0   400km
Scale

This division of Europe was referred to by British ex-Prime Minister Winston Churchill as an 'Iron Curtain' descending across Europe. As the years passed this Iron Curtain became more and more difficult to cross. Some rebellions from people in the East (East Germany 1953; Hungary 1956; Czechoslovakia 1968) were crushed ruthlessly by Soviet tanks. The West protested but did not interfere since Eastern Europe had been accepted as a Soviet zone of influence at Potsdam in 1945.

Between 1945 and 1989 the Cold War saw increases and decreases in tensions arising from crises all over the world. Several times things got really heated and threatened to erupt into a war using nuclear weapons.

ACTIVITY

1 Examine the Crisis Cards on pages 94–95. Place each Crisis Card on the temperature graph. The hotter the temperature – the more dangerous the conflict.

2 When did the Cold War nearly reach boiling point? What event have you identified as the most dangerous? Explain your answer.

Crisis 1 The Berlin Blockade

Under the 1945 Potsdam Agreement between the Allies, Germany was divided into four zones of occupation: Soviet, American, British and French. The capital city Berlin was also divided into four national sectors despite being situated deep in the Soviet zone of Germany. The USA, Britain and France began moves to join their zones together. The Soviet Union responded by blockading West Berlin (controlled by American, French and British forces). In order to cut off food and energy supplies to the city, Stalin surrounded its western half.

In response, America stationed B-29 long-range bombers in Britain, and in the event of the war, planned to drop atomic bombs on the Soviet Union. The Soviets had no nuclear weapons at that time. Some US generals recommended the use of force to open supply lines. President Truman rejected this option and supplies were flown in by air. The people received food, and Stalin re-opened supply lines in May 1949. But Berlin remained divided between East and West.

1950–1953

Korea had been divided into a communist North and a capitalist South when the Japanese withdrew at the end of the Second World War. After a dispute about elections across the whole country, the North, backed by Soviet money and advice, invaded the South. During three years of bitter fighting the South, backed by direct UN help (principally supplied by the US army), succeeded in preventing the invasion and the border settled down close to its original position. Korea remains divided to this day.

In the course of the war, the US army had approached too close to the Chinese border and this had triggered the entry of one million communist Chinese troops into the battle. General Douglas MacArthur of the USA recommended the use of nuclear weapons to stop the Chinese. President Truman rejected this advice and sacked MacArthur. Soviet troops also fought on the side of the North but used Chinese and Korean uniforms to conceal their identities.

Crisis 2 Korea

Crisis 3 The building of the Berlin Wall

By 1961, the existence of capitalist West Berlin deep in communist East Germany had become both an embarrassment and a real problem for the Soviet Union. By right, any person was allowed into any part of Berlin at any time. Many skilled East Germans, attracted by higher wages, used this right to emigrate to the West. Khrushchev, the leader of the Soviet Union, threatened war unless West Berlin was given up – but the USA refused to back down. On the night of 12/13 August 1961 a ring of barbed wire and guards sealed off West Berlin from East Berlin. No citizen of the East was permitted to cross. In the first few days the barrier was weak but gradually wire became concrete and the wall evolved into a sophisticated, almost impenetrable, barrier.

The USA protested but was secretly glad that Khrushchev had found a peaceful solution to the crisis. US tanks were brought up to the sealed border to insist that US and British soldiers could still cross to the East – and for a short time found themselves confronted by Soviet tanks. Both sides agreed to back off ten metres at a time and the wall stayed. Tension between the Superpowers had been reduced but the Berliners faced a divided city for the next 28 years.

MISSILE EQUIPMENT
MARIEL PORT FACILITY
4 NOVEMBER 1962

4 MISSILE TRANSPORTERS
OXIDIZER TRAILERS
OXIDIZER TRAILERS
FUEL TRAILERS

Crisis 4 Cuba

Base construction in Cuba was almost complete and some nuclear missiles had actually arrived before the USA realised what was happening. In October 1962 the world held its breath as the USA demanded that the missiles be removed. US generals were advising an attack on Cuba and we now know that, had this happened, the Soviet forces had orders to reply with nuclear weapons.

Instead, President Kennedy placed warships around Cuba and promised to search any ship approaching the island. War seemed likely as Soviet ships carrying missiles for the Cuban bases approached the US navy. The situation grew even more tense when a US spy plane was shot down over Cuba and its pilot killed. But Kennedy would not give the order for war and stuck to the blockade. At the last moment, on the orders of Khrushchev, the Soviet ships stopped and war was averted.

Talks then took place and a deal was reached. The Soviet Union agreed to remove the missiles from Cuba in return for a US promise never to invade that country. Cuba remains communist to this day. The US also agreed to remove its missiles from Turkey but insisted that this part of the deal was never made public.

In 1960 the USA had positioned nuclear missiles in Turkey. These were a direct threat to the Soviet Union but as no communist countries existed in the Western half of the globe it was not possible for the Soviet Union to threaten the USA in the same way. In 1961 the situation changed. Cuba, a country only 30 miles from the USA, became communist. Threatened by invasion from the United States, Cuba agreed to host Soviet missiles. Washington was in range of these missiles.

1965–1975

From the 1950s, South Vietnam faced a major communist-led revolt. The rebels, known as the Vietcong, were supported by the communist North Vietnamese government. The United States were worried by the so-called 'Domino Theory' – that communist victory in Vietnam would quickly lead to communists gaining control of other parts of South-East Asia. At first the US sent military 'advisers' to South Vietnam. From March 1965 they sent combat troops.

After 1965, the USA committed more and more troops to try to control the Vietcong but it proved impossible to fight them successfully. Bombing raids on North Vietnam came very close to the Chinese border and made the USA very unpopular. The Vietcong received training and supplies from both the Soviet Union and China but this time those countries did not fight directly against the USA. Eventually, after losing 55,000 soldiers and spending billions of dollars, the United States was forced to pull out of Vietnam. In April 1975 North Vietnamese forces overran South Vietnam.

Crisis 5 Vietnam

Crisis 6 Afghanistan

In 1979 the Soviet Union invaded the mountainous country of Afghanistan. They claimed that they needed to make their southern border secure against Islamic religious ideas. The Afghanistan tribesmen immediately stopped fighting each other and united against the foreign invader. These tribesmen were given weapons by the USA and knew the terrain of the country. Against such opposition the young and raw Soviet troops had little chance and were killed in thousands. Little progress was made by the Soviet Union in exchange for thousands of lives and at huge expense.

The money spent on the war nearly bankrupted the Soviet Union and led to its military withdrawal from Eastern Europe. During the 1980s, the Soviet Union started to realise that it could no longer compete financially with the USA. Communism was abandoned across the Soviet Union at midnight on 31 December 1991.

Has the end of the Cold War made the world a safer place?

The threat of a nuclear war did not stop with the ending of the Cold War. Both the United States and Russia still have nuclear weapons. Also, it was not just the United States and the Soviet Union who developed nuclear weapons after the Second World War. Britain became the third atomic power in 1952. France became the fourth in 1960. Since then China, South Africa, Israel, India and Pakistan have also developed nuclear weapons. Other countries are in the process of developing the capability to produce such weapons. Civilians all over the world still live under the threat of a nuclear war.

Why was the United States army forced to withdraw from Vietnam?

During the Cold War the United States fought communist forces in Vietnam. The United States was the most advanced industrial nation in the world. It was able to use the very latest technology in the war. Despite its superior resources the United States was defeated and forced to withdraw from Vietnam. Your task is to explain how this was possible.

> Half a million American soldiers, with 700,000 Vietnamese allies, with total command of the air, total command of the sea, backed by the huge resources and the most modern weapons … are unable to secure even a single city from the attacks of an enemy whose total strength is about 250,000.

▲ *Senator Robert Kennedy*

The 'enemy' Senator Robert Kennedy referred to was, in fact, two forces: the People's Army of North Vietnam (PAVN) and the People's Liberation Armed Forces: the 'Vietcong'.

The **PAVN** was the regular army of North Vietnam. They wore uniforms and were trained to fight normal set-piece battles, making the most of jungle conditions against US troops. The PAVN was inferior to the US army in terms of equipment and numbers. It was only used when careful planning could ensure that the US forces would be outnumbered and taken by surprise in a carefully chosen local area.

The **Vietcong** were largely a 'guerrilla' army. This meant that they did not wear uniforms but blended in with the local population in US-controlled South Vietnam. Vietcong units would come out of hiding and attack US bases or patrolling troops with hidden weapons. There were never more than 30,000 Vietcong fighters but these men and women were able to frustrate and demoralise over 500,000 US ground troops.

▼ *A Vietcong fighter*

The Vietcong was contemptuously referred to by the US troops as 'Charlie' or 'men in pyjamas'. The USA was confident of victory. They had more money, men and resources. They also controlled the air over Vietnam. Their B-52 bombers could fly at heights that prevented them being seen or heard. During the war, eight million tonnes of bombs were dropped on Vietnam – three times the amount of bombs dropped throughout the whole of the Second World War. However, the Vietcong were never defeated. This tiny force and its supporters among the South Vietnamese population did what no other army had ever been able to do – defeat the USA in a war. How was this possible?

Why are wars won and lost? What makes an army successful in a conflict?

Weapons, supplies and resources

- What type of weapons do they have? How effective are they?
- Are the troops well supplied? Do they have all the food and equipment they need?

Tactics

- How effectively are men and weapons used in the conflict?

Popular support

- How much support do the troops have in the country in which they are fighting?
- How much support do they have from other countries?
- If they are fighting abroad – how much support do they have back home? Do they feel that their country is supporting them?

Confidence and motivation

- Are the troops confident? Do they feel that they are going to win?
- How much do the troops want to fight? How much do they believe in what they are fighting for?

ACTIVITY

1 Look at the four factors above that decide the outcome of conflicts. Think back to previous conflicts you have studied. Are there any factors missing? If so, add them to the list.

2 Choose three conflicts from the list below. For each conflict place the factors **from above** in order of importance.
- The Battle of Hastings
- Agincourt
- The Spanish Armada
- The Battle of Trafalgar
- The First World War
- The Second World War

3 In which of the factors above might the USA have considered it had a definite advantage at the start of the Vietnam war?

4 Time to test out your hypothesis. Two soldiers (on pages 98–101) will guide you through the factors – one from an American point of view and the other from the Vietcong's point of view. Use pages 98–101 to fill in the table below. On each factor score both sides out of five.

Factor	US score	Explanation	Vietcong score	Explanation
Weapons, supplies and resources				
Tactics				
Popular support				
Confidence and motivation				

Weapons, supplies and resources

There is absolutely *no doubt* that our weapons and supply systems are superior in every way to those of the Vietcong. Every US soldier is armed with a light, powerful and fast firing rifle called the M16. We know for a fact that the Cong are using very crude rifles made in Russia. Those weigh over a kilogram more than ours and that makes a difference on a long march. What's more, they fire more slowly too.

In addition we want for absolutely nothing in the way of supplies here even though we are over 12,000 miles from the USA. On our bases we have cold beers, steaks, ice cream and all the comforts of home. We even have entertainment laid on for us by big stars from home.

Also we are very well supported from the air. Helicopters take us from our bases to our patrol points and then bring us back when the patrol's over to the comforts of the base. They also bring out the wounded very quickly so those guys get the best medical care.

We also see our huge bomber planes, called B-52s, flying high overhead to bomb the Vietcong's supply lines from North Vietnam. Each one of those planes carries 35,000 kilos of bombs, and travels at 650 miles per hour. The North Vietnamese and Vietcong can't do a thing about them most of the time since they don't really have an effective air force.

What puzzles me, though, is how these Vietcong soldiers always seem to find enough food to stay fit – and enough guns, rocket launchers and ammo to keep fighting us. If our B-52s are that good how come all these supplies keep getting through?

We do not have the supplies of the Americans, it is true. But sometimes I think they have so much it makes them soft. We can live on rice, vegetables and very little meat. Villagers in the south are either supporting us or afraid of us and, either way, they give us food. We also bring supplies by bicycle and trucks down the Ho Chi Minh trail from North Vietnam. This trail is a complex web of different jungle paths and is badly bombed but we keep moving it to keep the Americans guessing. It also runs through countries that are not at war with the USA, so they dare not bomb it in those countries.

Our Russian AK 47 rifles are crude and heavy and they don't fire as well as the M 16 but they are very tough and simple to fix. They are even able to fire after being kept in the damp and muddy supply hideaways we have all over the south. No M 16 could do that, so what use would such flashy guns be to us?

At first we used hand-made weapons such as spears, daggers and swords. However, over time we have built up a large supply of weapons that we have captured from the enemy. Most of the explosives we use for our mines and booby traps come from unexploded bombs dropped by the Americans. We have developed pineapple bombs that embed heavy plastic fragments into Yankee soldiers. These are impossible to spot by X-ray and many soldiers die slowly as doctors poke about inside them looking for bits of bomb. We have enough to hit them by surprise and to continue hitting them by surprise. Our soldiers know this land – which more than makes up for any disadvantage in equipment.

Tactics

We use guerrilla warfare to wear down the enemy. It is a bit like a flea attacking a dog. We bite, hop, and bite again, avoiding the foot that will crush us. We do not seek to destroy the enemy in one go. Instead we bleed him and feed on him, plague and bedevil him. When the enemy advances we retreat; when the enemy camps we harass them; when the enemy tires we attack. Our leaders tell us not to go into combat unless we outnumber the enemy. We tend to attack at night and concentrate on attacking small enemy patrols or poorly guarded positions.

We are always keeping the US soldiers guessing as to where we will hit them next. We have spies everywhere among people working on US bases and they help us plan our attacks. We move into position under cover of darkness then attack their bases hard. By the time they are ready to fight us we are gone. They never feel safe – we even attacked the US embassy in Saigon.

In the villages we control, we often build underground tunnels. These lead from the village out into the jungle. They also contain underground caverns where we can hide if US troops arrive. It is also where we store our equipment – medical supplies and weapons. The tunnels are usually too small for the American soldiers. Sometimes we lay in wait on trails we know they will use. We often kill or wound the whole American patrol without being seen. This means that even when we are not there the young Yankee soldiers are terrified of every tree! We are not silly enough to fight them in the open. They are too many and they are too well equipped.

We also dig big pits on the trails and place sharp bamboo stakes covered with poison or sewage inside. Then the whole pit is covered by palm leaves until a patrolling US soldier falls in. The stakes are angled so he can't be pulled out without being hurt even more. The sewage is designed to infect the wound.

We are sent on search and destroy missions into local villages. We are meant to find and kill members of the Vietcong but this is really difficult. You never know who your enemy is and who is your friend. They look alike and dress alike. Innocent people are sometimes killed by mistake.

Three months after being elected president, Lyndon B. Johnson launched Operation Rolling Thunder. The plan was to destroy the North Vietnam economy and to bomb territory controlled by the Vietcong in South Vietnam. For the next three years our planes dropped one million tonnes of bombs on Vietnam.

As well as explosives we have also dropped napalm. This produces a sticky gel that attaches itself to the skin and burns for a long time. Most victims are burnt through to the bone. Many die from the pain caused by the burning.

Then there is Operation Ranch Hand. This involves the spraying of chemicals from the air in an attempt to destroy Vietcong hiding places. In 1969 over one million hectares of forest were destroyed by a chemical called 'Agent Orange'. This chemical causes damage to chromosomes in the body as well as destroying trees. We have also sprayed chemicals on to crops. Huge areas of land have been sprayed with a chemical called 'Agent Blue' and this leads to very poor rice harvests.

But all this bombing hasn't worked. We have relied too much on superior technology. The key to defeating the Vietcong guerrillas is to win over the local population. But all we have succeeded in doing is turning many South Vietnamese against us, whilst the North Vietnamese seem even more determined to fight on.

Popular support

When the war started only a small percentage of the American population opposed the war. As the war has continued, more and more Americans have turned against it. Some people are upset by our use of chemical weapons such as napalm and Agent Orange. The International War Crimes Tribunal found the US guilty of using weapons that were banned by international law and of torturing innocent civilians. In 1971, Lieutenant William Calley was found guilty of war crimes for his part in the murder of 109 Vietnamese civilians at Mai Lai. The publicity created by the Mai Lai massacre turned the public even further against the war.

The US government has made no official attempt to censor the media. Every night people in America see colour television pictures of wounded and dead soldiers. By 1968 the war was costing 66 million dollars a day. Taxes have had to be increased in America. This has made the war even more unpopular. The more the war continues the more powerful and better organised the anti-war movement becomes.

Here in Vietnam things are just as bad. If we find evidence of the Vietcong being in a village, the local people are punished. US troops sometimes torture local people in order to get information from them. When they return to their village their homes have been wrecked, their animals killed and their rice taken – if they weren't Vietcong supporters before we arrived, they sure as hell are by the time we leave. We have totally lost the support of the local population.

We feel so strong. Many villagers in the south are secretly Vietcong or are helping the Vietcong. Even those who initially didn't want us are coming around to our point of view because of the murders and arrogant behaviour of the US soldiers. Never forget Mai Lai.

The USSR and China are supporting us and much of the world – even the non-communist world – admires us as the underdogs fighting the huge USA. The USA is losing its reputation and the longer it stays here the worse it will get for them. They are foreigners here and we are Vietnamese whether we live in the south or the north. Not all Vietnamese are communists yet, but many are beginning to hate the US soldiers.

Confidence and motivation

The United States has underestimated us. My fellow soldiers are well motivated – we are fighting for a cause we believe in. We want to unite Vietnam, we are fed up with interference from other countries.

It's only a matter of time. We will win for the good of Vietnam. Soon our people will live in a communist paradise without poverty. That is worth any sacrifice. We can carry on this war forever because we believe in what we are fighting for. Do the American soldiers?

There has been a collapse in American morale. Some men volunteered to fight but many young men like myself have had no choice. I was conscripted. I was called up to fight in the army at the age of eighteen. We serve in Vietnam for just over a year. Victory does not seem to be in sight. Our main aim is simply to survive the year. Most of us are counting down the days to the time when we can go home and try and forget about the whole thing.

We do not really understand this war. What are we fighting for? My family is not in danger and the US is not under threat of invasion. Many soldiers are angry that those conscripted tended to come from the poorer and less educated sections of society. Youngsters going to college have been able to avoid being drafted. Most of the soldiers here come from working-class homes. I don't see many sons of rich parents!

The climate here really wears you down. The heat can be incredible, it can wring the sweat out of you until you drop from exhaustion. Then there are the swarms of mosquitoes that can turn your face and hands into a mass of welts.

This fighting over here gives me the creeps. Even in our own bases we are afraid to salute an officer in case he is shot dead by a Vietcong rifleman hidden in the trees. How can we ever beat people we can't see? When out on patrol the Cong can be waiting for us anywhere – we never even see them when they're killing us. We can't go anywhere in South Vietnam without being in danger. Even when on leave in Saigon men have been killed by Vietcong terrorists. We can't carry on like this. Our men's nerves are shot to hell. Every step you take creates tension and fear. You constantly ask yourself where you should step next – that flat rock or the clump of weeds to the right. This step-by-step decision-making preys on your mind. We know that at any moment the ground we walk on can erupt and kill us or turn us into a blind, deaf and legless shell.

The average age of the soldier out here is just nineteen. I've seen many of my friends affected psychologically. Many suffer from some kind of stress disorder caused by the nature of the fighting. Suicide rates are high and large numbers have deserted.

DOING HISTORY: Causation

Use your completed table and the advice on this page to answer the Big Question:

Why was the United States army forced to withdraw from Vietnam?

Remember what you have already learnt about causes

- Most events have a number of causes – make sure you give more than one reason why the US were forced to withdraw.
- Causes are not equally important – make sure you make it clear which cause you think is the most important. Rank the causes in order of importance before you start.
- Looking for links between causes can help you do this.

ACTIVITY

Linking causes – producing a concept map

Look at the picture below. Four students are working together to find links between the factors that forced the US to withdraw.

1 Produce your own version of this diagram and fill in the missing speech bubbles to explain the links between the factors.

2 Can you find any other links? Make sure you can explain them.

3 Having completed this exercise, what factor do you think was at the root of the problems faced by the USA?

Remember how to structure your answer

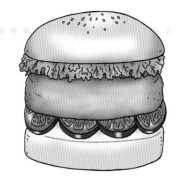

- Use the hamburger paragraph structure (see page 62).
- Support statements with specific examples.
- Use connectives to strengthen your explanations.

WARNING!

Do not simply **describe** what the US or the Vietcong did.

Look at the example below. The student **describes what happened** but does not **explain how** this weakened America's position in Vietnam and forced her to withdraw.

In answering causation questions the aim is to link events with their results.

WARNING

AVOID DANGER
USE CONNECTIVES

Student answer

The Vietcong had very clever tactics. In the villages the Vietcong often built underground tunnels. These led from the village out into the jungle.

American tactics were poor. They bombed and burnt down villages, killing innocent people.

So what? The student needs to explain why these tunnels were important. For example …

These tunnels meant that the Vietcong could take the US soldiers by surprise. The tunnels were also a useful secret storage space for weapons and supplies.

Once again the student describes but does not explain. Add a sentence to improve the answer.

This led to …

WARNING

ALWAYS LINK
WHAT YOU SAY
TO THE QUESTION

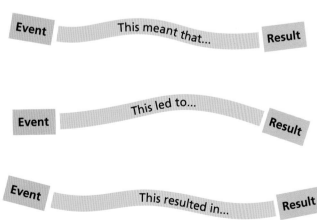

Event — This meant that… — Result

Event — This led to… — Result

Event — This resulted in… — Result

How has the nature of conflict changed and how could it change in the future?

The Vietnam War stands as a warning that countries with superior weapons and technology do not always win wars. It shows that the outcomes of conflicts are not always inevitable. However, can you draw any patterns from your study of conflicts?

Recent conflicts – the War on Terror

In 2000, 36 per cent of the world's military spending was by the United States but this did not make the country safe from attack. On 11 September 2001, terrorists hijacked four American passenger planes. The terrorists flew two of the planes straight into the twin towers of the World Trade Center in New York.

The two skyscrapers contained thousands of office workers, many of whom were killed when the planes hit the building or when the towers collapsed. A third plane was flown into the Pentagon building in Washington, the centre of the United States armed forces. The fourth plane crashed in a field after passengers fought with the terrorists. Over 3000 people were killed in the attacks.

The terrorists were members of al-Qaeda, an Islamic extremist group led by Osama Bin Laden, who believe that they are fighting a holy war against enemies of their religion. Their aim is to get rid of American influence in the Middle East. Al-Qaeda had already carried out terrorist attacks during the 1990s, bombing US embassies in Kenya and Tanzania.

DISCUSS

Think carefully about all the conflicts that you have studied during Key Stage 3.

1 Can you draw any general conclusions about why wars are won and lost? Have technology and resources usually played the key role?

2 Do you think that technology is going to become more or less important as a factor that decides future conflicts? Use the information and sources on pages 104–105 to help you to decide.

The early 21st century saw the world descend into a new war after the 9/11 terrorist attacks – the War on Terrorism. In 2002, an international force, led by the United States, invaded Taliban-controlled Afghanistan. The aim was to remove al-Qaeda bases in the country.

In 2003, the US and Britain attacked Iraq, without full UN authorisation, claiming that Saddam Hussein was capable of providing terrorist groups with chemical and biological weapons. Saddam's army was quickly defeated and eventually a new government was established. However, there were a growing number of attacks on US and British forces based in Iraq.

There were also further terrorist attacks by al-Qaeda. In Madrid (March 2004) and London (7 July 2005) transport systems were bombed. Al-Qaeda claimed that this was retaliation against countries whose governments had supported the Iraqi invasion.

The terrorist attacks on the United States on 11 September 2001 were carried out by a small group of well-organised terrorists. The aim was to create fear and confusion. These groups are not easy to identify or destroy. Multibillion-dollar weapons platforms, battle tanks and carrier task forces are not much help against terrorist organisations that carry out the acts of terrorism witnessed on 11 September, or suicide-bombing attacks.

Are civilians at greater risk than ever before?

The Vietnam War, like the Second World War, also resulted in massive civilian casualties. This suggests that during the twentieth century civilians began to be seen as 'military targets'. Only 5 per cent of deaths in the First World War were civilian deaths. Since then, in wars, the numbers of civilians slaughtered has become greater than that of soldiers fighting. In the Second World War, 66 per cent of deaths were civilians.

DISCUSS

- In the 21st century, can we expect this trend to continue? Are civilians at greater risk than ever before?
- Look at the information box below. What impacts could increasing terrorism have?

SOURCE 44 *Paul Kennedy in* BBC History Magazine, *November 2001.*

Defeating Japan was like shooting an elephant; defeating the terrorists who inflicted these wounds upon America will be like stomping on jellyfish.

SOURCE 45 *Gary Sheffield in* BBC History Magazine, *November 2001.*

Terrorism and guerrilla activity can be crushed by military action, if it is prolonged and ruthless. However, in the process, too often the seeds are sown of renewed conflict. Martyrs are made, reinforcing a sense of injustice to be handed down the generations. In a war fought in the shadows, intelligence is vital. Military force can be targeted only if the population is willing to share information.

How has terrorism changed in the last 100 years?

- During the nineteenth century and early twentieth century the targets of terrorism tended to be political leaders. A good example is the assassination of the Austrian Archduke Ferdinand by a nineteen-year-old Bosnian Serb student, Gavril Princip, in Sarajevo on 28 June 1914.

- Since the Second World War the nature of terrorism has changed. In many cases civilians have been deliberately targeted. Terrorists have increasingly attacked innocent civilians – often with the purpose of demonstrating that a

particular government is incapable of protecting its own people. One example is the attack on Israeli athletes at the 1972 Olympics.

- The scale of terrorism has also changed. The attacks on the World Trade Center shocked the world. Previously, it had been possible to believe that there were limits beyond which even terrorists would not go. After the thousands of deaths on 11 September, it was evident that at least one group would stop at nothing.

Comparing dictatorships: how similar were Joseph Stalin and Adolf Hitler?

During the first half of the twentieth century two men from relatively lowly backgrounds managed to become dictators of two of the most powerful countries in the world. How did Joseph Stalin and Adolf Hitler rise to power? Once in power, how did they change the lives of people living in the Soviet Union and Germany? How similar were the dictatorships they established?

JOSEPH STALIN

Family life
- Born in 1879 in Georgia, which was part of the Russian Empire.
- Original name was Iosif Dzhugashvili. Changed his name to Stalin (which means 'man of steel').
- His father was a shoemaker and alcoholic. He abandoned the family when Stalin was a young child.

Early political life
- Stalin made his name by taking part in violent bank raids to raise money for the Communist Party which was trying to overthrow the Tsar (the ruler of Russia).
- He was twice exiled to Siberia by the Tsar's secret police but he managed to escape each time.
- Stalin became a leading communist after playing an important role in defending the city of Tsaritsyn (later Stalingrad) during the Civil War.

Leadership qualities
- Not rated highly by Lenin (the leader of the Communist Party) or other leading communists. In 1923 Lenin had called for Stalin to be replaced. Stalin was seen as being slow, steady, dull and unimaginative. He was not a great public speaker.
- Ruthless and devious. He held grudges and was determined to make his enemies suffer.
- Hardworking and a clever politician. He was very good at using his power within the Communist Party. He took on many boring but important jobs such as General Secretary. He used this position to put his own supporters into important posts within the Party.

ADOLF HITLER

Hitler im Felde

Family life
- Born in 1889 in Austria. He got on badly with his father who died in 1903.
- Unhappy and lonely at school. He was moody, shy and poor at most subjects. Hitler left school with no qualifications.
- Hitler failed to get a place at art school. For the next few years he struggled to make a living on the streets of Vienna.
- In 1914 he joined the German army. He fought in the First World War and won a medal for bravery.

Early political life
- After the war Hitler was sent by the army to spy on a meeting of the German Workers' Party. He found himself agreeing with many of their ideas and joined the party. He was given membership card 555.
- The Party was renamed the National Socialist German Workers' Party (or Nazi Party). Hitler became leader of the Party in 1921. By the end of 1922 the Party had 20,000 members.
- In 1923, during the Munich Putsch, the Nazis attempted to overthrow the government by force. The Putsch failed and Hitler was sent to prison. However, he only received a short sentence and was soon back as leader of the Nazi Party.

Leadership qualities
- Energetic and charismatic. Hitler was a great public speaker. His timing, the style of his delivery and the content of his speeches captivated his listeners.
- Single-minded and very suspicious of others.
- Devious and ruthless.

How similar were Stalin and Hitler?

Although Stalin and Hitler had different political beliefs neither believed in democracy. By the mid-1930s they had both established dictatorships in their countries. The Soviet Union and Germany were not the only dictatorships in Europe. In 1922, Benito Mussolini (right), the leader of the Fascist Party, became leader of Italy. Mussolini quickly established a Fascist dictatorship. Other political parties were banned and nobody was allowed to criticise the government.

In contrast to Italy, Germany and the Soviet Union, countries such as Britain, France and the USA were run by a democratic style of government. As the table below shows, there were big differences between living in a dictatorship and living in a democracy.

In a democracy …	In a dictatorship …
A government has a limited time in power, after which voters can choose a different government.	No choice of government – there is only one political party.
Everyone, including the government, must obey the law.	The government is the law! The secret police and the army keep people under control.
People have the freedom to criticise the government and protest about its policies.	People who criticise the government may be imprisoned or tortured.
People can follow any religion they wish. They are allowed to join trade unions.	People are only allowed to follow beliefs that are approved by the government. Trade unions are banned.
Newspapers and the media can say what they like about the government.	The government controls the media. People are only allowed to see and hear what the government wants them to.

ACTIVITY

Some historians have argued that there were many other similarities between Stalin and Hitler. Other historians argue that these similarities have been over-exaggerated. As you work through this enquiry you need to compare Stalin and Hitler. Use the table below to record your findings.

- You should be able to fill in the first row of this table (Early life) already.
- Then use pages 108–121 to fill in the rest of the table.
- At the end of the enquiry you will need to reach a conclusion about how similar the two dictators were. Page 122 will help you.

Category	Stalin	Hitler similarities	Hitler differences	Similarity rating (out of 10)
Early life				
What did they believe in?				
How did they rise to power?				
How did they keep control?				
How did they change people's lives? (a) work (b) women and the family (c) young people				

What did Stalin believe in?

Joseph Stalin was a member of Russia's Communist Party. Karl Marx developed the idea of communism in the nineteenth century.

The world is run by capitalists, who own the banks and factories. They make huge profits and become very rich. The people who work in these factories have to put up with terrible working conditions and receive very little pay. Eventually these workers will not accept this situation any longer and there will be a revolution. The workers will rise up and take power themselves. This will lead to a communist society in which a workers' government will share out the wealth fairly. There will not be a division between rich and poor.

▲ *Karl Marx*

At the start of the twentieth century Russia was a large but backward country. It was ruled by a Tsar who had complete power. Factory and mine workers were badly paid and had to put up with poor working conditions. Most of the population were peasant farmers who were very poor and lived in dreadful conditions. In 1917 the Tsar was overthrown during the Russian Revolution. Eventually, after a civil war, the communists, led by Vladimir Lenin, seized power. Lenin made a number of changes to the way that the country was ruled.

The workers have been told to take control of the factories and to run them by committees. The peasants have been told to share out the land between themselves. Our government has taken control of the banks and the wealth of rich people has been confiscated. Houses have been taken from their rich owners and shared among the workers. No political parties are allowed, except the Communist Party. All newspapers are under our control. However, we are encouraging all classes to have access to the finest theatre and music – not just the rich. Women are equal to men and all titles and ranks have been dropped. Everybody is now called 'comrade'. The Tsar and his family have been shot. The old Russian Empire is now known as the Union of Soviet Socialist Republics (USSR or the Soviet Union).

▲ *Vladimir Lenin*

How did Stalin rise to power?

Lenin died in 1924. Stalin was one of several leading communists who were possible candidates to take his place. However, he was not the favourite to take over. Most people believed that Leon Trotsky would take Lenin's place as leader of the Soviet Union.

LEON TROTSKY

Family life
- Born in 1879 into a respectable Jewish farming family.
- Exceptionally bright at school and university.

Political life
- Worked closely with Lenin. The two men had met in London in 1902.
- Published two communist newspapers.
- Played a key role in the 1917 Revolution.
- Leader of the army during the Civil War.

Leadership qualities
- A brilliant writer and public speaker.
- Seen as the Communist Party's best political thinker, after Lenin.
- Very arrogant. Often offended other members of the Party.

DISCUSS

1 Look at the information on the left on Trotsky and compare it to Stalin's on page 106. What advantages did Trotsky have over Stalin?
2 Read the rest of the information on this page. What was the main reason Trotsky lost the leadership to Stalin? Was it luck, Trotsky's mistakes, or Stalin's tactics?

How did Stalin win the power struggle?

Trotsky underestimated Stalin. Unlike Stalin, Trotsky made little effort to build up support from members of the Communist Party. He also scared people in the USSR by arguing that as a country they should try and spread communism to other parts of the world. People in the Soviet Union were worried that this might bring them into conflict with other countries. In contrast, Stalin argued that the Party should concentrate on establishing communism in the USSR rather than trying to spread the revolution across the globe.

Trotsky was also unlucky. He fell ill towards the end of 1923. This was when it became clear that Lenin was dying and that Trotsky needed to rally support. Stalin also tricked Trotsky into not attending Lenin's funeral. Stalin told Trotsky that Lenin's funeral was going to take place on 26 January, when it was actually due to take place on the 27th. Trotsky was in the south of Russia and would not have had time to get back for the 26th; however, he could have returned in time for the 27th. So, at Lenin's funeral Stalin attended as chief mourner and was able to present himself as Lenin's closest friend.

Stalin was also a clever and ruthless politician. In 1924, Stalin worked with Kamanev and Zinoviev to keep power within the Party away from Trotsky and Bukharin. In 1926 he turned against Kamanev and Zinoviev and allied himself with Bukharin. After Kamanev, Zinoviev and Trotsky had been expelled from the Communist Party, Stalin attacked Bukharin. By 1929 Bukharin had also been expelled from the Party. Stalin was now the undisputed leader of the Soviet Union.

How did Stalin control the Soviet Union?

In the 1930s, Stalin's main aim was to turn the Soviet Union into a leading world power. He wanted to show the world that communism could succeed and that he could turn the USSR into a modern, industrial country that could match the capitalist countries of the West such as Britain and the USA. In order to achieve his goal, Stalin believed that he had to be in complete control of the country – opposition could not be tolerated. One of Stalin's aims was to control people to such an extent that they would be afraid to even consider opposing him.

Terror – how did Stalin use fear to keep people in line?

Stalin had a large secret police force, which he used to crush any opposition. People believed that there could be spies and informers everywhere. Children were encouraged to inform on their parents. People who criticised Stalin were arrested and often tortured before being sent to labour camps (known as gulags). The camps were often in the north of the Soviet Union where prisoners would be forced to work in freezing conditions for long hours and no pay.

Stalin was ruthless with political opponents or people he saw as a threat to his position of power. Stalin 'purged' all the people in the Communist Party who he thought might challenge his leadership. These people were arrested and put on 'show trials' in public where they would be forced to admit to crimes before being sentenced and executed. It is thought that around half a million members of the Communist Party were arrested and either executed or sent to the gulags. In addition, 25,000 army officers were removed from their positions. Later, the Purges were extended to teachers, engineers, miners, factory managers and workers. It has been estimated that, by 1937, 18 million people had been transported to the labour camps.

▲ SOURCE 1 *This mock travel poster was produced by people who had been exiled from the Soviet Union. The caption says, 'Visit the USSR's pyramids!'*

▶ SOURCE 2 *Forced labour on the Belomar Canal.*

Censorship and propaganda – how did Stalin control ideas?

People living in the Soviet Union only received the information that Stalin wanted them to. The government controlled all newspapers and radio stations. Communists did not believe in God so churches were closed and religious worship was banned. Instead, people were encouraged to worship Stalin. Belief in God was replaced by belief in communism.

▲ SOURCE 4 *Stalin at the Helm, a poster from 1933.*

▲ SOURCE 3 *The cover of a magazine from 1949. During the celebrations of his 70th birthday a giant portrait of Stalin was suspended over Moscow and lit up at night by searchlights.*

At the time, Stalin was popular and admired by the majority of people living in the Soviet Union. This was largely due to propaganda. Paintings, films, plays and posters were produced to show people that Stalin was the best person to lead the Soviet Union. Every town had a large statue of Stalin in the centre, a Stalin Square or a Stalin Avenue. Regular processions through the streets were organised in honour of Stalin and what he had achieved.

▲ SOURCE 5 *A 1937 photomontage of Stalin surrounded by a sea of children's faces.*

DISCUSS

Look at Sources 3, 4 and 5. What is the main message of each source?

111

How did Stalin change life in the Soviet Union?

Life for workers

The government ran all the main industries. A five-year plan was introduced that set targets for each of the key heavy industries (coal, iron, oil and electricity). Some of these targets were almost impossible to reach because of a shortage of raw materials. However, many people supported Stalin and were determined to reach the targets that had been set because they thought that they were working for a better future and helping to make the Soviet Union a leading world power. Propaganda posters like the one on the right played an important role.

Results during the first five-year plan were very impressive. Over 100 new industrial towns and 15,000 factories were built. Between 1927 and 1937 coal production rose from 35.4 million tons to 128 million tons; oil from 11.7 million to 28.5 million tons; and steel from four million to 17.7 million tons. By 1937, the Soviet Union had been transformed into a modern industrial power. Unemployment was virtually non-existent.

However, 'progress' came at a great human cost. People working in the factories had to work very long hours for very little pay (wages actually fell between 1928 and 1937). If they were late for work they could be sacked and lose their house or flat. Workers were fined if they failed to meet targets. If they made mistakes they were accused of sabotage and arrested. Overcrowding was a problem in the towns and the cities.

In the countryside, peasants were forced to join collective farms, under the control of the local communist leader. Land, animals and tools were not owned by individuals but by the collective. People were expected to work cooperatively. If they refused to join the collectives they were rounded up by the police and sent to labour camps. It took time for people to get used to the new system of farming and at first there were food shortages. In 1932–1933 there was a famine and millions died in Kazakhstan and the Ukraine – the Soviet Union's richest agricultural region.

How much did life change for women?

The Communist Party wanted to change the position of women in society. They thought that women should be more independent and not just fulfil the domestic role of caring for the home and family. Women played a key role in industry. The five-year plan revealed a shortage of workers so thousands of crèches and day-care centres were set up so that women could work in the factories. By 1937, 40 per cent of industrial workers were women. However, not enough childcare was provided by the government. Many children lived on the streets in gangs of orphans and survived by begging and stealing. Also, although the Communist Party stressed equality for women, few became actively involved in politics.

DISCUSS

What are the key messages in Sources 6, 7, 8 and 9?

▲ SOURCE 6 *This poster shows Stalin marching alongside Soviet miners. The text means, 'It is our workers who make our programme achievable'.*

▲ SOURCE 7 *Alexei Stakhanov – a Soviet coal miner, whose amazing productivity at work inspired others to work as hard as he did.*

▲ SOURCE 8 Woman Metro-Builder with Pneumatic Drill *by Aleksandr Samohvalov (1937).*

◄ SOURCE 9 Higher and Higher, *a painting by Serafima Ryangina (1934).*

Life for young people

The communists thought education was very important. Their aim was for each child to receive nine years of free education. However, schools often struggled for resources. Teachers were badly paid and many children left school early. At school, the aim was to combine education and political propaganda. During the 1920s:

- Religious teaching was replaced by an emphasis on communism and atheism.
- A large part of education focused on technical subjects and industrial training in order to prepare pupils for the world of work. There were visits to farms, factories and power stations.
- The history of the Soviet Union was rewritten in order to present Lenin and Stalin as the real heroes of the Revolution and the Civil War. Trotsky was given little credit. Like other old 'heroes of the Revolution' he was written and airbrushed out of Soviet history. Look at the two photographs on the right. Can you spot the difference?

Turning young people into loyal communists was not just left to teachers. Outside of school, students were expected to join the 'Pioneers' and promise to obey what the Communist Party taught them. In the Pioneers, children took part in activities like camping. However, they were also taught communist values. From the age of fourteen or fifteen young people could join the Komsomol. This was more serious and focused on politics. It was seen as an important step before becoming a member of the Communist Party.

▶ SOURCE 11 *After Stalin seized power, a very similar photograph was published with Trotsky and Kamanev painted out.*

▲ SOURCE 10 *A photograph of Lenin addressing troops in 1920, with Trotsky and Kamanev on the steps to the right of the platform.*

What did Hitler and the Nazi Party believe in?

THE PROGRAMME OF THE NAZI PARTY

This stated the aims of the Nazi Party. Hitler help to write this in 1920.

- Destroy the Treaty of Versailles. End reparation payments.
- Take over land in Eastern Europe in order to provide 'living space' for the growing German population.
- Only those of German blood may be members of the nation. No Jew may be a member of the nation.
- Provide generous old age pensions, help for small businesses and work for all.

KEY POINTS FROM *MEIN KAMPF*

Whilst in prison, after the failed Munich Putsch, Hitler wrote *Mein Kampf* ('My Struggle'). This book outlined his main ideas about how Germany should be ruled.

- Germany should have one strong leader. Debate and discussion produce weak government. Instead of democracy, decisions should be taken by one man.
- Communism is a threat to Germany. The Communist Party should be destroyed.
- The Aryans (white Europeans) are the Master Race. All other races (especially the Jews) are inferior.
- Rebuild the German army. Armed struggle is an essential part of life.

How did Hitler rise to power?

Adolf Hitler became leader of Germany in 1933. He did not seize power in the same way that Stalin became leader of the Soviet Union. After the First World War Germany became a democracy. Men and women living in Germany could vote in elections to choose who should run Germany. So, you need to find out how the Nazis became the most popular party in Germany.

The new government was known as the Weimar Republic. It soon faced many problems. The way that the government dealt with these problems made it unpopular.

DISCUSS

Today Hitler's ideas seem very extreme. Why, *in the 1920s and early 1930s*, might the German people have found some of his ideas attractive and wanted to vote for the Nazi Party?

Problem 1: The Treaty of Versailles

Key — Land lost due to Treaty of Versailles — Demilitarised area

The First World War ended in November 1918. By June 1919 the Allies (France, Britain and the United States) had decided on a peace treaty. This became known as the Treaty of Versailles. The new German government was not invited to take part in the discussions about the peace treaty and they had little choice but to accept the agreement. The German people hated the treaty and many blamed the new government for 'accepting' it.

The terms of the Treaty of Versailles:
- Germany was blamed for the war. It had to pay reparations to countries that had been damaged as a result of the war (mainly France and Belgium). In 1921 the sum that Germany had to pay was fixed at £6,600 million.
- The German army was reduced to just 100,000 men. The German navy was also reduced and Germany was not allowed to have submarines, tanks or an air force.
- Germany lost 13 per cent of its land. This included land that was rich in important raw materials such as coal.

Problem 2: Fear of communism

Communists living in Germany wanted to seize power for themselves. They did not believe that the new government would do enough to help working people. There were communist uprisings in 1919 and 1920. These uprisings scared many people living in Germany. Business owners and farmers were particularly concerned. They had seen what had happened in the Soviet Union where the communist government had taken over big industries and farmers' land. Groups like the Nazi Party and the German National Party hated communism. They often fought battles with the communists in the streets.

▲ Problem 3: Economic difficulties

Germany was also struggling to keep up with the reparation payments to the Allies. In 1923 French and Belgian troops marched into the Ruhr and seized control of all mines, factories and railways. This made the German government even more short of money. The government printed more money to pay German workers in the Ruhr who had gone on strike, and to help pay its debts.

However, the more money that they printed the less it was worth. Prices rose at an incredible rate and there was hyper-inflation. People needed more and more money to buy things. Workers found that wage increases did not keep up with rising prices. By November 1923 an egg cost 80 million marks and a glass of beer 150 million marks. People with savings were the biggest losers. Pensioners were badly hit. In 1919, 6,600 marks was a small fortune. By 1923 it would not even buy a stamp for a letter.

▲ *A camp for the homeless in a Berlin park.*

The German government was only able to get the economy back on track by replacing the old money system with a new currency called the Rentenmark. It also used foreign loans, mainly from the United States, to rebuild the economy. For a while people felt better off as new factories were built and new businesses were set up. But, in 1929, another economic disaster struck Germany. It became known as **The Great Depression**.

▲ *German children, in 1923, show how many German marks are equal to one US dollar.*

The problems started in the USA. Their stock market suddenly crashed and businesses went bankrupt. This affected many countries in Europe as the USA stopped buying foreign goods and loaning money to other countries. Germany was affected particularly badly because it relied so heavily on loans from the USA. Without the huge loans from the USA, German firms went bankrupt and unemployment rose to six million. Many German people lost their homes and millions lived in poverty.

The Great Depression made many people angry. They blamed the political parties that had been running the country and started to question the democratic way that Germany was governed. Support for the more extreme political parties like the Nazis and the communists grew.

The Nazi Party was well organised and it was able to take full advantage of the problems that the government faced. Hitler was a powerful and inspiring public speaker. He was able to make people believe that he alone could save them from the problems Germany faced. Nazi propaganda was also very effective. They used the latest technology – loudspeakers, slide shows and films – to spread their message. They also used powerful propaganda posters with simple slogans to spread their key ideas.

In the 1932 elections, the Nazi Party won 37 per cent of the vote. They became the most popular political party in Germany and the largest party in the German Parliament (the Reichstag). In January 1933, Hitler made a political deal with Franz von Papen (a well-connected politician). They agreed to form a new government with Hitler as Chancellor and von Papen as Vice-Chancellor. Hitler was now leader of Germany.

◄ SOURCE 12   *'Our last hope: Hitler'.*
A Nazi election poster from 1932.

Hitler becomes dictator

Opposition to the Nazis was weak and divided. The Nazis' two main rivals, the Communist Party and the Social Democratic Party, were not prepared to work together to stop the Nazis. Once in power, Hitler moved quickly to strengthen his position.

In February 1933, the Reichstag building where the German Parliament met was burnt down. A Dutch communist, Marinus van der Lubbe, was found at the scene. The Nazis claimed that this was part of a communist plot to take over the country. Hitler was able to persuade the German President to grant him emergency powers to deal with the threat. The Nazis used this extra power to attack their political opponents. Thousands of people were arrested, political meetings were banned, and opposition newspapers were closed down.

However, Hitler, like Stalin, wanted total power. On 24 March he was able to push through an Enabling Law. This law gave Hitler the power to pass any law he wanted without going through the Reichstag or the German

▲ SOURCE 13 *Nazi stormtroopers arrest suspected Communists, 1933.*

Parliament. The Reichstag had placed all the power in the hands of Hitler and his closest advisers. Germany was now a dictatorship.

By the end of 1933, all political parties except for the Nazis had been banned. In 1934, the entire army, the one group who had the power to overthrow Hitler, swore an oath of personal loyalty to Adolf Hitler.

How did Hitler control Germany?

Terror – how did Hitler use fear to keep people in line?

Hitler did not want any opposition within Germany. In order to achieve this, the Nazis used a mixture of propaganda, censorship and terror.

The man at the centre of the network of terror was **Heinrich Himmler** (right).

The SS

Himmler built up the strength of the SS (originally Hitler's personal bodyguard). By 1939 it had 240,000 members. Recruitment to the SS was very strict and they were trained to be ruthless and fiercely loyal to Hitler. The SS had the power to arrest people without trial and could search houses without permission from the courts. They also ran the concentration camps.

The Courts

The law courts were under Nazi control so a fair trial was impossible. All judges had to swear an oath of loyalty to Hitler. The number of offences carrying the death penalty increased from three, when the Nazis came to power, to 46. Even 'crimes' such as listening to a foreign radio station or telling an anti-Nazi joke could be punished by death.

Concentration camps

The Nazis set up concentration camps as soon as they came into power. At first, opponents to the Nazis were sent to makeshift prisons, set up in disused factories. Later, the camps were purpose-built and prisoners were forced to do hard labour. Food was very limited and discipline was harsh. Beatings and random executions were common and very few people emerged from the camps alive.

The Gestapo

The Gestapo were the secret police. They could open mail, tap telephones and arrest and torture people without going through the courts. The Gestapo set up a huge network of informers who reported on local people that they believed were 'anti-Nazi'. Every 30 or 40 houses had a Block Warden, a local Nazi, who checked up on people and reported back to either the Gestapo or SS.

Censorship and propaganda – how did Hitler control ideas?

Many Germans did not have to be terrorised into supporting Hitler. They went along with Nazi Party's policies because they believed that Germany was benefiting from the way that the country was being governed. Propaganda played an important role in convincing people that the Nazis were doing good things for the German people. The man who controlled Nazi propaganda was **Josef Goebbels** (right).

Goebbels made sure that the German people received one-sided information through the media. Nazi achievements were exaggerated; Nazi ideas were presented in the most attractive way possible, and Nazi failings were hidden from the public.

Rallies

Goebbels organised mass rallies, marches, torchlight processions and special celebrations. These made the German people feel that they were part of something special and exciting.

Books, newspapers and radio

As soon as the Nazis came to power, Goebbels organised public book-burnings. Books by political opponents, Jews, and anyone else the Nazis disapproved of were burned on huge bonfires. All new books were censored – nothing could be published without Goebbels' permission.

Two-thirds of Germany's newspapers were closed down. Those that remained received daily instructions about what to print. Display boards were set up in public places so that everyone could read these newspapers.

Goebbels quickly took control of all radio stations. Hitler's speeches were broadcast as were German music and programmes on German history. Cheap radios were made so that as many people as possible could listen to these programmes. In addition, loudspeakers were set up in workplaces, streets and bars so that people could listen to important speeches and programmes.

Films, art and posters

Goebbels controlled all the films made in Germany. Many were adventure stories, comedies or love stories, but newsreel films, full of the messages about the greatness of Hitler and the Nazi Party, were always shown before the main feature film. Some films were made on Goebbels' orders and carried very strong Nazi messages.

Artists were restricted in the same way as writers. Only Nazi-approved artists could publish their work or put on exhibitions. Paintings or sculptures showing heroic-looking Aryans, military figures or images of the ideal Aryan family were encouraged. Images of Hitler were everywhere.

▶ SOURCE 14 *A Nazi Party poster from 1936. The words at the top say, 'Young people serve the Führer'.*

DISCUSS

Look at Source 14. What key messages about Hitler is this poster putting across?

119

How did Nazi rule change life in Germany?

Life for workers

The Nazis were able to reduce unemployment by increasing the size of the armed forces from 100,000 to 1,400,000. All males between the ages of 18 and 25 had to do two years' military service. New tanks, aeroplanes and battleships were built and lots of jobs were created to build the weapons and equip the army.

Also, the Nazis put the unemployed to work on job schemes, helping to build new motorways, schools, hospitals and other public facilities. The Nazis stopped paying benefits to anyone who was unemployed or refused to join the job schemes. Workers on the job schemes were paid less than they had received from unemployment benefits.

Trade unions were abolished. All workers had to join the **German Labour Front**, which was run by the Nazis. Schemes such as **Strength Through Joy** gave workers cheap theatre and cinema tickets, and organised leisure activities, which included holidays, trips, courses and sports events. Better meals and facilities were also provided. But in the factories working hours increased and wages remained low.

How much did life change for women and the family?

The Nazis believed that women should be mothers and housewives – not workers. Lots of women employed as lawyers, doctors, teachers and civil servants were sacked. Hitler believed that women had no role to play in politics or government.

The Nazis did not want women to stay single. Marriage and having children were encouraged. Loans were offered to married couples. The more children they had the less they had to pay back. However, not all women were allowed to have children. Women with inherited diseases had to be sterilised.

Slimming was frowned upon as the Nazis wanted women to be strong and solid in order to have lots of babies. Women were encouraged to wear simple rather than fashionable clothes. Wearing trousers or high heels, having permed or dyed hair, using make-up or smoking in public were all discouraged.

▲ SOURCE 15 *Workers ready to start work on building the first motorway in 1933.*

▲ SOURCE 16 *A poster showing the Nazis' view of the ideal German family.*

DISCUSS

What message is being put forward by the Nazis in Source 16? *Think* about how each role within the family is portrayed.

Life for young people

The Nazis knew that they could never be sure that they had the support of all adults, but Hitler believed that if they could control young people then they could control the future. As Source 17 shows, Hitler had very clear ideas on how young people should be educated.

Education

Hitler wanted all young people to become loyal Nazis. This was to be achieved both inside and outside of school. The school curriculum was used to teach what the Nazis wanted young people to think. Teachers who refused to teach Nazi ideas were sacked. Here's an overview of what lessons were like:

- Lots of physical exercise – to make youngsters fit and tough. Boxing was compulsory for boys.
- Lots of German history – to teach pupils about Germany's military victories in the past and how Adolf Hitler was the saviour of Germany.
- Girls were taught home-making and childcare.
- In biology, pupils were told that they were special and that the 'Aryan race' was superior in intelligence to other races. To keep the Aryan race strong you would be taught about the 'danger' of mixing with other races.
- Maths was used to help young people understand guns and artillery.

The Hitler Youth

Outside of school all children aged between ten and eighteen were pressurised into joining the Hitler Youth. By 1939, nearly all young Germans had joined the Hitler Youth. All other youth movements were banned.

The Hitler Youth provided holidays, camping and sports activities for young people. Most Hitler Youth meetings also contained a short lecture on Nazi ideas, and members would be expected to be able to answer questions on Nazi achievements and military history. The main aims of the Hitler Youth were to make sure that young people grew up to be loyal Nazis and to prepare young men for a life in the army.

Boys spent a lot of their time doing physical activities that would make them brave, fit and tough soldiers. They were expected to be able to complete a one-and-a-half-day cross-country march, do close combat exercise, learn how to use weapons and even jump out of a first-floor window wearing full army battledress.

▶ SOURCE 18 *Hitler Youth members jumping over fire to demonstrate their bravery.*

SOURCE 17
Hitler's words on youth, from Hitler Speaks *by Herman Rauschning, 1939.*

In my great educational work I am beginning with the young. My magnificent youngsters! With them I can make a new world!

My teaching is hard. Weakness has to be knocked out of them. The world will shrink in alarm from the youngsters who grow up in my schools: a violent, masterful, brave, cruel, younger generation. I will have no intellectual training. Knowledge is ruin to my young men.

DISCUSS

What can you learn from Sources 17 and 18 about Hitler's attitude towards educating young people?

Making effective comparisons

Historians often make comparisons between events in different countries or across different time periods. This can be quite a difficult skill to master.

WARNING!

It is easy to fall into a trap. Many students describe one event in detail. They then describe the other event in detail. Finally in their conclusion they analyse similarities and differences between the two events. It is only in this last section of their answer that they really make *effective* comparisons.

Let's take the question:

How similar were Stalin and Hitler?

A bad way to tackle this question would be to follow **Plan A** (above right).

The problem with this approach is that the first two paragraphs (which could be very long) do not really answer the question.

To be able to answer this type of question effectively you need to make direct comparisons. You need to plan your paragraphs very carefully. In each paragraph take a theme that will allow you to make direct comparisons. Use **Plan B** (right) to help you.

Within each paragraph use the *double hamburger paragraph* structure and clever connectives to make sure you answer the question.

- Use the top bun to clearly signpost the theme you are exploring.
- Then include a section where you explore similarities related to this theme.
- Followed by a section where you explore differences related to this theme.
- Finally, use the bottom bun to reach a mini-conclusion. In terms of the theme of the paragraph – how similar were the two dictators/dictatorships?

PLAN A

Paragraph 1: Write everything you know about Stalin! Describe Stalin's early life, his beliefs, how he got into power, how he controlled the Soviet Union and how he changed people's lives.
Paragraph 2: Write everything you know about Hitler! Describe Hitler's early life, his beliefs, how he got into power, how he controlled Germany and how he changed people's lives.
Paragraph 3: Reach a conclusion – how similar were they?

PLAN B

Paragraph 1: Compare their early life and beliefs.
Paragraph 2: Compare how they got into power.
Paragraph 3: Compare how they controlled their country.
Paragraph 4: Compare how their dictatorship changed people's lives (remember to explore workers, women and young people).
Paragraph 5: Reach an overall conclusion – reach a judgement on how similar they were – were they almost exactly the same, very similar, quite similar or not really similar at all? Make sure you give your key reason(s) for reaching this judgement.

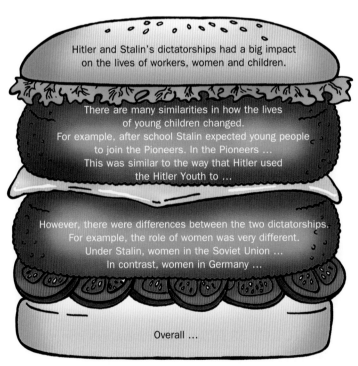

Hitler and Stalin's dictatorships had a big impact on the lives of workers, women and children.

There are many similarities in how the lives of young children changed.
For example, after school Stalin expected young people to join the Pioneers. In the Pioneers …
This was similar to the way that Hitler used the Hitler Youth to …

However, there were differences between the two dictatorships.
For example, the role of women was very different.
Under Stalin, women in the Soviet Union …
In contrast, women in Germany …

Overall …

Puzzle

DISCUSS

What type of source is this?

    Why do you think it was produced?

        When do you think it was produced?

            Where was it produced? Which country?

                Who are these people?

Do you notice anything unusual?

CLUE

Think about an important event that happens in the
UK every year on 27 January.

What can the story of Frank Bright and his classmates tell us about the Holocaust?

The photograph on page 123 was taken in a Jewish school in Prague in May 1942. The children in the photograph are about the same age as you. The country in which they were living, Czechoslovakia, was one of the countries occupied by Nazi Germany during the Second World War. How were they affected by Nazi rule? What can their story tell us about the Holocaust?

Before Hitler came to power there were around eight million Jews living in Europe. Between 1939 and 1945 six million Jewish men, women and children were murdered in the parts of Europe occupied by Nazi Germany. This attempt to wipe out the Jewish population is usually known as the Holocaust. Jews were not the only victims – other groups of people that the Nazis thought 'undesirable' were also affected. Hundreds of thousands of Gypsies, homosexuals and mentally and physically handicapped people (particularly children) were murdered as Nazi Germany took control of much of Europe.

In this enquiry we are going to focus on what happened to Jews living in Europe under Nazi rule. In 2007, whilst preparing resources for Holocaust Memorial Day, I was fortunate enough to meet Frank Bright, one of the pupils in the photograph. Frank is in the middle of the back row.

Frank survived the Holocaust and has spent many years trying to find out what happened to all the pupils in his class. It is a remarkable story that will enable you to build up your own knowledge of the Holocaust in a unique way. Too often when we study history we fail to register that the past is about human action and that the events studied affected people's lives, often in devastating ways. History is not the story of strangers, aliens from another universe; if we had been born a little earlier, it could have been our history.

▲ *Frank Bright in 1946, above, and in 2007, top.*

Frank's story: Introduction

Frank was born Franz Brichta on 7 October 1928. His early years were spent in Berlin, the capital of Germany. Frank was the only child of Hermann and Toni Brichta. Frank's father (right) was born in Moravia (now part of the Czech Republic) and had fought for Austria-Hungary on the German side during the First World War, as had Frank's uncle, who was killed.

Frank's mother was born in Berlin. Her twin brother Fritz served in the German navy during the First World War and was awarded the Iron Cross. Fritz was one of thousands of Jews who fought bravely for Germany during that war. This did not stop such Jews being persecuted as soon as Hitler came to power – their names were even removed from war memorials. In 1935, Frank started to attend a Jewish school in Berlin. Jews were not allowed to attend 'Aryan' schools. As you will see this was one of many restrictions placed on Jews living in Germany.

The photograph below (right) is from Frank's first day at school, aged six and a half. The cone in his hand was filled with sweets to make up for the first day away from home.

In June 1938 Frank and his mother and father left Berlin and moved to Prague, where he attended another Jewish school. Frank was thirteen and a half at the time the class photograph (on page 124) was taken in May 1942.

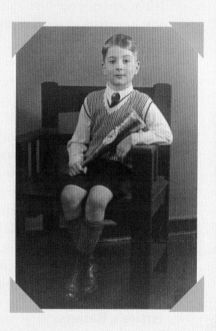

Why is everyone in the class photograph wearing a star?

When you first looked at the class photo, did you notice anything unusual about what the pupils were wearing? If you look closely you will notice that most pupils in the photograph are wearing a star. Those who are not would have had the star sewn on to their jackets. The star was yellow, six-sided and had the word 'Jude' (Jew) inside it. In 1941 a law was introduced that forced all Jews to wear it. If they did not they would be punished. Only a few stars were issued to each person. It had to be firmly fixed to clothes and kept in good condition. Every time clothes were washed the star had to be taken off and then put back on again. The law was designed to humiliate the Jews and make them easy to identify. Non-Jews were not expected to mix with Jews. This is just one example of how the Jews were persecuted in Prague and the rest of Nazi-occupied Europe.

Frank's family had hoped to escape the dreadful persecution that Jews had to endure in Germany. But, on 15 March 1939, Germany invaded the Czech and Moravian part of Czechoslovakia. By the summer of 1940 they occupied nearly all of Europe (Sweden, Switzerland and Spain remained neutral) and Britain faced the very real threat of invasion. During the Second World War the Nazis would push their anti-Jewish policy to new extremes.

DOING HISTORY:
Organising your research

ACTIVITY

In the UK, on 27 January every year, we hold a Holocaust Memorial Day. Your task, as you work through this enquiry, is to prepare a presentation on the Holocaust for this important day.

You need to use the story of Frank and his classmates to explore **four key questions**:

1 Why did the Nazis persecute the Jews and other groups of people?
2 How did the Nazis persecute the Jews?
3 How should the Holocaust be remembered?
4 Why is the Holocaust so significant?

Key Question 1: WHY DID THE NAZIS PERSECUTE THE JEWS?

Frank was just over four years old when Adolf Hitler became leader of Germany. Hitler was not the first leader in Europe to attack the Jews and he did not invent anti-Semitism (hatred of Jews) – nor was he the first ruler to force Jews to wear a yellow badge.

Jews had suffered religious prejudice for many centuries. In Europe during the Middle Ages, Jewish communities were attacked and, during the Crusades, Jews were murdered or driven out of many countries. In England, in 1275, all Jews were made to wear a yellow badge. In 1290, Edward I expelled Jews from England and seized all their land and money. It was not until the seventeenth century that Oliver Cromwell allowed Jews to return to England. In 1648 there were savage attacks (called pogroms) on Jews in the Ukraine and up to 100,000 Jews were massacred. There were further pogroms against the Jews in Russia during the nineteenth century.

The Nazis took anti-Semitism to a new extreme. As a young man Hitler had lived on the streets of Vienna, where anti-Semitic ideas were very common. Hitler became obsessed with the Jews. He did not try to hide his hatred of the Jews from the German people.

Hitler's Beliefs

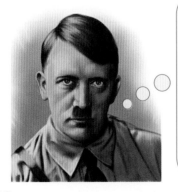

I believe:

• The Germans are 'Aryans' – a superior race of people. Aryan men should be workers and fighters; women should have babies and look after the family.
• Other races are inferior. There are many inferior races, such as Slavs and black people – but the lowest of them all are Jews.
• The Aryan race should be kept pure. Aryans should not marry or have children with other races. German blood has been polluted by other races.

As you can see, for your research into the first key question, there isn't very much information for you to read. However, the second key question is a bit different. The information you need can be found on pages 127–136. 'How did the Nazis persecute the Jews?' is a **big question** and will form a large part of your presentation for Holocaust Memorial Day. Make sure that you use **sub-questions** or sub-headings to break down your research notes and structure your presentation. For example, for this opening section you could use:

• 'How were Jews treated in Germany when the Nazis first came to power?' or
• 'How were Jews persecuted in Germany from 1933 to 1938?'

As you work through pages 127–136 you can use the sub-headings and questions suggested by us or, even better, think of your own.

126

As soon as he got into power Hitler started to persecute the Jews. The Nazis used false research to suggest that Jews were an 'inferior' race. They blamed Jews for the problems in Germany and encouraged ordinary Germans to hate Jews. There were about half a million Jews living in Germany. For a young Jewish child living in Berlin it must have been a frightening time.

ACTIVITY

How is Frank's story supported by Sources 19–21?

What can Frank's story tell us about how Jews were treated in Germany when the Nazis came to power?

Frank's Story Part 1: Berlin 1928–1938

I remember the horrible cartoons of Jews in the official Nazi newspapers, displayed behind glass in showcases fixed at eye level to walls at street corners. They showed the most ugly Jews with the most enormous noses. They were often shown profiting from exploiting good-looking innocent Germans. These cartoons were obviously designed to foster hate.

The park had wide paths with benches. Jews could only sit on one bench, reserved for Jews, somewhere in the middle. We did sit on it but it was risky, one felt conspicuous, uncomfortable and vulnerable. This was what they wanted.

This sign, that Jews were not welcome, was in the entrance door of all German restaurants and bars. I felt, and was, a second-class citizen.

I started to attend a Jewish school set up to offer an education to the many children who had been expelled from the local state schools or where their stay had been made impossible by bullying, threats and intimidation by their German classmates and teachers.

▼ SOURCE 19 *This bench is marked 'For Jews only'.*

▼ SOURCE 21 *This sign in a small German town says 'Jews not wanted in this place'*

▼ SOURCE 20 *Illustration from a Nazi children's book.*

What can Frank's story tell us about how Jews were persecuted in countries that the Nazis occupied?

By the mid-1930s many Jews had fled Germany. However, emigration was not easy. It certainly wasn't a matter of 'pack up and go'. There were two main obstacles. One was getting a visa to enter another country – most countries had a strict quota system that limited the number of people (we would call them political asylum seekers) that they accepted. The second obstacle was money. The Germans demanded a large sum of money before they would give Jews an exit visa.

Frank's family were one of the families who were able to escape. In 1938 they moved to Prague in Czechoslovakia. However, it was not long before they once again found themselves living in a country under German control – the Germans occupied the western part of Czechoslovakia in March 1939.

Frank attended a Jewish school. He was not allowed to attend a Czech or German school. Frank, his classmates and their families faced very similar restrictions to Jewish children living in Germany.

Frank's Story Part 2: Prague (1938–1942)

There are many restrictions which I remember vividly. The afternoon shopping hour when there was nothing left. The handing in of radios and the absence of newspapers, which left us completely uninformed. The ban on using public transport, no clothing coupons, the curfew from 8 p.m. The wearing of the star, the disconnection of telephones, the confiscation of sewing machines, bicycles and cameras. The handing in of musical instruments, as well as radios, which meant that our lives were without music. Jews had no rights. The police would not act, no lawyer would defend you and the word of a Jew in court counted for nothing. The Germans confiscated Jewish people's bank accounts, savings, life insurance policies, shares and everything of gold, silver and pearls.

For Frank and his classmates these restrictions had very real consequences. There is more to the text than reading the bare words. The confiscation of sewing machines might not seem like a big deal to us but for Jewish families living in Prague it created real difficulties.

ACTIVITY

Study the restrictions and consequences cards on page 129. Look at the list of **restrictions** placed on Jews living in Prague. Think carefully about the **consequences** for Jewish families of the laws that were passed.

1 Try and match each restriction to a consequence card like the example below:

2 Can you think of other consequences? Produce your own consequence cards and link them to laws that were passed.

3 Which laws do you think had the greatest impact on Jews living in Prague? Select three laws and explain your reasoning.

4 Use this information to add to your presentation for Holocaust Memorial Day. Remember to think of a good sub-heading.

23.10.1941: It is an offence to sell to Jews: fruit of any sort, including nuts; also marmalade, jams, cheese, sweets, fish of any sort, as well as poultry and game of any sort.
02.03.1942: Aryan doctors are not permitted to prescribe additional food for sick Jews.

led to

People went hungry. They also became sick because they did not get vitamins and nutrients they needed.

Restrictions placed on Jews

10.10.1940: Jews not eligible to obtain clothing coupons.

20.12.1941: Confiscation of sewing machines.

10.01.1941: Collection of articles of fur and woollens.

20.02.1941: The shopping period for Jews limited to between 15:00 and 17:00 hours.

24.09.1941: Jews are excluded from all but one post office, access limited to between 13:00 and 15:00 hours.

17.09.1941: Distribution of distinguishing Jewish yellow star.

22.09.1939: Handing over of radio receivers.
01.05.1942: The sale to Jews of German newspapers is a punishable offence.

16.03.1939: Jews excluded from being lawyers, teachers, members of juries, engineers. Jews cannot be vets, chemists, artists. Jewish doctors may only treat Jewish patients.

September 1939: Jews are forbidden to be out of doors after 20:00.
20.02.1940: Jews are forbidden to visit cinemas, theatres and sports events.
17.05.1940: Jews are forbidden to enter Prague's public parks and gardens.
July 1941: Jews are to hand in pets, such as dogs, cats and birds.

October 1941: All synagogues and prayer rooms are to be closed.

Consequences

This meant that clothing, if it was spare, could not be easily altered at home or by Jewish dressmakers and tailors.

The one post office open to Jews for the whole of Prague could mean a walk of several miles for a stamp to send letters to keep in touch with relatives.

This was a real problem with growing children who grew out of their clothes and shoes.

The winters in Prague are long and cold, without woollens they were made harder to bear.

This made you feel as if you stood out. It made you more aware than ever that you had no civil rights. Also, people avoided you.

This together with the fact that their savings and valuables had been taken from them meant that many Jews struggled to survive and lived in poverty.

This was a period of extreme food shortages and meant that by the afternoon there was nothing left on the shelves to eat.

This meant living on rumours. The fear of being called up for transportation to unknown places from which no one ever returned made for stress, which it is impossible to convey.

Jews were made to feel like second-class citizens. All personal freedoms had been taken away. It was very difficult to have any kind of social life.

Jews found it difficult to pray together.

What happened to the pupils in the photograph after their school was closed down?

The Jewish school that Frank and his classmates attended in Prague was closed down in the summer of 1942. Between July 1942 and July 1943 the majority of Frank's class were sent to Theresienstadt ghetto. Frank was one of the last children to be sent to the ghetto. In July 1943, Frank and his parents were sent to Theresienstadt, an old fortress town about 60 km from Prague.

How did the Nazis' treatment of the Jews change during the Second World War?

After Germany invaded Poland on 1 September 1939, another 3.5 million Jews were trapped under Nazi rule. In Poland, Jews were also forced into special sections of cities and towns, called ghettos. The largest ghetto in Poland was the Warsaw ghetto. The ghetto was shut off from the rest of the city – if Jews tried to escape they were executed. It was also impossibly overcrowded. Food was very limited and people had to survive on just 300 calories a day (the equivalent of two and a half slices of bread a day). Jews who could work were used for slave labour. Those who could not were left to die from hunger and disease. Over half a million Jews died in the Warsaw ghetto.

During the war Jews were also forced into ghettos in other countries. Theresienstadt was the nearest ghetto to Prague. However, one of Frank's closest friends never made it to the ghetto. In June 1942, Reinhard Heydrich (a high-ranking SS Officer) was assassinated in Prague. In retaliation the Germans burned to the ground two Czech villages. Many other Czechs were executed too and so were Jews. On 10 June 1942 one thousand Prague Jews were sent on transport 'AAh' to Ujazdow and then shot on arrival. Among those Jews taken from Prague to Ujazdow were **Kurt Herschmann** (left) and his mother. Only one month after the class photograph was taken, Kurt and his mother, Wilhelmina, had been murdered.

ACTIVITY
Use the information on page 130 to add to your research notes for Holocaust Memorial Day. Make sure that you explain how the Nazis' persecution of Jews started to change during the Second World War.

▲ SOURCE 22
Photographs of young children in the Warsaw ghetto, 1941.

What can Frank's story tell us about life in the ghetto?

Theresienstadt – a model camp?

The Nazis claimed that Theresienstadt was a model camp. They even used it as propaganda to show that Jews were living in good conditions in ghettos! When the Red Cross visited the ghetto of Theresienstadt on 23 June 1944, the Nazis were able to convince them, or they were too easily convinced, that Jews lived a comfortable life in the ghetto.

The Red Cross followed a route that had been carefully planned by the Germans. The fronts of houses along the official route were painted to give them a fresh look. A band was playing in the park, which had been constructed for the day of inspection only, and when the SS commander of the camp gave chocolate to children playing in the playground, they had to say: 'Chocolate again, Uncle Rahm?'. The Red Cross inspection team only stayed a few hours and did not question the details given to them by the SS. The Red Cross delegation did not speak to a single inmate. The Red Cross report spoke of the ghetto in glowing terms, as if it were a health resort with a happy population without a care in the world.

Frank's Story Part 3: Theresienstadt Ghetto (1943–1944)

Theresienstadt ghetto was surrounded by walls about 30 feet high. I think that the very first item the Germans put up in the ghetto were multiple gallows. One young man who had lived in our block of flats and had been sent with the very first transport of 342 men from Prague on 24 November 1942 to establish the ghetto, was hanged there. His crime? He had posted a postcard to his girlfriend. He was one of sixteen executed for the same offence of trying to keep in touch with their nearest and dearest.

Families were separated. My mother was allocated a bunk bed in a huge room with two-tier bunks as far as the eye could see. There was no privacy whatsoever and not even a chair or table or anywhere to put her belongings. My father was placed in a loft of another old barracks. I was moved to a small room with three-tier bunks, which I shared with six other boys in an old house. We had never been separated before. For the first few days we met at a mealtime, what there was of it, and were surrounded by old people begging for food. If you gave your small allocation away it was you who went hungry. The Germans considered those too old or too weak to work as being 'useless mouths'. These people received only starvation rations with the result that they died only a few weeks after arrival.

The place was vastly overcrowded. Into a space designed for ten soldiers were now crammed between 50 and 70 people. It was difficult to keep clean. Soap was in short supply, disinfectants were unheard of. Disease spread rapidly, particularly typhus. This disease caused fever, delirium and, if the body was weak, death.

The overcrowded conditions were also the ideal breeding ground for bed bugs. Bedbugs are small, evil-smelling, round insects, say 5 mm in diameter, which at night crawl along the ceiling and drop on to a sleeper's face. They never miss, they have an uncanny instinct. They would then suck blood, gorge themselves and inflate to several times their original size. As it went from one victim to another it would spread infections. While I was there houses which had a particularly bad infestation would be debugged using Zyklon-B gas. This was the gas that would later be used to murder Jews in gas chambers, only we didn't know that at the time.

ACTIVITY

The reality of life in the ghetto for people like Frank and his classmates was very different to the report written by the Red Cross.

1 Use Part 3 of Frank's story to challenge the report. Select three pieces of evidence to prove that Theresienstadt was far from a model camp.

2 As a class, decide on five words to describe life in the ghetto.

3 Use these words and the key pieces of evidence you have selected to add to your research notes. Choose a powerful sub-heading and make sure that you vividly describe the reality of life in the ghetto for people like Frank.

What happened to the pupils in Frank's class after they left the ghetto?

The majority of people who were sent to Theresienstadt did not remain there for very long. The constant coming and going was a feature of the ghetto. Only three children from Frank's class remained in Theresienstadt throughout the war: **Hana Ginz**, **Jiri Kavan** and **Ruth Weber**. The rest of the class were among the tens of thousands of Jewish people who were sent east from the ghetto to the extermination camps in Latvia, Poland and Russia. Most of them were sent to their deaths. Of the 139,517 men, women and children sent to the ghetto, 33,521 died there, 87,063 were sent to the east – and of those only 3,097 survived.

By the end of 1941 the German army had invaded Poland and a large part of Russia. Six million Jews were now living in territory controlled by the Germans. As the German army advanced through Eastern Europe it was followed by special SS units called **Einsatzgruppen**. The job of these units was to round up and shoot Jews and other 'undesirables'. By the autumn of 1941, mass shootings were taking place all over Eastern Europe.

It was not just Jews from Poland and Russia who were killed in mass shootings in Eastern Europe. **Eva Wachtl** (left) and her younger brother Ota were both in Frank's class. Together with their father, Emil, and mother Ignacia, they were sent to Theresienstadt on 20 July 1942. They did not stay very long. Just over a week later, on 28 July, the whole family was sent to Baranowicze (near Minsk in the Soviet Union) on transport 'AAy'. There were no survivors from that transport.

Alfred Handel (below left) was sent to Theresienstadt on 10 August 1942 only three months after the class photograph was taken. Just ten days later, on 20 August, he was moved to Riga, in Latvia, on transport 'Bb'. None of the 1000 people on the Riga transport survived. In total, 2000 Jews from Theresienstadt were taken to Riga and murdered. Of the 20,000 Jews sent from Germany to Riga, fewer than 1000 survived.

On reaching Riga, Jews were sent into a ghetto, from which they were either sent to slave labour camps or to their death. Thousands of innocent human beings were driven to pits and then shot, their bodies falling on to those below. The shooting was often done by local Latvian SS troops, praised by the Germans for their strong nerves in carrying out executions.

ACTIVITY

Use the information on the following pages to continue your research into how the Nazi treatment of the Jews changed during the war. Make sure your notes cover:

* The Einsatzgruppen and the face-to-face killings that took place in Eastern Europe (page 132).
* The Final Solution and the death camps (pages 133–135).

▼ SOURCE 23 *Photograph of an execution of Romanian Jews carried out on 14 September 1941 by members of an SS Einsatzgruppe.*

132

The 'Final Solution'

On 20 January 1942, leading Nazis (representing all the ministries of the German government – not just the SS) met at Wannsee (a suburb of Berlin). They met to plan what they called a 'Final Solution' to 'the Jewish Question'. This meant the complete extermination of all Jews under German control. Executions and the ghettos were seen as 'inefficient' ways of killing millions of people, so modern industrial methods were introduced. Six special death camps were built, with gas chambers capable of killing 2000 people at once, and large ovens for disposing of the bodies.

The death camps

The most famous death camp is Auschwitz, in Poland. However, transports from Theresienstadt to Auschwitz did not begin until late 1942. By this point some of Frank's classmates had already been murdered at other death camps.

Alfred Popper (left) and his family were moved to Theresienstadt on 27 July 1942. A few days later on 4 August 1942 the family was sent to Maly Trostinets (near Minsk, in the Soviet Union) on transport 'AAz'. The journey could take anything from two to six days. Alfred and his father, mother and brother were all killed on arrival. Tens of thousands of Jews were murdered in specially constructed gas vans where the exhaust pipe was connected to the inside of the van. Four other classmates and their parents were also killed at Maly Trostinets during the August and September of 1942: **Hanus Stein**, **Harry Pick**, **Ervin Herskovic** and **Jiri Feuerstein**.

Marketa Fischer (left) was fifteen years old when the class photograph was taken. She left Prague for Theresienstadt on 3 August 1942. Just a few weeks later she was moved to Treblinka, in Poland. 2,018 people were on Transport 'Bx' to Treblinka, including Marketa's

▲ SOURCE 24 *Map showing the location of the main concentration and death camps.*

mother and father. None survived. Treblinka was a death camp that had been set up in a secluded wood, just over 40 miles from Warsaw. Almost everyone who was sent to Treblinka was murdered. In less than a year, an estimated 750,000 Jews (half a million of them from Warsaw) had been killed by gassing.

From October 1942 onwards the transports that left Theresienstadt had one destination: Auschwitz in Poland. Frank's research has revealed that of the 25 children from his class who had been sent to Auschwitz between 6 September 1943 and 28 October 1944 (the very last transport), only six survived. Of the eleven children sent earlier to other death camps, none survived.

In addition, one of Frank's teachers, **Dr Georg Glanzberg** also died at the camp. Frank's other teacher, **Dr Jakub Rand**, was also sent to Auschwitz. He was one of the few people to survive. He worked as a slave labourer in a plant that manufactured poison gas for use by the German army. On arrival at Auschwitz, Jewish prisoners faced a selection. Some prisoners were chosen for slave labour, around 80 per cent of arrivals were sent straight to the gas chambers. If those chosen for slave labour later became too ill to work, they would also be sent to the gas chambers.

What can Frank's story tell us about the death camps?

On 12 October 1944, Frank and his mother were sent to Auschwitz. Frank's father Hermann had left Theresienstadt for Auschwitz on transport 'El' two weeks earlier, on 29 September. Frank did not have an opportunity to say goodbye. Of the 1,500 people on that transport only 79 survived. Frank's father was not one of them. Like many of Frank's classmates' parents, he was murdered at Auschwitz.

Frank's Story Part 4: Auschwitz (October 1944)

▲ SOURCE 25 *Guards at Auschwitz selecting who would work and who would die.*

In nearly all cases people were transported to the camps in covered cattle trucks, which was bad enough. If they were unlucky and the German railways didn't have any covered trucks they were put into open cattle trucks. In winter that would spell death.

However, there were exceptions. When my mother and I were taken from the ghetto to Auschwitz, on transport 'Eq', it was in a third-class railway carriage with a central gangway and wooden seats and windows. All I remember of the departure is the locking of the train's doors. Now I had been on trains in pre-war days but never one that had been locked, and there had never been the unease, the apprehension, the foreboding that comes from sitting in a sealed compartment not knowing one's destination, not knowing what to expect.

We arrived the next morning. We were put into two long columns, one made up of men, the other of women, some six abreast. In the mêlée of leaving the train and being put into one of the two columns I became separated from my mother. She saw me and left her place in the other column, walked over to me, shook my hand and returned to her place. Her column went forward first, one at a time until they came across an SS officer with several assistants either side of him. I couldn't see exactly what was happening but some of us went to the left and some to the right. Two, maybe all of three seconds was all that it took them to weigh up whether a man or woman or sixteen year old was or was not fit to carry out heavy work.

When it was my turn I walked forward until I got to the SS officer in charge. I had seen my mother go to the left and so I simply turned left too. I was called back. Obviously the officer's assistant had watched his finger and saw it point to the right even if I had not. So I was called back and told to go to the right. I had been chosen to live or rather, not so much to live, as to work.

On the right I waited for further directions with the others who had also been told to turn right. There weren't many of us. From records I now know that out of our transport of 1,500 who left the ghetto of Theresienstadt on 12 October 1944 only 78 survived. Of course, a few more may have survived this first selection and died, or were put to death later – but there were very few anyway.

▶ SOURCE 26 *A gas chamber in Auschwitz death camp.*

Those of us who had had been selected to work were now marched to the next stage where we undressed, put our clothes on a heap, showered, had all our hair shaved off and were issued with prison clothes. In our case it was not the striped clothing. I received no shirt, instead I was handed a thin blanket to wrap around me and to tuck into the trousers. The trousers too were ill-fitting, made for a short but wide man and held up with string. The jacket was black, very old and had been worn by many others before it was handed down to me. It had a very large cross in dark red and now crumbling paint on the back. We were then marched off to an empty wooden hut.

I didn't stray far. It was dark outside by then apart from the gloomy light given off by the bulbs attached to the concrete posts with bent tops to which the high-voltage barbed wire was attached. I saw just one man in the wire, his body twisted by the electric shock. Presumably he couldn't take it any more.

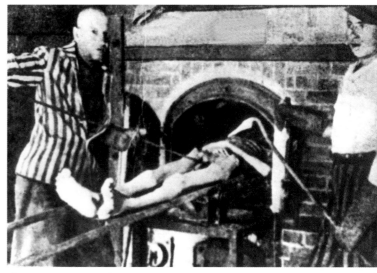

▲ **SOURCE 27** *Prisoners putting a dead body into the oven at Auschwitz.*

I didn't have far to go or to look to see the squat rectangular chimney belching black smoke. By that time I had heard what had happened to those who had been directed to the left by the moving finger. I stood there by the flickering flames licking above the top of the chimney and thought to myself, 'Which of these flames is my mother?'

She had thought of herself as German until 1933, had played her part for Germany in the 1914–1918 war, had been proud of her brother in the German navy being awarded the Iron Cross. It also occurred to me that my father, who must have arrived at the very same place a fortnight earlier, would have suffered the same fate and that from now on I was on my own.

The first night was horrific. It was cold, as was the concrete floor on which we had to lie with one thin blanket covering about five people. We were not permitted to leave the block at night and had to relieve ourselves into a huge tub or wide half barrel with two holes. Unfortunately I, and another fellow, were ordered to lift it and carry it to the cesspit and empty it. As it was full to the brim, spilling was unavoidable and some of it went over us.

◀ **SOURCE 28** *Inside the barracks (prisoners' building) in Auschwitz.*

What can Frank's story tell us about the slave labour camps?

Many German firms used death camps like Auschwitz as a source of slave labour. Just a few days after arriving at Auschwitz, Frank was selected for work in a slave labour camp. On 19 October 1944, Frank was among 165 prisoners who left Auschwitz for a place called Friedland (at the time in Germany – it is now in Poland and is called Mieroszow).

Slave labour was used by the Germans on a huge scale. German industry benefited from slave labour. Jewish prisoners in concentration camps or death camps such as Auschwitz were hired out to German firms by the SS. These firms paid the SS at very cheap rates and made a good profit by employing slave labour. Jewish workers did not get paid at all.

ACTIVITY

Use Part 5 of Frank's story to make notes on how Jews were treated in slave labour camps. This is an important part of your presentation. It is often forgotten that at least half a million Jews died while serving as slave labourers.

Frank's Story Part 5: Friedland Slave Labour Camp (1944–1945)

I travelled in a cattle truck from Auschwitz to Friedland with 164 other prisoners, standing room only. We had been selected because we were, or looked, fit and we were pleased to leave Auschwitz. Anywhere else could only be better. Friedland was a branch camp of a major concentration camp at Gross-Rosen. We were slave labourers, hired from the SS by a firm that produced aircraft propellers for the German Air Force. We were paid no wages. The rent the manager paid to the SS for our labour amounted to a few pence.

We were in Friedland for the last seven months of the war. During that time we had no change of clothes. We worked, marched and slept in the same rags, bits of thin blankets wrapped round us for vest and shirt; bits of thin blanket wrapped round my feet for socks; a coat which had survived several wearers and was falling apart. We had running cold water but no soap – certainly no towel; my shoes were solid wooden clogs. We had very little to eat. I could count my ribs – I had a hollow where there is now a stomach.

We had no resistance to infections. I had the beginnings of TB in one lung and the war came to an end just in time. I lost the nails on all my fingers. When infection set in, against which we had lost all resistance, others developed blood poisoning, which turned into internal complications, like kidney failure. It wasn't a bullet or gas that killed them but the result was the same.

The working conditions were meant to exhaust. We worked twelve-hour shifts, far too long, we didn't have the strength to operate heavy machinery and carry around heavy propeller blades for so many hours. To make matters worse we were made to stand on the Appellplatz, the barrack square, for hours on end. I have frostbite in both heels as a result and to remind me of those days.

The weeks dragged on. Interrupted sleep due to nothing but liquid food, a difficult march to and from the works on a slippery, icy road with smooth, wooden clogs. People died of starvation. I had made friends with **Hans Karl Levi**. He had emigrated from Germany to Holland, had been taken to camp Westerbork during the German occupation of Holland, had been sent from Westerbork to Theresienstadt, and from there to Auschwitz where he joined our transport to Friedland. The many years of homelessness had left him weak to begin with. One night I found him in the sickbay, a room with something like three beds, a prisoner acting as a nurse and a doctor.

He died a day or two later on 3 March 1945.

ACTIVITY

You need to use pages 137–139 to consider a new key question: How should the Holocaust be remembered?

- Make sure you that you make research notes on other groups persecuted by the Nazis and on Jewish resistance. These are often forgotten. Make sure your presentation does not leave these themes out.
- You need to decide whether to explore: 'Who was to blame for the Holocaust?' in your presentation. Debate the issues then decide as a group whether to include it as part of your presentation.

Of the 38 children in the photograph who Frank has been able to trace, only nine survived, including Frank. It is also important to remember that many of the children who survived lost fathers, mothers, brothers and sisters during the Holocaust. After the war ended Frank returned to Prague. All the flats and houses of the deported had been emptied of absolutely everything by the Germans. Those few, like Frank, who did return, now had nothing to call their own. He may have been free but he was now homeless. Frank found that all of his family were dead, including all relatives on his father's side. Of the 33 fathers and stepfathers of the classmates who were identified on the class photo and who Frank has been able to trace, 29 were murdered and only four survived. Of the 33 mothers, 28 were murdered and only five survived.

You have studied the Holocaust through the story of what happened to Frank and his classmates from the Jewish school in Prague. It is important to remember that each of the six million Jews who were killed during the Holocaust was an individual, each with their own story. The victims of the Holocaust were not just those who were killed. We need to remember the suffering of the survivors – many of whom were used for slave labour and separated from family members who they would never see again.

Who else did the Nazis persecute?

The Jews were not the only group of people that the Nazis persecuted. It was soon very clear that there was no place in Germany for people the Nazis viewed as 'undesirables'.

- Those who wouldn't work. Habitual criminals, tramps, beggars, alcoholics and others like them were regarded as socially useless. They were rounded up in 1933 and 500,000 of them were sent to concentration camps.
- Those who couldn't work. The physically disabled, mentally ill and handicapped were also regarded as a burden. From 1938 onwards, the Nazis began to put such people to death in gas chambers. Between 1939 and 1941, 72,000 mentally ill patients were gassed, including children.
- Those who didn't fit into 'normal' families. This included homosexuals. About 15,000 were arrested and sent to concentration camps; many were castrated or used in medical experiments.
- Those who were not 'Aryans'. This included black people and Gypsies as well as Jews. 500,000 Gypsies were murdered in the Holocaust.

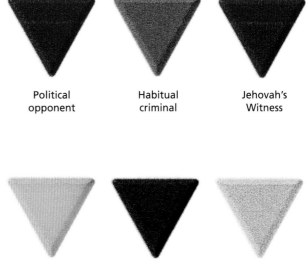

Political opponent

Habitual criminal

Jehovah's Witness

Homosexual

Gypsy

Jew

How did the Jews resist?

RESISTANCE FIGHTERS

It is important to remember that Jews did resist what was happening to them. Jewish resistance groups took to the countryside. In Poland there were at least 28 groups of Jewish fighters. These resistance fighters blew up railway lines and attacked German soldiers. During 1942 as many as 40,000 Jews escaped from the ghettos of Poland into the forests. They had hardly any weapons and no food apart from what the forests could provide. The German army was forced to use large numbers of men and even aircraft against them.

▲ SOURCE 29 *Members of the Jewish partisan unit in the Parczew Forest.*

UPRISINGS IN THE CAMPS

There were even uprisings in the camps. In Treblinka, in 1943, one of the prisoners managed to get into the weapons store. He handed out grenades and guns to other prisoners. The camp was set on fire, fifteen guards were killed and 150 prisoners escaped. In October 1943, 600 Jews escaped from Sobibor camp. In Auschwitz, towards the end of the war, Jews who were forced to become Sonderkommandos (the people who emptied the bodies from the gas chambers) managed to blow up two of the gas chambers.

INDIVIDUAL DEFIANCE

Jewish resistance could take other forms. Individual defiance was to escape the round-up of Jews by the Germans and try to merge into the population. That could only be done successfully with the help of the non-Jewish population, and was a huge risk.

Families fought hard to stay together for as long as possible. To survive was a victory of the human spirit. A young Jewish resistance fighter, Chaim Lazar wrote: *'Struggling to stay alive another day was a form of resistance. Escaping from the ghetto and hiding in a bunker was resistance. Resistance was giving birth to a child in the ghetto, sharing food with others, praying together, singing in a chorus, studying the Bible, planting flowers, keeping a diary under the shadow of death.'*

JEWS IN THE ALLIED ARMIES

It should also be remembered that Jewish soldiers, sailors and airmen fought in all the Allied armies. Polish Jews fought in the defence of Poland. In the battle for Poland more than 60,000 Polish soldiers were killed in action, among them were 6000 Polish Jews. The Germans shot all Polish prisoners of war who were Jewish.

Belgian, Dutch and French Jews fought against the German army in 1940. British Jews served in all branches of the armed forces and a Jewish brigade was established as part of the British army in 1944.

GHETTO REVOLTS

Armed uprisings took place in many of the ghettos. In 1943, in the Warsaw ghetto, 15,000 Jews armed with makeshift weapons held out for four weeks against fully equipped German forces twice their number. The Jews had just two machine guns and fifteen rifles. In contrast, the Germans had 135 machine guns and 1,358 rifles. Despite this, on the first day of the fighting the Germans were forced to retreat. The next day the Germans broke into the Jewish hospital and killed all the sick and wounded as they lay in their beds. They then set fire to the building. Many doctors and nurses hiding from the soldiers died in the fire. Street by street the Germans set fire to or dynamited buildings until the ghetto was reduced to rubble. Some 7000 Jews were killed in the fighting.

▲ SOURCE 30 *Jews from the Warsaw ghetto surrender to German soldiers after the uprising.*

Who was to blame for the Holocaust?

Hitler	It is unlikely that he ever personally killed any Jews nor are there any written orders signed by Hitler for the extermination of the Jews. However, Hitler was very anti-Semitic, made speeches in which he talked of annihilating the Jews and passed laws against the Jews. His closest supporters (men like Himmler and Goering) believed that they were carrying out his instructions.
Goebbels	Controlled Nazi propaganda. He used newspapers and films to spread anti-Semitic ideas. Goebbels was also behind Kristallnacht (a night of large-scale, organised violence against the Jews in which many died).
Herman Goering	Marshal of the Reich, head of the Gestapo and one of Hitler's closest advisers. In 1941 he gave a written order for leading Nazis to develop what he called 'the Final Solution to the Jewish problem'.
Heinrich Himmler	Ran the SS and was put in charge of implementing 'the Final Solution'.
Reinhard Heydrich	Assisted Himmler. He had organised the ghettos and the Einsatzgruppen. It was Heydrich who led the planning of the death camps and the methods of killing in the gas chambers.
Camp commandants	Men like Rudolph Höss, the Commandant at Auschwitz, controlled what happened in the concentration, slave labour and death camps.
SS camp guards	The orders for the Holocaust came from senior Nazis. However, these orders were carried out by the SS. It was the SS guards who ran the camps. Apart from Germans, camp guards included Austrians, Ukrainians, Latvians and Estonians. The SS recruited men from the countries that Germany occupied.
Clerks and civil servants	Collected and stored information about the Jews and wrote the lists of the Jews that were to be transported.
The police	Rounded up the Jews in Germany and in other countries the Nazis controlled. Many victims were actually taken from their homes by the local police, rather than by the Gestapo or SS.
Engine drivers, firemen, train guards	Drove the trains to Auschwitz, Chelmno, Treblinka and Maly Trostinet, knowing the fate of their cargo. Also, the other railway employees who organised the cattle trucks to take Jews to the slave labour and death camps.
Engineers	Designed the huge gas chambers and crematoria and the chemical firms who produced tens of thousands of Zyklon-B poison gas containers, all of whom knew the purpose of their work.
Businesses	Used slave labour and made huge profits during the war.
The German people	Some Germans did speak out against the persecution of the Jews or tried to help individuals. They were living under a ruthless dictatorship that persecuted anybody showing the slightest sympathy towards Jews. Most closed their eyes to what was happening and did not protest. Many benefited when they took over homes, shops, factories and valuables that had been taken from Jews.
Governments of other countries	Who placed restrictions on the number of Jews that they would allow in and didn't bomb the railway lines to camps such as Auschwitz.

ACTIVITY

Look at the list of people in the table who contributed to the Holocaust.

1 Are all these people to blame?
2 Are there such things as different levels of blame? If so, who is at each level? Use a Ripple Diagram to show your ideas. Place the person or people you think were most responsible at the centre of the diagram. Who could have stopped the Holocaust?
3 Look at Sources 31 and 32. Who would each writer blame for the Holocaust?

SOURCE 31 *Ian Kershaw, an historian, writing in the 1990s.*

The road to Auschwitz was built by hatred but paved with apathy.

SOURCE 32 *Laurence Rees, an historian, writing in 1977.*

Nazism brought into the world new knowledge of how low human beings can sink.

Hitler did not do this on his own.

DOING HISTORY: Significance

The Holocaust is seen as one of the most significant events in history. In Britain, since 2001, Holocaust Memorial Day has taken place on 27 January. The Holocaust is one of the few events named in the Key Stage 3 National Curriculum for History. Why do you think it is so significant?

Proving historical significance

Remember what you have already learnt about historical significance. **People use different criteria to decide what is significant and this leads to debates and arguments.**

One criterion is usually that it had **far-reaching consequences** – it changed people's lives. Make sure you prove that the Holocaust was important at the time. Consider:

- How many people were affected?
- How deeply did it affect them?

However, it is also crucial to prove that the Holocaust is **still important today**. Consider:

- Is it still relevant to our lives today? What lessons are relevant to today's society? For whom are they relevant?
- Is it possible for people to connect with the experiences of the people involved?
- Have there been any similar events in the world since the Holocaust?

SOURCE 33 *Karl Jaspers, German-born philosopher, writing just after the Second World War.*

That which has happened
  is a warning.
To forget is guilt.
It must be continually
  remembered.
It was possible for this to
  happen,
and it remains possible for
  it to happen again at
  any minute.
Only in knowledge can it
  be prevented.

SOURCE 34 *Pastor Martin Niemoller, First World War German submarine commander and concentration camp survivor.*

First they came for the Communists,
  – and I did not speak out –
  Because I was not a Communist.
Then they came for the Socialists,
  – and I did not speak out –
  Because I was not a Socialist
Then they came for the trade unionists
  – and I did not speak out –
  Because I was not a trade unionist
Then they came for the Jews,
  – and I did not speak out –
  Because I was not a Jew
Then they came for me,
  And there was no one left
  To speak out for me.

ACTIVITY

Use the key questions on the left and the information on the following pages to help you explain the historical significance of the Holocaust. You need to finish your presentation by demonstrating the significance of the Holocaust to your audience. Why do we remember the Holocaust with a special memorial day every year? Why should all young people learn about the Holocaust?

DISCUSS

Look at the sources (left). How does each writer argue that the Holocaust will remain relevant to people in the future? Is it because …

- It acts as a clear warning of where racism and other forms of prejudice can lead.
- It allows us as individuals to reflect on our own responsibility to tackle racism, prejudice and discrimination in our own society.

Genocide – a never-ending story?

Genocide is the systematic murder of all members of a particular race or group. After witnessing the horrors of the Holocaust, and the death of all his family except his brother, Raphael Lemkin campaigned to have genocide recognised as a crime under international law. In 1948, the United Nations passed the Prevention and Punishment of the Crime of Genocide Resolution. Despite this, since 1945, millions of people across the world have been killed in genocides.

❶ 1975–1978 Cambodia

Between 1975 and 1978 Cambodia's communist rulers, the Khmer Rouge, murdered approximately two million people (about 25 per cent of the population). Different ethnic and religious groups were targeted.
- The Vietnamese community was entirely destroyed.
- The ethnic Chinese population fell from 425,000 to 200,000.
- Buddhism was eliminated.
- Many Muslims were murdered for their refusal to eat pork.
- The Khmer Rouge also executed political opponents.
- Many people who lived in the cities were removed to the countryside and forced to work on farms. Many died from exhaustion or starvation.

❸ 1999 Kosovo
- Armed Serbs massacred several thousand unarmed Kosovan Albanians.
- As many as 600,000 people fled the country as villages were looted and burned.

❹ 1990s Bosnia
- Only one year after the world watched the events in Rwanda, genocide occurred in the Bosnian city of Srebrenica.
- 8000 Bosnian Muslims were killed by members of the Serbian army whose campaign in July 1995 included deportations and mass murder.
- This was the first legally established case of genocide in Europe.

SOURCE 35 *A letter sent by the principal of an American high school to all the teachers on the first day of term.*

Dear Teacher,

I am a survivor of a concentration camp. My eyes saw what no man should witness:

Gas chambers built by learned engineers.

Children poisoned by educated doctors.

Infants killed by trained nurses.

Women and babies shot and burned by high school and college graduates.

So I am suspicious of education.

My request is: Help your students to become human.

Your efforts must never produce learned monsters, skilled psychopaths, educated Eichmanns.

Reading, writing and arithmetic are important only if they serve to make our children more human.

❷ 1990s Rwanda
- In 1994, militiamen from the majority Hutu population massacred the minority Tutsi people.
- Approximately one million Tutsis and a number of moderate Hutus were murdered in just 100 days. Two million people fled the country.
- This was an attempt by extremists from the Hutu majority to remove Tutsis from the country.

❺ 2003 Darfur
- Since 2003, a fierce civil war has raged in the Darfur region of western Sudan.
- It is estimated that within the first four years of the conflict, between 200,000 and 400,000 civilians had been killed – targeted by the Sudanese government and the Janjaweed militia.
- Both the American and French governments described the situation in Darfur as genocide.
- By 2008, 2.5 million people were living in refugee camps.

Throughout history people have often protested about the way in which their country is run. Do you recognise some of the people below? What links them is that they all tried to change the way that their country was governed. However, they used different methods to campaign for change. In this section you will explore how human rights were fought for during the twentieth century.

Do you recognise all the people on this page? You should have recognised some of them from previous sections in this book and from your work in Years 7 and 8.

All of them protested in order to change the world in which they were living. They have campaigned for either their own or other people's human rights. They used different methods to campaign for change. This section continues the story of how people have had to fight for equal rights throughout history. You will study three different case studies from the twentieth century:

- the fight of women to achieve the vote in Britain
- the Civil Rights Movement in the United States
- the campaign against apartheid in South Africa.

As you work through each case study you will focus on three key questions.

Question 1: What were they fighting for?
Question 2: How did people protest?

- What methods did they use?
- How similar were they to methods that had been used in the past?
- Did their methods change over time?
- Did people disagree about the best way to protest?

Question 3: How successful were they?

- To what extent did people's lives change as a result of each protest movement?

The Universal Declaration of Human Rights

In 1948 the United Nations set out the Universal Declaration of Human Rights. Some of the main points are summarised below. All countries had to sign the Declaration before being allowed to join the United Nations.

ACTIVITY

Read through the Declaration. Which rights do you think are the most important?

1 Can you spot key themes? Which rights are to do with the following themes:
   a) Equal treatment under the law.
   b) Political power – the right to influence the way in which a country is run.
   c) Equal opportunities in the world of work.
   d) The right to a decent standard of living.
   e) Equal opportunities in education.
2 Which of these rights were denied people in the past? Take each individual from page 142. Which rights were they fighting for?
3 Look at the three new case studies you will be studying in this section. What rights do you think these individuals were fighting for?

All human beings are born free and equal in dignity and in rights.

Everyone has the right to life, liberty and security of person.

No one shall be held in slavery.

No one shall be tortured or punished in a cruel, inhumane or degrading way.

Everyone has the right to equal protection of the law.

Everyone has the right to a fair trial, in public.

Everyone is presumed innocent until proved guilty.

Everyone has the right to marry, without limitation due to race or religion.

Everyone has the right to own property.

Everyone has the right to freedom of thought and religion.

Everyone has the right to freedom of opinion and expression.

Everyone has the right to meet freely in peaceful organisations.

Everyone has the right to take part in the government of their country. There will be genuine elections with a secret vote.

Everyone has the right to work, to free choice of employment, to just and favourable conditions of work. Everyone has the right to equal pay for equal work.

Everyone has a right to a standard of living adequate for the health and well-being of themselves and their family, including food, clothing, housing and medical care.

Everyone has the right to education. Education shall strengthen the respect of human rights and promote understanding, tolerance and friendship among all nations, racial or religious groups.

How did women in Britain campaign for the right to vote?

At the start of the twentieth century there was a lot of disagreement about the best way for women to campaign for the right to vote. Many women followed the more radical approach taken by Sylvia Pankhurst and her sisters. In this enquiry you will study their methods and decide whether their actions advanced or held back the struggle to gain votes for women.

'A dictatorship of angels?'

Did the militant actions of the Pankhursts advance or hold back the struggle to gain votes for women?

Sylvia's story

In October 1912, a young woman climbed a ladder outside a newly-leased shop in Bow, East London, and began to paint a slogan in gold letters on the exterior. Passersby in this desperately poor area were open mouthed that a middle-class woman would do such work in public. They were even more amazed when, outside the same shop and from the top of a flimsy wooden frame, she began to speak (see photo above). Sylvia, at first treated with suspicion, had begun to catch the imagination of the area.

In February 1913, again in Bow, Sylvia climbed on a cart placed by the wall of a school and began to speak. This time the day was very cold and passersby paid scant attention to the passionate voice of the speaker. Frustrated by this and by Parliament's failure to help her cause, she took up a stone, jumped down from her cart and threw it through the window of a newly opened undertaker's shop. Emboldened, her companions joined in, smashing the window of a public hall and a Liberal club. Soon she was under arrest and in jail. She immediately began a hunger and thirst strike.

On the third day, two prison doctors examined her and said that they had no alternative but to feed her by force. Six wardresses flung Sylvia on her back on the bed and held her down. Her mouth was forced open and she felt a steel instrument pushed into it. The screw was turned to prise open her jaws. A feeding tube was then thrust down her throat. She vomited as the contraption was removed.

This routine of tube feeding continued day after day. As soon as she could pull herself together after the forced feeding she would struggle to bring up what they had forced into her. After some days the flesh around her eyes became increasingly painful and she shrank from the light. Friends described her eyes as two pools of blood staring out from a thin white face.

Later in the year Sylvia was forced to arrive at public meetings in disguise to avoid arrest. Once, addressing an audience from a stage in Bow Baths Hall, she was alerted by the crowd shouting 'Jump, Sylvia, jump'. She turned, half-dazed with shock, to see policemen with truncheons striking the people who were crowded on the platform and smashing the chairs. The people in the gallery retaliated by throwing chairs down on the police. People in the audience then stole up behind Sylvia, put somebody's hat and coat on her and hurried her out in order that she might speak in nearby Poplar Town Hall that night. Quite a demand after such a narrow escape!

Why was Sylvia so angry? Why was she so willing to risk arrest and even her own life?

In Britain at this time, women were not allowed to vote for members of Parliament. During the nineteenth century the right to vote had been extended to all men.

Parliament was the main law-making body in the country. Women saw the right to vote as the key to changing the law and gaining equal rights. As late as 1866, women were held back from making a full contribution to society by laws and customs such as the ones below.

- Everything a woman owned passed on to her husband when she married.
- A woman was expected to give up any paid work upon marriage.
- A woman was expected to hide herself away during pregnancy.
- A woman could be forced to stay in a husband's home against her will.
- The husband made the key decisions about how children were raised.
- A woman had sole responsibility for a child born outside of marriage.
- A woman could only divorce a husband by proving that two of the following acts had been committed: cruelty, desertion or adultery.
- A woman could be divorced for committing any one of the acts of cruelty, desertion or adultery.
- A woman could claim no maintenance money from a husband after divorce or separation.
- If walking in a garrison town (a town with an army or navy base nearby) any woman could be forcibly inspected by a male doctor to see if she had a sexually transmitted disease.

By 1900, women's pressure groups had made a little progress in gaining rights for women. For example, in 1870 and 1882 laws were passed that allowed women to keep their own income and property after they married. This limited progress had been made by persuading male members of Parliament to pass laws for them – but women were still not permitted to vote in elections let alone become MPs in their own right! This outraged women like Sylvia who felt that they were subjected to 'The Laws that Men had Made'.

On 21 June 1908, at least 250,000 people marched peacefully to Hyde Park in London. Their objective was to persuade the British Prime Minister to allow women to vote in parliamentary elections. At the time this was the largest political demonstration ever seen in Britain but the Prime Minister refused to act.

By late 1908, supporters of votes for women were mounting stone-throwing attacks on public buildings. By 1913 they were undertaking violent acts against members of the government. Sylvia believed that her willingness to take risks and to suffer would create the mass support needed to win women the vote. Clearly she was ready to break the law (and windows) to gain the vote.

SOURCE 1 *Sylvia Pankhurst, March 1914. NB You can see a photo of Sylvia on the cover of this book.*

It is necessary for women to fight for the vote because by means of the vote, we can win reforms for ourselves by making it plain to governments that they must either give us the things we want or make way for those who will.

Disagreements over tactics

In 1903 the women's movement was split by differing opinions about how to protest.

Suffragists

The National Union of Women's Suffrage Societies (known as the **Suffragists**) had been founded in 1896 from many already-existing women's groups. It was led by the intelligent and determined Millicent Fawcett. When attacked for moving too slowly she defended her patient tactics. Millicent Fawcett saw her movement as being like a glacier – slow by its very nature yet mighty and irresistible in the long run. The group largely relied on the tactics of influencing MPs through logical argument.

Suffragettes

The Women's Social and Political Union (known as the **Suffragettes**) had been founded in 1903 by Emmeline Pankhurst (Sylvia's mother) after persuasion by her eldest daughter Christabel. The WSPU felt that women had already waited too long for the vote and were determined to speed up the process. They felt that it was a woman's right to demand the vote – not to ask for it as a gift from men. Many of the more extreme members of the NUWSS joined the WSPU but some retained membership of both organisations.

Sylvia Pankhurst had been raised in an atmosphere of radical politics and a tradition of protest. Sylvia's tactics were not the most extreme in her family.

DISCUSS

Can you think of other groups who achieved success through tactics similar to the Suffragists?

ACTIVITY

Suffragist or Suffragette?
Use the information above to help you match the quotations on page 147 to the leaders of the two organisations.

Millicent Fawcett – Suffragist (NUWSS)

Christabel, Emmeline and Sylvia Pankhurst – Suffragettes (WSPU)

Deeds not words.

Suffragettes have done more in twelve months than I and my own followers have been able to do in the same number of years.

Women's nature is different and more pure than men's. To adopt violence as men have done to gain their vote would bring us down to their level. Women have something new to add to politics.

We can work with men in gaining the vote.

Kill me or give me my freedom.

Our concern was not in the numbers of women to be given the vote but in the removal of stigma (shame at being considered inferior) from women.

Men of any party are not true allies of women. The struggle for the vote is a battle of the sexes.

This movement needs not democracy but military discipline.

Our leaders apart from me are arrested or in hiding. I will run the movement from Paris. Your orders are to supply our members with materials to cause fires.

I do think these personal assaults perfectly abominable and above all extraordinarily silly.

Parliament were more impressed by the demonstrations of well-off women than by those of poor workers.

A dictatorship of angels?

By 1907, the Pankhursts ruled the Suffragette WSPU as virtual dictators without any form of election or say for its members. There wasn't even a constitution or set of rules. Some thought this very worrying in an organisation aimed at allowing women to take full part in parliamentary democracy! Many talented members, such as Teresa Billington Greig, left the WSPU in protest.

Emmeline Pankhurst replied with the argument that the WSPU needed military discipline since it was in a war for the vote. Armies did not vote on decisions so why should the WSPU?

SOURCE 2 *Teresa Billington-Greig, 1907.*

I do not believe dictatorship can be right ... even if it is a dictatorship of angels.

ACTIVITY

1 Read Source 2. What do you think Teresa Billington-Greig meant by 'a dictatorship of angels'?
2 What are the advantages and disadvantages of Emmeline Pankhurst's view and Teresa Billington-Greig's view of the movement?

Work in pairs. In the discussion one of you should be Emmeline Pankhurst and the other Teresa Billington-Greig. Point out why your view is right and attack the other point of view.

147

Did the militant tactics of the Suffragettes advance or hold back the struggle to gain votes for women?

The 'militant spectrum'

Any organisation that adopts militant (shocking, confrontational or violent) tactics takes a risk. Those tactics can bring the organisation publicity and increased membership but, if taken too far, can turn public opinion against the cause.

This is what we will call the 'militant spectrum'.

Helps the cause		Some problems		Danger	
Public begin to notice the organisation. Its leaders become celebrities. Membership rises.		Some people begin to worry that the organisation is breaking or challenging the law. Moderate support is lost.		The actions are so extreme that the organisation carrying them out becomes disliked if not hated. Sympathy goes to those being attacked.	
Zone 1A	Zone 1B	Zone 2A	Zone 2B	Zone 3A	Zone 3B

Generally the Suffragist NUWSS avoided illegal or really shocking tactics. After 1908 it condemned all illegal acts and called itself a 'constitutional' movement – one that respected the law. As you have probably worked out, the Suffragette WSPU was a very different type of organisation!

ACTIVITY

1 In threes, discuss the potential **publicity, shock** or **horror** of each incident on pages 149–151. Then decide where each incident should be placed on the militant spectrum. Sometimes the consequences of the actions taken by the Suffragettes are not stated and you will need to think carefully about where to place the incident.

   Remember that people in the early 1900s were more easily shocked than people are today – so if you are in any doubt put an action into a higher zone rather than a lower zone.

2 Now look at where you have placed the incidents on your militant spectrum. In the view of your group do you feel that the militant tactics of the Pankhursts:
   - always harmed the cause of 'votes for women'
   - always helped the cause of 'votes for women'
   - helped and harmed in roughly similar amounts
   - changed in its effect over time?

   Remember that however much they disliked the fact, the Suffragettes were relying on male politicians and government ministers to pass a law for them. Does this affect your view?

3 Prepare a case for a class debate on the issue: *Did the militant tactics of the Suffragettes advance or hold back the struggle to gain votes for women?*

1905

On the evening of 13 October, Christabel Pankhurst and Annie Kenney were seated towards the back of the Free Trade Hall. Sir Edward Grey (a member of the Liberal government) was urging the return of the Liberals to office, when Annie Kenney shouted the question, 'Will the Liberal government give women the vote?'

Uproar ensued, as Liberal stewards and plain-clothes police tried to remove the women from the hall. Christabel and Annie struggled against their ejection. Christabel spat in the face of Superintendent Watson, and then spat in another officer's face and struck him in the mouth, saying that she wanted to assault a policeman. The women were then ejected into South Street.

1906

On 9 March, about 30 women went to 10 Downing Street and asked to see the Prime Minister. Irene Fenwick Miller pounded on the door of Number 10, and Mrs Drummond managed to open it and rush inside. They were both arrested. Annie Kenney then jumped onto the Prime Minister's car, and began to address the crowd. After refusing to climb down, she too was arrested.

Suffragette membership rose dramatically between 1906 and 1907.

▲ *Sylvia Pankhurst being arrested.*

1907

A procession of about 400 women was formed. Mrs Pankhurst's cry 'Rise up, women!' was answered by shouts of 'Now!' and some of the marchers sang, to the tune of 'John Brown's body':

Rise up, women! for the fight is hard and long;
Rise in thousands, singing loud a battle song.
Right is might, and in its strength we shall be
*   strong,*
And the cause goes marching on.

When the first groups reached the green beside Westminster Abbey, the police announced that the procession could continue no further. The women refused to halt. As they went forward, mounted policemen began to ride through their ranks, in an attempt to break up the march, and constables on foot seized women and shoved them down side streets and alleys. The struggle continued for several hours, as bedraggled women hurled themselves again and again against the police.

Fifteen women managed to get inside Parliament, where they were promptly arrested. By 10 p.m. the trouble had ended. Over 50 women had been arrested, including Sylvia and Christabel Pankhurst.

1908

On 21 June a protest rally was held in Hyde Park. *The Times* thought there were from 250,000 to 500,000 people present. Some supporters claimed: 'it is no exaggeration to say that the number of people present was the largest ever gathered together on one spot at one time in the history of the world.'

On 2 July, Marion Wallace Dunlop was sentenced to one month in prison for defacing the wall of St Stephen's Hall on 24 June. She asked to be treated as a political prisoner. Her request was denied. Three days later, without the knowledge of the Suffragettes' leaders, she began a hunger strike. After refusing all food for 91 hours, she was released from prison.

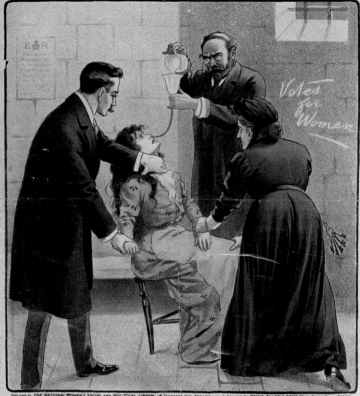

TORTURING WOMEN IN PRISON

Votes for Women

Produced by THE NATIONAL WOMEN'S SOCIAL AND POLITICAL UNION 4 Clements Inn Strand w.c. & Printed by DAVID ALLEN & SONS Ld. 133 Fleet St E.C.

VOTE AGAINST THE GOVERNMENT

Later, hunger strikers were force fed by prison doctors and warders in a brutal process involving tubes and steel mouth clamps. This shocked the public greatly and aroused great sympathy for the Suffragettes who were very good at using this for propaganda purposes.

Emmeline Pankhurst later declared that: 'the argument of the broken pane of glass is the most valuable argument in modern politics'. However, window breaking caused many women to leave the Suffragettes, including Dr Elizabeth Garrett Anderson, the first British female doctor.

1911

Armed with bags of stones and hammers supplied to them at the Suffragette shop, the women went to break windows at government offices and business premises. Windows were smashed at the Home Office, Treasury, National Liberal Federation, Guards' Club, two hotels, the *Daily Mail* and *Daily News*, Dunn's Hat Shop, as well as at a chemist's, a tailor's, a bakery, and other small businesses. Two hundred and twenty women and three men were arrested.

1912

On 18 July, in Dublin, Mary Leigh threw a hatchet (small axe) into a carriage in which the Prime Minister, was riding. She escaped. That evening, she and Gladys Evans tried to set fire to the Theatre Royal, where the Prime Minister had just seen a performance. The two women ignited the curtains behind a box, threw a flaming chair down into the orchestra, and set off small bombs made out of tin cans. They did not try to evade arrest, and were subsequently sentenced to five years in prison.

January 1913

On the last day of January, the Suffragettes began an organised campaign of destruction of public and private property. Within the next three weeks, slogans were burned on to putting greens; the display case containing the crown jewels was smashed at the Tower of London; telegraph and telephone wires were cut; an orchid house was burned at Kew Gardens; windows were smashed at London clubs; the refreshment house at Regent's Park was destroyed by fire; and at Harrow a railway carriage was set ablaze. Most of those responsible escaped arrest but Suffragette leaders made it clear that their organisation was responsible.

February 1913

At 6 a.m. on 18 February, a bomb set by Emily Wilding Davison and accomplices wrecked five rooms of a partly-completed house that the Chancellor was having built near Walton Heath.

Suffragette membership seems to have gone into quite steep decline in 1912–1913.

June 1913

In June, Emily Wilding Davison and her flatmate attended the Derby horse race. Emily dashed on to the course and was run down by the King's horse, Anmer. Her skull was fractured, and she died five days later without having regained consciousness. The funeral was a large and public spectacle. The WSPU had gained its first martyr.

1914

On 22 May, King George V was attending the theatre when Suffragettes publicly insulted him. The following day a woman who had managed to gain entrance to a Court function suddenly fell on her knees before the King, and cried in a loud voice, 'Your Majesty, won't you stop torturing the women?'

How did women finally gain the vote?

When the war broke out in 1914, Sylvia Pankhurst refused to stop working for women's rights. She condemned the war but recognised that it was causing great hardship for women. Women were frequently unable to work because they needed to find childcare, and those working in munitions factories found that their health suffered. Sylvia did not ignore this. She took over an old pub called the Gunmakers' Arms and re-named it the 'Mother's Arms'. She ran it as a nursery, school and crèche, thereby allowing women to work without worrying about their children. Sylvia ran a cheap health-food restaurant, the Suffragette HQ (even though the women hated strange beans and unpeeled potatoes). Sylvia also continued to keep the government aware of how women were working under great strain in order to allow men to fight in what she considered was a man's war. Her tactics had moved away from militancy.

Millicent Fawcett and the Suffragists supported the war but didn't stop looking for chances to pressure the government. When she realised that the government had to introduce a new voting law to allow all the soldiers and sailors serving abroad to vote, she insisted that the price of her continued support for the war was inclusion of women's votes in that law.

In 1918 women over the age 30 who owned property were given the right to vote. The rest gained the vote in 1928 – the year Emmeline Pankhurst died.

ACTIVITY

Read the information below, then in groups of three sort the factor cards into a diamond nine. Place the most important factors towards the top of the diamond. Make sure you can explain your decisions to other groups in the class.

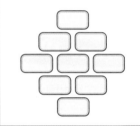

A Sylvia Pankhurst and other women publicised women's war work and the hardships they were undergoing.

B In the war women showed themselves capable of doing jobs previously done by men – and doing them just as well as men.

C Soldiers and sailors posted abroad would not have had the right to vote under the old law. So a new law was urgently needed to ensure that they were not denied the vote.

D Emmeline Pankhurst said that women's votes should wait until the question of giving votes to all fighting men had been settled. This led to her being left out of negotiations with the government.

E Millicent Fawcett coolly told the Prime Minister that women would not tolerate being left out of a new law on voting having done so much for the war.

F The Suffragists had helped support a number of Labour MPs in elections. The Liberal Party was worried that failure to adopt votes for women might lead to even more Labour MPs.

G The Conservative Party (the Liberals' main rivals) had been aware for a long time that it had nothing to fear from giving some women the vote.

H The fear that women's violence might return after the war was real. Only the war seemed to have stopped that violence running totally out of control.

I The Suffragists were prepared to accept that only women with property and over the age of 30 would initially be given the vote. It accepted that men would worry if women immediately became the largest electoral group.

Would Sylvia Pankhurst be disappointed at the position of women in Britain today?

Campaigners such as Sylvia Pankhurst did not regard getting the vote as an end in itself. They believed that greater political power for women would lead to major social changes and an improvement in the position and status of women. To what extent has this been the case? Has getting the vote brought equality? Are women treated equally in Britain today?

Equal political power?

Before the First World War many men believed that women would take over Parliament if they got the vote. In the short term, this did not happen. In the 1918 elections , only 17 women stood as candidates and only two were elected as MPs. In 1928, Parliament gave all adult women over the age of 21 the vote. This meant that women had the same voting rights as men. It also meant that for the first time in British history the majority of voters were women. Today, women still make up more than 50 per cent of voters. What percentage of MPs are women today?

In 1979 Britain elected its first female prime minister, Margaret Thatcher. She claimed that, 'The battle for women's rights has largely been won.' Do you agree?

Equality at work?

During the First World War women had shown that they could do jobs that had previously been viewed as 'men's jobs' just as well as men. Most women did not want to return to the poorly paid jobs that they had done before the war. However, within the space of a few years the majority of women were back doing the jobs they had done before the war. A similar pattern took place during the Second World War. Women filled the jobs left by men who went away to fight. When the men returned, women were demoted.

By the 1960s, more women than ever before were attending university. They became increasingly frustrated that despite equality in education the top jobs were still closed to them. The 'women's liberation movement' campaigned for change and managed to put pressure on the government to introduce new laws:

- In 1970 it became illegal to pay women less than men for the same work.
- In 1975 the Sex Discrimination Act outlawed discrimination in jobs, housing and other areas.

What has been the impact of these laws? Look at the evidence around you. Do women have equal opportunities? Are there still jobs that are dominated by men? Has pay become more equal?

SISTERHOOD is POWERFUL!

SOURCE 3 *A recent survey showed that:*

- Less than 20 per cent of MPs are women.
- Women still earn less than men.
- Since 1975 the pay gap has fallen from 29 per cent to 17 per cent.
- In the food and drink industry male managers earn 46 per cent more than female managers. In careers in human resources, pensions and insurance the gap is also over 40 per cent.
- Only 95 women were listed in *The Sunday Times* richest 1000 people in the country (56 of those were half of male–female partnerships).

ACTIVITY

Carry out your own research – what other measures of equality can you think of? Debate as a class: to what extent are women treated equally today?

153

How did black Americans campaign for equal civil rights?

The United States of America won freedom from British rule in 1783. The American Declaration of Independence stated that 'all men are created equal' and promised to protect the rights and freedoms of the people of America. The Declaration helped to create an image of the United States as a land of freedom and democracy. Was this really the case for everyone living in the country? What about black Americans like Jesse Owens? In this enquiry you will explore how black Americans had to fight for equal civil rights.

What can Jesse Owens' story tell us about how black Americans were treated in the 1930s?

The Jesse Owens Story: Extract 1 – Germany 1936

The 1936 Olympic Games were held in Germany. Hitler believed that the Games would show that the Aryan race was superior to all other races. He believed that Aryan Germans were part of a 'Master Race' and that black people and Jews were inferior. Hitler must have been very disappointed when Jesse Owens, a black athlete from America, became the star of the Games. Jesse Owens won four gold medals – setting a world record of 10.3 seconds for the 100 metres, an Olympic record of 20.7 seconds for the 200 metres, jumping 8.06 metres to win the long jump and helping to set another world record in the 400-metre relay.

The racism, prejudice and discrimination that existed in Germany at this time is well known. However, what was life like for black Americans such as Jesse Owens back home in 'the land of the free' – the United States of America?

PUZZLE

1 Look at the cropped photo on the left. In the 1930s, H.L. Mencken, an American newspaper columnist, called this pastime:
'a replacement for the merry-go-round, the theatre, the symphony orchestra'.
What was he describing? Using Mencken's description, complete the missing part of the photograph or discuss what you think is happening.

2 Read Extract 2. Does this help you solve the picture puzzle?

Using sources part 1 – making inferences

You have already learnt that using sources well means finding out things from a source that it does not obviously tell you. This is called **inference**.

ACTIVITY

What does Extract 2 tell us about how black people were treated in the United States during the 1930s? Fill in the first two columns of the table below. The first step is to look for obvious clues as to how Jesse was treated. Then think carefully about what you can *infer* from this information. What do Jesse's experiences suggest about America in the 1930s?

OBVIOUS CLUE (How was Jesse treated?)	INFERENCE (What does this suggest?)	SUPPORTING EVIDENCE
Jesse could not eat at the Blue Moon restaurant	This suggests …	This is supported by …

The Jesse Owens Story:
Extract 2 – Columbus (Ohio) Thursday 23 May 1935

Just after dawn on Thursday 23 May 1935, Jesse Owens swallowed a moan as they hoisted him into the car. He had seriously injured his back playing touch football with a couple of friends just a few days earlier. In addition to a slipped disc, his vertebrae were swollen and out of joint. On Saturday Jesse hoped to compete in the Western Conference athletics championship in Ann Arbor, Michigan. Before then, he was in for a long and agonising ride. Sixteen athletes and two coaches were squeezed into three old cars and the journey from their home town of Columbus to Ann Arbor would take six hours.

As the three cars drove down the empty High Street they passed the Blue Moon restaurant where you could order a T-bone steak with dessert to follow for just 45 cents. However, the offer did not extend to Jesse and his fellow black athletes. Like every other restaurant on the High Street, the Blue Moon was only open to white customers. The old Union Building, where hot dogs, not steak, were always the special of the day, was the only place where blacks could eat in public.

Within a few minutes Jesse's car had also passed the three main movie theatres in the town. When they opened that evening all three would be reserved for 'Whites Only'. The only cinema that would admit black people was the crumbling Rex, on the far side of town, which sold 'cullud seats' in the top six rows of its dingy balcony.

None of Jesse's white team-mates seemed to notice. 14,000 people attended Ohio State University, yet there were fewer than a hundred black students and they were not allowed to stay on campus. Jesse and his friend, Dave Albritton, were forced to share the top floor of a boarding house well away from the University. Dave often moaned about how they were treated in Columbus but Jesse had experienced even worse places travelling to athletics meetings in other parts of the country.

In 1933, he had driven through Indiana, stopping at a town called Kokomo. Jesse did not stay long once he heard that a young black man had been lynched the day before. The body had been strung up and left to dangle in the breeze as the citizens of Kokomo picnicked around the tree.

Halfway between Columbus and Ann Arbor, Jesse and his fellow athletes stopped for breakfast at a place called Finlay. The diner was half empty and there would have been enough seats for all the athletes. However, like most places on the road this was a 'White Only' restaurant and Jesse and his fellow black athletes had to remain in their cars as the white athletes sat down inside the diner.

DISCUSS

Read Extract 3. Why were Jesse Owens' performances in Ann Arbor so incredible? List the mental and physical obstacles he had to overcome.

The Jesse Owens Story: Extract 3 – Ann Arbor (Michigan) Saturday 25 May 1935

At just after eight on a warm Saturday morning, Jesse carefully lowered himself into a steaming bath. The heated pads that had been placed on his back during the night had only slightly eased the pain. He arrived at the athletics stadium, packed with 12,000 people, just after noon. The pain had moved from his back to his upper right leg. At 2.15 p.m., Jesse pulled on his running gear but did not go through his normal warm-up routine. Jesse did not feel even close to normal. He sat down on the grass and leaned against a pole as he watched the other athletes warm up. His first race, the 100-yard final, was at 3.15 p.m. Jesse decided not to risk

moving until the last possible moment. At three o'clock Jesse's coach walked briskly towards him.

'I don't think we should chance it today,' Snyder said. 'It's not worth the risk.'

'Please, coach,' Jesse said, 'let's try the 100. If I look bad you can pull me straight out of the jump and the 220.' After a brief discussion the coach finally gave in and Jesse made his way to the starting line.

A stillness settled across the stadium. Everyone always stopped to watch Jesse Owens run. The starter pulled the trigger. The blank fired. They were away first time. Owens accelerated away with astonishing ease and finished the race five yards clear of the second placed athlete. Jesse's time was 9.4 seconds. He had equalled the world record set by Frank Wykoff in 1930.

After a brief celebration, Jesse turned quickly to the long-jump pit. His 220-yard final was less than 30 minutes away and the 220-yard hurdles just fifteen minutes after that. His bad back would probably only last one jump. Hundreds of people surrounded the long-jump pit and hundreds more lined the thin grassy runway down which he would sprint. At 3.22 p.m., less than seven minutes after his 100-yard dash, Jesse set off, running faster and faster past the rows of screaming faces. Suddenly, his front foot hit

the board and he landed in an explosion of sand and noise. He knew it was a huge jump but the official announcement made even Jesse Owens shake his head in astonishment: 26 feet, $8\frac{1}{4}$ inches. He had shattered the world record by 6 inches.

Jesse hugged his friends but once again there was little time to celebrate. Athletes were being called for the start of the 220-yard final. Jesse quickly made some footholds in the cinder track to help his start and then settled into position. On the starter gun he flew from the holes and was over the line in 20.3 seconds, three-tenths of a second faster than the world record set in 1924.

Larry Snyder, Jesse's coach, knew that he had no chance of persuading Owens to pull out of his final event, the 220-yard hurdles. However, Snyder was still worried about the back injury.

'OK, Jesse,' he murmured. 'Take it easy in the hurdles.' At four o'clock, Jesse joined the five other finalists. He had been placed in the outside lane, the worst possible draw, and lacked experience at an event that was still relatively new to him. It didn't matter. By the end of the race Owens was six yards clear. His time of 22.6 seconds was another world record. The spectators in the stadium had witnessed the most incredible string of individual performances ever seen in athletics. In the space of just 45 minutes, Jesse Owens had broken three world records and equalled another.

ACTIVITY

Read Extracts 4 and 5. Use them to continue filling in the first two columns of your table from page 155.

The Jesse Owens Story: Extract 4 – Life before the Olympics

Jesse Owens was born on 12 September 1913 on a small farm in Oakville, Alabama. His grandparents had been slaves. Jesse's parents, like many black Americans in the South, were sharecroppers. Being a sharecropper meant that a family rented land, and received a house, tools and sometimes seed. In return they had to give the landlord who owned the land (usually a white farmer) one-half or sometimes two-thirds of the crop. Living conditions for Jesse and his family were very harsh. Jesse later described their house as: 'wooden planks thrown together'. The roof leaked and it was very cold in winter. The family had no money for doctors or medicine. When a large lump appeared on Jesse's leg his mother cut it out with a hot kitchen knife.

When Jesse was nine his family moved to Cleveland, Ohio. In 1927, Jesse started to attend Fairmount Junior High School where he became a member of the athletics team. Jesse had to train before school started because he worked in the afternoons – sweeping floors, shining shoes and delivering groceries.

The Jesse Owens Story: Extract 5 – Life after the Olympics

When Jesse returned to America from the Olympics he rode through New York at the head of the parade of the American Olympic team. There was also a parade to welcome Jesse back to Cleveland. However, Jesse soon encountered prejudice and discrimination again. In Germany, during the Olympic Games, Owens had been allowed to travel with and stay in the same hotels as white athletes. When he returned to America he found that he could not ride in the front of a bus or live where he wanted.

Despite his amazing achievements Jesse had very little money. Athletes were amateurs and were not allowed to make any money from the sport. When Jesse started to take up offers to make money from his new-found fame, athletics officials were furious and withdrew his amateur status. This ended his athletics career.

In 1938 Jesse set up a dry-cleaning company but it went out of business a year later. By the end of the 1930s, Jesse Owens, the world's greatest athlete, was running in exhibition races against baseball players, dogs and horses. He felt that he was now more of a spectacle than an athlete.

DOING HISTORY: Evidence

Using sources part 2 – cross-referencing

You have already learnt that using sources well means checking sources against each other to find ways in which they agree or disagree before deciding on your answer. This is called **cross-referencing**.

How typical were the experiences of Jesse Owens?

In this enquiry we have been focusing on the story of one black American, Jesse Owens. From his story you have been able to infer what life was like for black Americans in the United States during the first half of the twentieth century. However, at the moment your inferences are based on the experiences of just one person.

As you have learnt, it is dangerous to make generalisations based on just one piece of evidence. Historians always need to ask: **How typical is the source?**

It is now time to check the inferences you have made from Jesse Owens' story against other sources. This is called cross-referencing.

ACTIVITY

Use Sources 4–13 and the information boxes on pages 159–161 to cross-reference the inferences you have made in the second column of your table from page 155.

- In the third column of your table (see below) record evidence that *supports* the inferences you have made.
- Record any evidence that *challenges* the inferences you have made in column four.
- Use your table to answer the question:

How typical were Jesse Owens' experiences of how other black Americans were treated?

Obvious clue (How was Jesse treated?)	Inference (What does this suggest?)	Supporting evidence	Evidence that challenges
Jesse could not eat at the Blue Moon restaurant	This suggests that black Americans were discriminated against in their leisure time. They could not use the same public facilities as white Americans	This is **supported** by Source X, which shows … It is also supported by …	
Jesse was not allowed into some cinemas	This indicates that …		This is challenged by Source X, which suggests that …

158

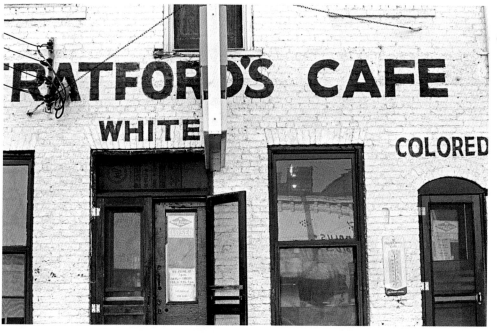

◄ SOURCE 4
Segregated café in Atlanta, Georgia, 1962.

◄ SOURCE 5
A woman enters a segregated launderette in Louisiana, New Orleans.

From Slavery to Segregation and Discrimination

Slavery did not end in the United States until 1865 – after the American Civil War. However, black Americans were not made free and equal by the abolition of slavery. Black Americans continued to be treated like second-class citizens. Many states, particularly in the South, chose to persecute black people and limit their rights. They passed what became known as **'Jim Crow' laws**, designed to **segregate** blacks and whites in daily life.

These **'segregation laws'** meant that black people were forced to live separately from white people. They were given separate seats on buses and cinemas. Public benches, toilets and water fountains were labelled for use by 'white' people or 'coloured' people. Black children had to attend different schools to white children and the best universities were closed to black students. In 1958, a black teacher was sent to a mental asylum for applying to the University of Mississippi.

In many Southern states it was also made very difficult for black people to vote. Violence, intimidation and unfair tests were used to stop black people from voting. Georgia, for example, introduced a tax of two dollars on citizens wanting to vote. Most black voters were too poor to pay.

▲ SOURCE 6 *Separate drinking fountains were an example of the deliberate public discrimination against black citizens.*

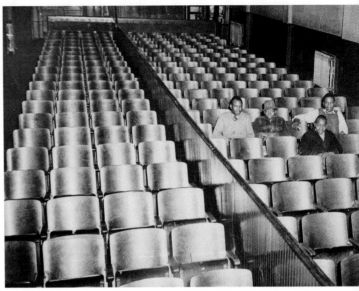

▲ SOURCE 7 *A segregated cinema in the USA, c.1940.*

SOURCE 8 *Timuel Black (quoted in* The Good War *by S. Terkel) joined the army in 1943. The army kept units segregated. Black Americans found promotion difficult and were often given the worst jobs. When black soldiers were injured, only blood from black soldiers could be used. The Red Cross was forced to segregate the blood of white and black people.*

We were shipped overseas. On board, blacks had their quarters and the whites had theirs. We didn't associate with one another. We stayed in Wales, getting ready for the invasion [of Normandy]. Black soldiers and white soldiers could not go to the same town. The ordinary British were absolutely amazed, looking at these two armies.

SOURCE 9 *The following account is adapted from* In Black & White – The untold story of Joe Louis and Jesse Owens *by Donald McCrae.*

America was divided into two separate and unequal worlds. 'Negroes' were barred from white schools, restaurants, hotels, parks and benches. They sat in the 'coloured' carriages of trains and the back seats of buses. It was the same in sport. In the 1932 Los Angeles Olympics, only four black athletes were picked for the American track team (in 1928 the Olympic team had been exclusively white). No black American was allowed to play major league baseball until Jackie Robinson in 1947. The ban against black players in American football lasted until 1946; and in basketball to 1950.

◄ SOURCE 10 *The lynching of Abram Smith and Thomas Shipp, outside the jail in Marion, Indiana. The photograph reveals what was missing from the photograph at the bottom of page 154). As you can see from H.L. Mencken's description on page 154 and the sources on page 161, lynchings were often major social events, many of which were attended by children.*

▶ **SOURCE 11** *The Ku Klux Klan were involved in many of the lynchings that took place. This was a secret organisation of white Southerners who used parades, beatings and lynchings to intimidate black people, Jews, Catholics and foreign immigrants. The attacks usually took place at night and members of the Klan often left behind a burning cross as their calling card. Their aim was to keep whites in control of the Southern states. The Ku Klux Klan was banned in 1872 but the organisation continued and by the 1920s membership had reached nearly five million.*

Violence against African-Americans

During the late nineteenth and early twentieth century, lynching of black Americans became increasingly common. Lynchings were horrific executions and included hanging and burning victims alive. They were carried out by members of the public against people who were said to have committed a crime. Sometimes, simply looking or whistling at a white woman was enough for a black person to be lynched.

Victims of lynchings did not get a chance to defend themselves in court and were often cruelly tortured before being killed. The authorities did nothing to stop them taking place. It is estimated that between 1889 and 1940, 3,833 people were lynched. Ninety per cent of these people were murdered in the Southern states of America. Eighty per cent of those killed were black, including more than 50 black women, some of whom were pregnant.

SOURCE 12

The Daily Mirror *newspaper's account of an event in Owensboro (1936).*

15,000 people – a typical country carnival crowd – saw Rainey Bethea, a Negro, hanged here shortly after dawn. They had been invited by the authorities. Many Owensboro citizens gave all-night 'hanging parties' at which beer and sandwiches were consumed, and just before the hanging many were drunk. When the trap door opened and he dropped to his death, they cheered and yelled.

PUZZLE

Read the clues in the source line of Source 13 and read the lyrics carefully or listen to the song. Can you work out what the song is about?

SOURCE 13

This song was written in 1936 by Abel Meeropol, a Jewish teacher. It was made famous by the well-known black American singer Billie Holiday.

STRANGE FRUIT
Southern trees bear a strange fruit,
Blood on the leaves and blood at the root,
Black body swinging in the Southern breeze,
Strange fruit hanging from the poplar trees.

Pastoral scene of the gallant South,
The bulging eyes and the twisted mouth,
Scent of magnolia sweet and fresh,
And the sudden smell of burning flesh!

Here is a fruit for the crows to pluck,
For the rain to gather, for the wind to suck,
For the sun to rot, for a tree to drop,
Here is a strange and bitter crop.

The background to 'Strange Fruit'

Abel Meeropol wrote 'Strange Fruit' in 1936 after having seen a picture of a lynching in a civil rights magazine. Meeropol said, 'I wrote "Strange Fruit" because I hate lynching and I hate injustice and I hate the people who perpetuate it.'

The song became widely known when it was sung and eventually recorded by Billie Holiday who, in the 1930s, was one of America's most famous singers. Like Jesse Owens, Billie Holiday had faced many obstacles in her career. In the 1930s it was tough for anyone who wanted to make it as a musician. In September 1935, when Billie was hired to sing at New York's 'Famous Door', she was told that she was not allowed to mingle with the guests between sets or even sit at the bar. When she wasn't on stage Billie was forced to hang around outside the toilets.

In 1938 Billie landed a job with Artie Shaw's big band, becoming one of the first black women to work with a white orchestra. It was a big step forward in her career. Shaw was hired to play at Manhattan's Lincoln Hotel. The owner told Billie that she could only use the tradesmen's entrance and that she had to use the freight elevator rather than the guest lifts. The rest of the band were outraged and Shaw complained to the owner. The owner refused to change her mind.

After leaving Shaw's band, Billie got a job singing at Café Society in New York. The owner wanted to create a club in New York where people of all colours and creeds could eat without harassment and listen to good jazz played by the best musicians. The club's slogan was, 'The Wrong Place for the Right People'.

The song 'Strange Fruit' was brought to Billie whilst she was working at Café Society. She always closed her set with the song. Before she started to sing the song all service stopped and the staff stood still. The room went dark – the only light available was a spotlight on Holiday's face. When the song finished Holiday never returned for an encore, walking off into the darkness. When her mother asked her why she sang the song 'Strange Fruit' Holiday said, 'Because it could make things better.'

'But you'll be dead,' replied her mother.

'Yeah, but I'll feel it,' Holiday said. 'I'll know it in my grave.'

ACTIVITY

1. Look at the lyrics to 'Strange Fruit'. Why are the trees specifically 'Southern trees'? What does this tell the listener?
2. The horrific image of 'blood on the leaves and blood at the root' is very powerful. Why is the blood not just on the 'leaves' but also 'at the root'?
3. Do you think the song is more powerful, or less powerful, because its topic (lynching) is implied instead of stated?
4. Listen to a recording of the song. What does the song make you feel?
5. Why do you think that Billie Holiday thought that the song 'could make things better'?

How important was the role played by Martin Luther King in the Civil Rights Movement?

As you have seen, throughout the first half of the twentieth century racial discrimination was a feature of everyday life in the USA. America claimed to be 'the land of the free' but in a fair, free and democratic country surely every citizen should have equal civil rights. This was not the case for America's black citizens. Black Americans had to fight hard for equal civil rights. Which individuals played the key role in the Civil Rights Movement and what forms of protest were most successful?

Martin Luther King is often presented as the key figure in the Civil Rights Movement. His birthday (15 January) is now a national holiday in the USA. King was certainly an important individual in the fight for equal civil rights. However, he was not the only individual. Nor were his methods the only ways that people campaigned. As you will see, different groups used different methods to campaign for equal civil rights. You will be able to make up your own mind about how important Martin Luther King was in the Civil Rights Movement and whether or not it was his methods and tactics that proved most successful.

ACTIVITY

Use the photographic history of the campaign for equal civil rights on pages 164–169 to answer three key questions:

1 Which groups/individuals played an important role in the campaign?
2 What tactics did they use?
3 How successful were they?

Use a table like the one below to record your findings.

Individual/Group	Methods/Tactics	Impact – How successful were they?

4 Using your completed table, place each group or individual on the political protest spectrum on the right.
5 Is there any link between the way people protested and the success or failure of their methods? Discuss your answers to the questions below:

- Did the use of violence tend to achieve more than non-violent campaigns?
- How important was direct action? Did this achieve more than campaigns that kept within the law?
- Did Martin Luther King's methods prove to be more successful than those of other campaigners?

Campaigning within the law
- Legal challenges – trying to change the law
- Boycotts

Violent direct action
- Riots
- Sabotage
- Armed revolution
- Guerilla warfare
- Terrorism

1   2   3

Non-violent direct action (that breaks the law)
- Passive resistance (sit-ins)
- Civil disobedience (non-violent actions that break the law in order to challenge laws that are seen as unjust)

The campaign for equal civil rights: a photographic history

Martin Luther King was not the first person to campaign for equal civil rights for black Americans. Individuals such as Booker T. Washington, Marcus Garvey, Paul Robeson and Thurgood Marshall fought hard to try and improve the lives of black Americans before King became famous during the 1950s

Booker T. Washington (1856–1915)

Washington set up the National Negro Business League to help and support the development of black businesses. He wanted to create more equal opportunities so that black Americans could improve themselves. Washington believed that African-Americans should concentrate on developing their practical skills and improving their education – by doing this, they would become accepted by white Americans.

Marcus Garvey (1887–1940)

Garvey founded the Universal Negro Improvement Association, which helped black people to set up their own businesses. By the 1920s there were some UNIA-funded grocery stores, restaurants and laundries. He also urged black Americans to be proud of their race, colour and cultural heritage. This message had a major impact on ordinary black people, especially those living in poor areas of the northern cities. Some of his ideas and slogans, such as 'Black is Beautiful', were used by civil rights leaders in the 1960s.

Paul Robeson (1898–1976)

At college Paul Robeson was a talented American footballer. He qualified as a lawyer before becoming a highly successful singer and actor. Robeson spoke out against lynchings and at one rally compared the Ku Klux Klan to the Nazis. Robeson tried to persuade the American President to introduce a law that would make lynching illegal.

How much had been achieved by 1950?

All of the above individuals were very important but by 1950 little progress had been made. In the Southern states, the 'Jim Crow' laws that segregated black Americans from white continued. There were still separate schools and hospitals. Lynchings also continued. One of the most well known is the case of Emmett Till who was murdered in 1955 because he had allegedly wolf-whistled at a white woman. Those accused of his murder were found not guilty.

The NAACP

The National Association for the Advancement of Colored People (NAACP) was set up in 1909 and campaigned against lynching and the 'Jim Crow' laws. In the 1950s the NAACP tended to focus on challenging discrimination through the law.

The **NAACP** and the black civil rights lawyer **Thurgood Marshall** used the law courts to challenge segregated schools. They brought a case against the Board of Education in Topek, Kansas. They argued that a black student, **Linda Brown**, should be allowed to attend a whites-only school near her home rather than have to travel several kilometres to a school with black students. In 1954, the Supreme Court ruled in favour of Brown and the NAACP. Integrated schools were introduced quickly in some states. However, as you will see below, in states like Arkansas, there was bitter resistance to integrated schools.

Little Rock, Arkansas (1957) – Elizabeth Eckford's first day at school

In 1957, the Supreme Court ordered the Governor of Arkansas, Orval Faubus, to let nine black students attend what had been a white-only school in Little Rock, Arkansas. The photograph shows **Elizabeth Eckford** making her way to school. The black children were meant to arrive together but Elizabeth did not get the message and was forced to march up the street alone with people shouting insults such as, 'Lynch her' and 'Tie her to the tree'. Violence broke out when the children entered the school and they were forced to leave for their own safety. Troops had to be sent to make sure that the students could attend school safely. Eight of the students completed their course but the soldiers had to remain in Little Rock for a year. Through their tremendous courage these children became heroes and heroines for many black Americans in the South.

The Montgomery Bus Boycott

Montgomery in Alabama had a law that black people were only allowed to sit in the back seats of a bus and they had to give up those seats if white people wanted them. **Rosa Parks** was a civil rights activist who decided to make a stand against this law. Tired after a long day at work, she refused to give up her seat to a white man when the bus became full. The driver called the police and she was removed from the bus and arrested. The photograph shows her fingerprints being taken for police records.

In response, civil rights campaigners set up the Montgomery Improvement Association (MIA). **Martin Luther King** was chosen to lead the MIA. He was an effective organiser and brilliant public speaker who was able to inspire people. The MIA organised a boycott of the buses. This method of protest proved to be very successful. The black community organised a car pool to help people get to work and the bus company lost 65 per cent of its income. The bus boycott lasted 381 days.

Throughout their campaign the leaders of the bus boycott were placed under enormous pressure to end the protest. Martin Luther King was arrested twice and churches and homes were set on fire. Throughout the campaign King urged the black community to stick to non-violent means of protest.

Even after his own house was firebombed, King urged his supporters not to retaliate.

At the same time, civil rights lawyers fought Rosa Parks' case in court. They too were successful. In December 1956, the Supreme Court ruled that Montgomery's bus laws and similar bus laws in other states were illegal.

How much had been achieved by the end of the 1950s?

There had been some progress in desegregating schools and the Montgomery bus boycott had raised black pride and shown that peaceful mass protest could be effective. However, in many Southern states black Americans still faced segregation and were treated as second-class citizens.

Senate chaplain Barry Black later said that Parks' courage served as an example of 'the power of fateful, small acts'. What do you think he meant by this?

Martin Luther King and the SCLC

After the success of the Montgomery bus boycott, Martin Luther King formed the Southern Christian Leadership Conference (SCLC). Martin Luther King believed in taking direct action as a means of protesting. King was prepared to break what he saw as unjust and immoral laws. However, he also passionately believed in non-violent protest, favouring methods such as boycotts and sit-ins. The SCLC ran conferences and trained civil rights activists in non-violent direct action as a means of protesting. Martin Luther King argued that black Americans should not hate white Americans, instead they should:

'Meet the forces of hate with the power of love. Our aim must never be to defeat or humiliate the white man, but to win his friendship and understanding.'

The Student Non-violent Coordinating Committee (SNCC)

Black and white American students played an important role in the Civil Rights Movement. They set up the Student Non-violent Coordinating Committee (SNCC). In the early 1960s the way in which they protested followed the non-violent direct action approach taken by Martin Luther King and the SCLC.

In 1960, in Greensboro, North Carolina, four black students demanded to be served at a whites-only lunch counter. When staff refused to serve them they remained seated at the counter and refused to move until the shop closed. The next day more students joined their protest and the sit-ins spread to other shops. Sales dropped and segregation ended.

'Sit-in' protests soon spread to other towns and cities. The photograph shows black and white SNCC protesters at a sit-in at a segregated restaurant in Jackson, Mississippi. By September 1961, it was estimated that there had been 50,000 black and white students involved in this type of protest. (There were also 'wade-ins' at beaches, 'read-ins' at segregated libraries and 'sleep-ins' at motels.) By the end of 1961 hundreds of towns and cities had desegregated public areas. However, in many places in the Southern states segregation remained as strong as ever.

The Congress of Racial Equality and the Freedom Rides (1961)

The Congress of Racial Equality (CORE) had been established in the 1940s by James Farmer. In 1961, CORE activists began a form of protest that they called 'freedom rides'. They wanted to show that any person should be able to travel anywhere in the USA by public transport without having to use segregated facilities. The first group of freedom riders set off from Washington in May 1961 and travelled south. The black Americans used whites-only facilities to challenge segregation.

The freedom riders were attacked by white mobs and beaten with bicycle chains, clubs and baseball bats. In Anniston, Alabama, a bus was attacked and burned (see photo). There was little police protection for the freedom riders. When the riders arrived in Jackson, they were arrested when they tried to use the whites-only waiting room. The campaign gained a lot of media coverage and did a great deal to raise awareness of how black Americans were treated in the Southern states. It also put pressure on the government and Robert Kennedy (the US Attorney-General) organised the desegregation of all inter-state travel.

James Meredith enters Mississippi University (1962)

The photograph shows James Meredith entering Mississippi University. The university did not want any black students and Meredith was prevented from registering as a student. In 1962, the Supreme Court ruled that the university had to accept Meredith. President Kennedy had to send troops to make sure that Meredith arrived safely on campus. There were riots in which two people were killed and 70 injured. The troops had to remain at the University until Meredith received his degree three years later. On campus Meredith was segregated from other students and was forced to eat alone. However, his refusal to give in was an inspiration to many other black Americans.

Birmingham, Alabama (1963)

In April 1963, Martin Luther King and the SCLC organised a series of demonstrations in Birmingham, Alabama. The city had not desegregated. In order to avoid desegregating public facilities such as parks, playgrounds and swimming pools, Birmingham had closed them all.

King knew that the local police would react violently to any demonstrations. And this proved to be the case. In the full view of TV and newspaper cameras, the police used electric cattle prods, dogs and powerful fire hoses to attack peaceful protesters (see photo). Many of the protesters were children and students. A group of children, some as young as eight or nine, were fire hosed as they came out of church to begin a demonstration. The police arrested King and over 1000 other protesters. The scenes shocked many Americans and put even more pressure on the government to act on civil rights. In May 1963, President Kennedy ordered the Governor of Alabama (George Wallace) to force the police to release all the protesters and to make Birmingham desegregated.

The March on Washington (August 1963)

The March on Washington in 1963 is perhaps the most well known of the events that were organised during the civil rights campaign. Over 250,000 people marched on Washington, including well over 50,000 white protesters. The aim of the march was to put pressure on President Kennedy to introduce a civil rights bill. King closed the rally with his famous 'I have a dream' speech (right). Both the speech and the event as a whole had a major impact on American public opinion, increasing support for the Civil Rights Movement. Read the extracts from the speech (right). Why do you think it had such a powerful impact?

Let us not wallow in the valley of despair. I say to you today, my friends, so even though we face the difficulties of today and tomorrow. I still have a dream. It is a dream deeply rooted in the American dream. I have a dream that one day, on the red hills of Georgia, the sons of former slaves and the sons of former slave owners will be able to sit down together at the table of brotherhood. I have a dream that one day even the state of Mississippi, a state sweltering with the heat of injustice, sweltering with the heat of oppression, will be transformed into an oasis of freedom and justice.

I have a dream that my four little children will one day live in a nation where they will not be judged by the colour of their skin but by the content of their character. I have a dream today. I have a dream that one day down in Alabama, with its vicious racists, with its governor having his lips dripping with the words of interposition and nullification, one day right down in Alabama, little black boys and black girls will be able to join hands with little white boys and white girls as sisters and brothers. I have a dream today.

This is our hope. This is the faith that I go back to the South with. With this faith we will be able to hew out of the mountain of despair a stone of hope. With this faith we will be able to transform the jangling discords of our nation into a beautiful symphony of brotherhood. With this faith we will be able to work together, to pray together, to struggle together, to go to jail together, to stand up for freedom together, knowing that we will be free one day.

Changes to the Law

By 1963 civil rights was a major political issue. The government could no longer ignore it. In 1963 President Kennedy introduced a Civil Rights Bill. But he was assassinated in November 1963. His successor, Lyndon Johnson, was able to push through the Bill and on 2 July 1964. He signed the **Civil Rights Act** (see photo).

- Segregation in public places was banned.
- The Attorney-General could use the law to speed up desegregation in schools.
- Racial discrimination was banned in employment.

President Johnson also introduced a **Voting Rights Act**. The Act ended literacy tests and made illegal the kind of barriers and intimidation that had prevented black people from registering to vote in large numbers. It also allowed government agents to inspect voting during elections and make sure there was no discrimination.

How much had been achieved by 1965?

By 1965 the non-violent direct action methods of protest used by Martin Luther King and his followers had achieved a great deal. Segregation was now illegal, a Civil Rights Act had been introduced, and increasing numbers of black people were registering to vote.

However, despite the changes to the law, many black Americans remained frustrated. Those who lived in the overcrowded ghettos that existed in many of the major cities saw little improvement in their living conditions. They were also angry at high unemployment rates and the continuing discrimination and poverty they faced. This discontent resulted in riots in many of America's cities and increased support for groups such as the Nation of Islam and individuals such as Malcolm X who rejected Martin Luther King's principles of non-violence.

The Nation of Islam

Some campaigners thought progress in civil rights was too slow and that Martin Luther King's non-violent tactics were the wrong approach. They felt that force was justified in order to achieve equality for black Americans. The Nation of Islam (or Black Muslims) argued for separatism (keeping the races apart). Members of the Nation of Islam rejected their 'slave surnames' and called themselves 'X'. The Nation of Islam attracted followers such as Malcolm X and the boxer Muhammad Ali, who spoke out against racial discrimination.

Malcolm X (1925–1965)

- Born in Nebraska in 1925 as Malcolm Little. His family had to move several times because of threats from the Ku Klux Klan, who burned down the family home in Michigan.
- His father was murdered and his mother became mentally ill. The family was split up. Malcolm was fifteen when he left school and moved to Boston. Here he was sent to prison after becoming involved in drug pushing and burglary.
- In prison he was drawn to the ideas of the Nation of Islam movement. On leaving prison he changed his name to Malcolm X, joined the movement and became leader of a mosque in Harlem, New York.

- Malcolm X was the most powerful spokesperson of the Nation of Islam. He encouraged black people to take pride in their own heritage and culture. He gained a strong following, particularly in the major cities, where he argued for improvements in housing and education and drew attention to the appalling living conditions of many black Americans.
- In the early 1960s, Malcolm X was very critical of Martin Luther King's methods. Malcolm X argued that violence had to be met with violence and that black people should defend themselves in the face of white violence.

'If you're interested in freedom, you need some judo, you need some karate – you need all the things that will help you fight for your freedom. You don't need a debate. You need some action. So what you and I have to do is get involved. You and I have to be right there breathing down their throats. Every time they look over their shoulders, we want them to see us.'

- He also believed that if violence was necessary to bring about real progress in how black Americans were treated then it should be used.

'I am for violence if non-violence means we continue postponing a solution to the American black man's problems. If we must use violence to get the black man his human rights in this country then I am for violence.'

- Towards the end of his life Malcolm X left the Nation of Islam, became less extreme in his views and began to argue against black separatism. Malcolm X set up the Organisation of Afro-American Unity to promote closer ties between Africans and African-Americans. He was assassinated by a member of the Nation of Islam in 1965. Malcolm X's ideas lived on and influenced many of the protesters of the late 1960s, particularly those involved in the Black Power movement.

The Riots of 1965–1968

From 1965 to 1968 riots took place in most of the USA's major cities. One of the most serious riots was in 1965 in the Watts area of Los Angeles (see photo). Large numbers of people were involved and the riots caused nearly US$40 million worth of damage. An investigation into the causes of the riots showed that black people felt unprotected by the police and were frustrated with their living conditions.

Stokely Carmichael and Black Power

Stokely Carmichael was elected chairman of the SNCC in 1966. Like Malcolm X, he was very critical of the methods used by Martin Luther King. He argued that the USA was 'racist from top to bottom' and that love and non-violence would not change the country. Instead he argued for 'Black Power'. He wanted black Americans to take responsibility for their own lives and to reject white help. Carmichael encouraged African-Americans to have pride in their heritage, adopting the slogan 'Black is Beautiful'. The Black Power Movement gave black Americans a greater confidence and pride in their race, heritage and culture. However, it also caused divisions in the civil rights movement and lost some of the public support that Martin Luther King had worked hard to gain.

The Black Panthers

The Black Panthers were even more radical than Stokely Carmichael. They were formed in California by Huey Newton and Bobby Seale and by the end of 1968 had around 5000 members. The Black Panthers wanted decent jobs, housing and education for black Americans. The Panthers wore uniforms and were prepared to use weapons. They patrolled the ghettos in order to keep an eye on the police. In 1967, Huey Newton was shot whilst being arrested and two policemen were killed. In 1969, 27 members of the Black Panthers were killed in confrontations with the police.

The Assassination of Martin Luther King (4 April 1968)

The Black Power movement had an influence on Martin Luther King. In his later speeches he emphasised that black Americans had plenty to be proud of and he began to place a greater importance on tackling social and economic conditions. King also spoke out against the Vietnam War. Martin Luther King was assassinated in Memphis in 1968. He had travelled to Memphis to support black dustmen who were on strike, campaigning for equal treatment with white dustmen. James Earl Ray, a white racist, was convicted of the crime although it was unclear if he had fired the fatal shot.

Summary: How much had been achieved by the early 1970s?

By the early 1970s, the proportion of black people in segregated schools had fallen to just under 10 per cent. The number of black registered voters in the south trebled from one million before the 1965 Voting Rights Act to 3.1 million by 1968. More black people were becoming involved in politics. The 1970s saw a steady increase in the number of black

Pulling it all together – how should the story of the campaign for equal civil rights be told?

ACTIVITY

Imagine that the photographic history of the Civil Rights Movement on pages 164–169 is being turned into a published book. You have been asked by the publisher to make a number of important decisions.

Work in groups to decide on the best approach the publisher should take.

Be prepared to justify your decisions to other groups who may have different ideas.

DECISION A – Title
- **What should be the title for the book?**

Think carefully about the way that people protested and which methods were the most successful. Can you get this across in the title of the book?

DECISION B – Front cover

- **What pictures should go on the front cover?**

The publisher suggests one individual and one key event. Which ones would you choose? Can you think of a better design for the front cover?

DECISION C – Chapter headings

The publisher wants to divide the book into four chapters. The working titles for each chapter are: 1900–1950, The 1950s, The 1960s, 1970 to the present.

- **Can you think of more interesting headings?**

Think of a heading for each period that sums up the nature and extent of change in each period. Think carefully about the pace of change in each period. During which period was the pace of change the quickest?

Look at the examples below. Do you agree with these phrases or do they mislead people about what really took place during these years?

1900 –1950: Disappointment and failure

The 1950s: The turning point in the struggle

At the moment the book has been organised chronologically. Can you think of a better way to organise the book?

DECISION D – The final chapter

The publisher is very keen to bring the story of the struggle for equal civil rights up to the present day.

- **How do you think the story should be brought up to date?**

Do you agree with the title below?

1970s to the present: Equality at last!

Start by reading Sources 14–17. Use a traffic light system to help you reach a decision.

- Colour code red any evidence of inequality that still exists.
- Colour code amber any statements that you are unsure about. Carry out some extra research using the internet to help you find out more about these issues.
- Colour code green any evidence that supports the view that there is equality today.

SOURCE 14 *Josephine Boyd, the first black student to enrol at an all-white high school in the Southern states, interviewed in 2004.*

There has been some progress. There are ten times as many black Americans with high school degrees as in 1957. But almost everywhere, schools have started to re-segregate. Black and white students rarely share classrooms, and social segregation is deeply entrenched. I don't see that the masses of black kids have benefited at all.

Many black kids are still in the same place they were when this whole thing started ... I thought there was going to be this dramatic change in white folks because they were going to see that we were just like them. That was my biggest disappointment, that this magical place I envisioned never came to be.

A never-ending story? To what extent has life really improved for black Americans?

SOURCE 15 *Gary Younge from the* Guardian, *28 April 2007.*

Martin Luther King had stated clearly that '1963 is not an end but a beginning'. In an interview just before he died he explained that overcoming economic deprivation was essential to making the dream a reality. His wish that 'sons of former slaves and sons of former slave owners will be able to sit down together at the table of brotherhood' was sincere, but not the whole story. Integration had won African-Americans the right to eat in any restaurant. Only equality could ensure that they could pay the bill. Integration was not an end in itself but the means towards that still-elusive goal. In King's words, black Americans 'came to the nation's capital to cash a cheque ... that will give [them] the riches of freedom'. They are still waiting for America to honour it.

SOURCE 16 *Ruth Owens (Jesse Owens' wife) interviewed in 2000.*

I switch on my television now and whenever a game comes on I see black fellers in starring roles. Black men look like they rule sport in this country now. It is the only area where they are right on top. It was nothing like that in the 1930s. America was white and that was that. Like everyone, I just knew it didn't do you no good to dream of making it to the big time. It was impossible.

SOURCE 17 *Extracts from Barack Obama's speech: 'We the people, in order to form a more perfect union', 18 March 2008. Obama was campaigning to become the Democratic presidential candidate. He went on to be elected as the first black President of the USA.*

I am the son of a black man from Kenya and a white woman from Kansas ... I've gone to some of the best schools in America and lived in one of the world's poorest nations. I am married to a black American who carries within her the blood of slaves and slave owners – an inheritance we pass on to our two precious daughters. I have brothers, sisters, nieces, nephews, uncles and cousins, of every race and every hue, scattered across three continents, and for as long as I live, I will never forget that in no other country on earth is my story even possible.

But race is an issue that I believe this nation cannot afford to ignore right now – a part of our union that we have yet to perfect. Understanding this reality requires a reminder of how we arrived at this point. As William Faulkner once wrote, 'The past isn't dead and buried. In fact, it isn't even past.' We need to remind ourselves that so many of the disparities [inequalities] that exist in the African-American community today can be directly traced to inequalities passed on from an earlier generation that suffered under the brutal legacy of slavery and Jim Crow.

Segregated schools were, and are, inferior schools; we still haven't fixed them, 50 years after *Brown* v. *Board of Education*, and the inferior education they provided, then and now, helps explain the pervasive achievement gap between today's black and white students.

Legalised discrimination – where blacks were prevented, often through violence, from owning property, or loans were not granted to African-American business owners, or black homeowners could not access FHA mortgages, or blacks were excluded from unions, or the police force, or fire departments – meant that black families could not amass any meaningful wealth to bequeath to future generations. That history helps explain the wealth and income gap between black and white, and the concentrated pockets of poverty that persist in so many of today's urban and rural communities.

The legacy of discrimination – and current incidents of discrimination, while less overt [obvious] than in the past – are real and must be addressed. Not just with words, but with deeds.

Nelson Mandela: how did a prisoner become leader of his country?

Nelson Mandela was sent to prison in 1964. At the time South Africa was ruled by a white minority who did not allow the black majority to have any say in how the country was run. The government introduced apartheid laws, which meant that black and white people lived separate lives, and were given different rights. In this enquiry you will explore how Nelson Mandela and other campaigners protested against apartheid. What methods did they use? Why did apartheid end? How did a prisoner become President of South Africa?

Nelson Mandela – from prisoner to president

Prisoner

▲ SOURCE 18 *Prisoners on Robben Island where Nelson Mandela was imprisoned.*

As a young man, Nelson Mandela left his home in the South African countryside and travelled to the city of Johannesburg. Here he joined the African National Congress (ANC) and began to campaign for equal rights for all South Africans.

In 1964, at the age of 45, Mandela was sent to prison on Robben Island by the South African government for his role in organising protests against apartheid. Mandela remained in prison for the next 26 years. He was held in isolation for the first eighteen months, and not even allowed to whistle let alone talk to other prisoners. His cell was four metres square and only contained a mat, a bedroll and two blankets. On Robben Island the prisoners were forced to do hard labour, breaking rocks or working in the quarry. They were chained together at the ankles and badly treated by some of the guards.

President

▲ SOURCE 19 *Nelson Mandela at his inauguration in 1994.*

Nelson Mandela's wife, Winnie, was forced to travel 1,600 km to visit him in prison – she was not allowed to take their children to see him. Mandela made sure he kept himself mentally and physically strong whilst he was in prison. He would get up at 3.30 a.m. and do two hours of exercise before work. In the evening he studied law, history, literature and politics.

People did not forget Nelson Mandela. The work of the ANC and campaigners from around the world kept Mandela's name in the news. On 11 February 1990, one billion television viewers watched Nelson Mandela being released from prison.

In 1994, as a result of a free election in which all races took part, Nelson Mandela was elected as the new President of South Africa. Twenty million people voted – most of them for the first time in their lives.

What can Nelson Mandela's speech tell us about South Africa under apartheid?

Later in this enquiry we will explore why Nelson Mandela was released from prison and how apartheid in South Africa ended. But first let's look at why he was sent to prison in the first place. At his trial in 1964, Nelson Mandela described what life was like in South Africa at the time of his arrest and defended the tactics that he and many others had used to protest about the way that the country was governed. However, his speech (see extracts on pages 174–175) also gives us a real insight into Nelson Mandela's character and his beliefs.

▲ SOURCE 20 *Nelson Mandela on release from prison in 1990.*

ACTIVITY

You're going to consider three key questions.

1 How did Nelson Mandela and the ANC protest and why did their methods change?
Use Extract 1 (page 174) to find out how the ANC protested against the South African government.

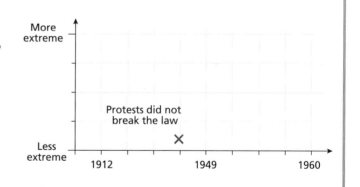

a) Use a Living Graph to summarise your findings. Plot how extreme you think the protest methods used by the ANC were at the following points:
- before 1949
- after 1949 and up until 1960
- in the early 1960s
- at the time of Mandela's arrest in 1964.

b) What reasons does Nelson Mandela give for the ANC changing its tactics to more extreme methods of protest?

2 What type of character was Nelson Mandela and what did he believe he was fighting for?
a) Decide on five words that best sum up Nelson Mandela's character.
b) Summarise, in three bullet points, what Nelson Mandela believed he was fighting for.

3 What was South Africa like under apartheid?
a) Use Extracts 2 and 3 (on pages 174–175) to make notes on what South Africa was like under apartheid.
b) Choose five words that best sum up what life was like for black South Africans like Nelson Mandela under apartheid.

Extract 1

The African National Congress was formed in 1912 to defend the rights of the African people, which had been seriously reduced. Until 1949 it adhered strictly to a constitutional struggle [protesting within the laws of the country]. But white governments remained unmoved, and the rights of Africans became less instead of becoming greater.

Even after 1949, the ANC remained determined to avoid violence. At this time, however, the decision was taken to protest against apartheid by peaceful, but unlawful, demonstrations. More than 8,500 people went to jail. Yet there was not a single instance of violence.

In 1960, there was the shooting at Sharpeville, which resulted in the declaration of the ANC as an unlawful organisation.

Fifty years of non-violence had brought the African people nothing but more and more repressive laws, and fewer and fewer rights. I came to the conclusion that, as violence in this country was inevitable, it would be unrealistic to continue preaching peace and non-violence … the decision was made to embark on violent forms of political struggle.

We felt that planned destruction of power plants, and interference with rail and telephone communications, would scare away investors from the country, thus forcing the voters of the country to reconsider their position.

Extract 2

South Africa is the richest country in Africa, and could be one of the richest countries in the world. But it is a land of remarkable contrasts. The whites enjoy what may be the highest standard of living in the world, whilst Africans live in poverty and misery. Poverty goes hand in hand with malnutrition and disease.

The government has always sought to hamper Africans in their search for education. There is compulsory education for all white children at virtually no cost to their parents, be they rich or poor. African children, however, generally have to pay more for their schooling than whites. Approximately 40 per cent of African children

in the age group seven to fourteen do not attend school. For those who do, the standards are vastly different from those afforded to white children.

All the better jobs of industry are reserved for whites only. Menial tasks in South Africa are invariably performed by Africans. When anything has to be carried or cleaned the white man will look around for an African to do it for him, whether the African is employed by him or not. Because of this sort of attitude, whites tend to regard Africans as a separate breed. They do not look upon them as people with families of their own; they do not realise that they have emotions – that they fall in love like white people do; that they want to be with their wives and children like white people want to be with theirs; that they want to earn enough money to support their families properly, to feed and clothe them and send them to school.

Extract 3

Africans want to be paid a living wage. Africans want to perform work that they are capable of doing, and not work which the government declares them to be capable of. Africans want to be allowed to live where they obtain work. Africans want to be allowed to own land in places where they work. Africans want to be part of the general population, and not confined to living in their own ghettoes. Africans want to be allowed out after 11 o'clock at night and not to be confined to their rooms like little children. Africans want to be allowed to travel in their own country and to seek work where they want to and not where the labour bureau tells them to.

Above all, we want equal political rights. It is a struggle of the African people, inspired by their own suffering and their own experience. It is a struggle for the right to live. During my lifetime I have dedicated myself to this struggle of the African people. I have fought against white domination, and I have fought against black domination. I have cherished the ideal of a democratic and free society in which all persons live together in harmony and with equal opportunities. It is an ideal which I hope to live for and to achieve. But if needs be, it is an ideal for which I am prepared to die.

DOING HISTORY: Evidence

Using sources part 3 – evaluating sources

What makes a source useful?

You have already learnt that using sources well means selecting sources that are most useful for investigating a particular enquiry or telling a particular story.

Being able to evaluate a source and reach a decision about how useful it is for an enquiry is a very important skill. Follow the steps below to help you evaluate Nelson Mandela's speech.

 **Evaluate the content of the source – does the source contain useful information?**

Always be very clear on what you are trying to find out.
Always ask … *Useful for what?*
A source is never 100 per cent useful or completely useless all of the time! It depends on what you are using it for and what you are trying to find out.

 **Evaluate the reliability of the source – should we trust what the source tells us?**

Always ask yourself how much you can trust the information contained in the source. Use the three Ws below to help you.

- **What** type of source is this? (You are using a speech. Are other sources likely to be more useful for your research into the three key questions? How does it compare to a newspaper, letter or diary account?)
- **Who** produced it? (Is it the view of an eyewitness? What are the advantages and disadvantages of this? Is Mandela likely to give a one-sided view of events? If so, how much does it affect the usefulness of the source?)
- **Why** was the source produced? (Why is Mandela giving this speech? What is his purpose? What is he trying to achieve? Who are his intended audience?)

 **Use other sources of information to help test the accuracy of the source**

It is also important to see if the key messages contained in the source are supported by other sources. It is time to carry out two tests:
Test 1: Was life for black South Africans under apartheid really as bad as Mandela describes? (Use page 177 to carry out this test.)
Test 2: Why did the ANC change their tactics and use more violent forms of protest? (You will carry out this test on pages 178–179.)

ACTIVITY

You have already used the speech to explore three key questions:

- How did Nelson Mandela and the ANC protest and why did their methods change?
- What type of character was Nelson Mandela and what did he believe he was fighting for?
- What was South Africa like under apartheid?

1 Look at your notes. Did the source contain useful information that helped you answer your key questions?

2 How reliable is the speech? To what extent should we trust everything that Mandela tells us?

3 Read pages 177–179. Do you think that Nelson Mandela's speech gives a fair and accurate account of:

a) life for black Africans under apartheid.

b) why the ANC changed their methods of protest.

Was life for black South Africans under apartheid really as bad as Mandela describes?

FILE 1– Political Power

- South Africa had been part of the British Empire. In 1910, the Union of South Africa was formed. The majority of white South Africans were Boers, or Afrikaners as they became known. Afrikaners were allowed to vote. Africans and Indians had no voting rights at all.
- In 1948, the Nationalist Party won the general election and Dr Daniel Malan became Prime Minister of South Africa. He appointed a cabinet made up entirely of Afrikaners. In their election campaign, the Nationalists had promised to bring in a policy of apartheid (which means separateness).
- The police had the power to arrest anyone and hold them without trial. Political opponents could be arrested, beaten, tortured and even murdered. People like Nelson Mandela who spoke out against apartheid were banned from meeting others and from writing, broadcasting and moving around the country.

FILE 2 – Living Conditions

- Black people were given their own 'homelands' to live in (also known as Bantustans). However, these were always the poorest areas. They only covered 13 per cent of the country despite black South Africans making up 70 per cent of the population.
- Life for people in the black homelands was very harsh. They were overcrowded and land could not be farmed effectively. They became worse over time as more and more black people were forced to move from white areas.
- Whilst white people in South Africa enjoyed one of the highest standards of living in the world, black people in the Bantustans suffered one of the lowest. Poverty, malnutrition and disease were common.
- Many black people worked in mines and factories in 'white' areas but were forced to live outside these cities. It often meant travelling huge distances from the Bantustans to the cities.

FILE 3 – Laws

The government introduced a series of laws that tried to make sure that blacks and whites lived entirely separate lives.
- Marriages between people of different races were illegal.
- Pass Laws forced black South Africans to carry a pass book, which said who they were and where they were meant to be. If they were found in a town or city without permission they were fined and sent to a black 'homeland'.
- Public spaces and public services were divided according to race. This meant separate parks, beaches, post offices, buses, toilets and cinemas.

FILE 4 – Education

- All schools were brought under the control of the government who placed strict controls on what was taught. Black children were taught about white superiority.
- Black children were not expected to continue their education past primary level. The government believed that they only needed the skills for lower paid jobs.
- Less money was spent on black pupils. In 1953 nearly 64 Rands was spent per white pupil, whilst just under 9 Rands was spent on each black pupil.

Why did Nelson Mandela and the ANC change their tactics and use more violent forms of protest?

Part 1 – the early years of the ANC

1912–1948

In 1912 the South African Native National Congress was formed. It became the **African National Congress (ANC)** in 1923. **Sol Plaatje** became its first secretary. Plaatje, like many black Africans, had worked for the British during the Boer War. He believed that Britain would extend a share of political power to educated Africans after the war. When this did not happen Plaatje set up a newspaper to campaign for political rights.

ANC members travelled to London to try and persuade the British government to introduce voting rights for all South Africans. They believed that the best way of achieving their aims was to keep on good terms with the whites and win their respect. They did not agree with breaking or disobeying the law.

1949–1959

Part 2 – a change in tactics?

From 1948 onwards the ANC began to change its tactics as younger figures such as Nelson Mandela and Oliver Tambo started to play a leading role in the movement. Mandela realised that the ANC could learn a great deal from the way that the Indian National Congress protested. He was impressed by their use of mass non-violent protests.

The Defiance Campaign

In 1952 Mandela was put in charge of organising a campaign of defiance against apartheid. ANC supporters all over South Africa refused to follow the apartheid laws. They travelled in 'Whites Only' compartments in trains, sat on 'Whites Only' benches and queued at 'Whites Only' post offices. By October over 2000 protesters had been arrested. Black South Africans were inspired by their actions and membership of the ANC rose from 7000 to 100,000.

The Freedom Charter

In 1955 the ANC called a nationwide meeting, bringing together all groups in South Africa that were campaigning for change. Nearly 3000 people attended the meeting at Kliptown, near Johannesburg. Before the meeting ANC members travelled across South Africa asking people what their demands were. The demands were listed in a Freedom Charter and read out at the meeting. The crowd greeted each point by calling out 'Africa!' or 'Mayibuye' (which means 'Let us return').

Part 3 – a more violent approach?

Sharpeville

In 1959 the ANC begun a campaign against the Pass Laws (see page 177). The ANC announced single-day anti-pass marches. ANC protests were not the only ones to take place. In 1960, the newly formed Pan-African Congress (PAC) decided to hold a mass civil disobedience demonstration at Sharpeville. They planned to refuse to carry passes and go to the police station and demand to be arrested. When the crowd arrived outside the police station the police suddenly opened fire, killing 69 people and wounding 180 others. The police claimed that they had come under attack from the protesters. Other reports stated that the protesters had been unarmed and peaceful.

Huge crowds attended the funerals of those killed and there were protests all over South Africa. The government made no apology for what had happened and tried to justify what the police had done. Both the PAC and ANC were banned and thousands of people were arrested. World opinion started to turn against the South African government. The UN called for sanctions against South Africa and anti-apartheid groups were set up in many countries, including Britain.

Umkhonto We Sizwe

Sharpeville and the reaction of the South African government to the tragedy changed the way that many members of the ANC viewed the struggle against apartheid. Some members of the ANC, such as Albert Lutuli, continued to believe in non-violent protest. Nelson Mandela argued that violence had already been started by the government and that the ANC should change its tactics. The ANC set up Umkhonto We Sizwe to carry out an armed struggle against apartheid.

Umkhonto We Sizwe did not support all-out war against the white community and wanted to avoid killing innocent people. At first they chose the tactic of sabotage and key targets such as electricity pylons were blown up. Nelson Mandela travelled around South Africa secretly organising Umkhonto We Sizwe.

Oliver Tambo had left South Africa in 1960 and the government had banned him from returning. Tambo spent the next 30 years trying to persuade foreign governments to put pressure on the South African government to end apartheid. Nelson Mandela also visited other countries, talking to political leaders.

Umkhonto We Sizwe continued its acts of sabotage. By mid-1963, around 200 attacks had been carried out. However, in the same year the police uncovered the headquarters of the movement. Papers were found giving the names of the organisers and several were arrested. In 1964 those involved in organising Umkhonto We Sizwe, including Nelson Mandela, were put on trial and charged with treason. They were sentenced to life imprisonment on Robben Island.

Why did apartheid finally end?

ACTIVITY

1 A number of factors combined to weaken and eventually end apartheid in South Africa. Use pages 180–181 to produce a concept map (see page 102) to show how some of these factors are linked.
2 Which three factors do you think were the most important?

Factor 1: Steve Biko and Black Consciousness

During the 1960s it was very difficult to resist apartheid. The PAC and ANC had been banned and their leaders were either in exile or in prison. However, during the 1970s a new form of resistance emerged, which became known as the Black Consciousness movement.

A key figure in this movement was Steve Biko, who was influenced by the campaign for civil rights in the USA and the writings of Martin Luther King and Malcolm X. In 1969, Biko set up a students' union for blacks only, the South African Students' Organisation (SASO). Through the student newspaper Biko started to spread his ideas. For Biko, Black Consciousness was about:

- taking pride in being black
- knowing about history and the black African heroes of the past
- refusing to accept white superiority
- refusing to accept help – black Africans could achieve by themselves.

Steve Biko travelled all over South Africa and became known as a powerful and inspirational speaker. He died shortly after being arrested in 1977. The government claimed that he died as a result of a hunger strike. However, a policeman later admitted that Biko had been brutally beaten and before being taken to hospital had spent at least a day in an unconscious state, chained to a grille.

Factor 2: The Soweto uprising and student protest

Biko's ideas inspired many young South Africans. In 1976 the school pupils of Soweto started an uprising, which quickly spread to other townships. In Soweto there were often over 60 pupils in a class and the facilities were run down. Also, the government announced that half of the subjects that pupils studied in school would be taught in Afrikaans. For the South African students it was the language of the government they hated. It was spoken only by South African whites.

In June 1976, 15,000 students held a demonstration in Soweto. The police fired at them, killing two young students. Images appeared in newspapers across the world and changed many people's attitudes towards apartheid.

Demonstrations were held in other parts of South Africa. Students boycotted classes and burned schools. The police continued to use more force against the protesters and many more students were killed. By the end of the year, nearly 1000 protesters had died. Despite this, student protests continued. Eventually, the government did make some changes and during the 1980s spending on black education tripled.

Factor 3: Archbishop Desmond Tutu and the role of black church leaders

Black church leaders such as Desmond Tutu also played an important role in the campaign against apartheid. Church leaders saw apartheid as un-Christian and regularly spoke out against apartheid. Tutu became General Secretary of the South African Council of Churches in 1978. He used this position to criticise apartheid. He was a highly skilled public speaker who became internationally famous, winning the Nobel Peace Prize in 1984. Tutu tried to persuade black South Africans to join protests and use non-violent methods to resist apartheid.

Factor 4: The role of the United Nations

In 1962 the United Nations put forward a plan to introduce economic sanctions against South Africa. This involved cutting off all trade links with the country. The United Nations hoped that the South African government would realise that their economy could be ruined and therefore they would end apartheid.

However, for the plan to work, the United Nations needed the support of the main countries that traded with South Africa. Countries with strong trading links with South Africa (such as the USA, Britain, Germany and Japan) did not want to place tough economic sanctions on South Africa.

Factor 5: Uprisings in black townships

By the late 1980s, black opposition seemed impossible to crush. Sabotage attacks were increasing and there were a series of uprisings in black townships. There were rent strikes and in some cases councillors' houses were burnt. In 1987, in the town of Tumahole, the thirteen-year-old Stompie Moeketsie led an 'army' of 1,500 under-14s who burned down the town hall. The government continued to use force against the protesters but they never really regained control over the black townships.

Factor 6: The anti-apartheid movement

Many ordinary people in Europe and the USA were opposed to apartheid. Anti-apartheid groups were formed all over the world. When the South African rugby team arrived in Britain in 1970, the anti-apartheid movement set up a 'Stop the tour' campaign. They disrupted games and several matches had to be abandoned. It was the last time that a South African sports team played in Britain until apartheid was ended in the 1990s. The anti-apartheid movement also encouraged people not to buy South African goods and demonstrations were held outside British companies that traded with South Africa.

Factor 7: Trade unions

During the 1980s the black workers were allowed to join trade unions. Different unions joined together to form the Confederation of South African Trade Unions (COSATU). The unions used organised mass strikes as their main weapon to force change. In 1982, over 365,000 working days were lost as the result of strikes. Striking workers were supported by the black community and boycotts of the shops or goods of the company the unions were striking against were organised.

Factor 8: Economic problems

By the end of the 1980s, South Africa was in chaos. It seemed to be heading towards a major civil war. There was increasing violence and big businesses had started to pull out. The cost of the large army that was needed to keep control added to the government's economic problems. Taxes were increased and the income of white South Africans began to fall.

Factor 9: A new government

In 1989, F.W. de Klerk became President of South Africa. He realised the need for urgent and major changes. In February 1990, in his first speech to Parliament, he outlined a series of new measures that signalled that apartheid was at an end. He stated that:
- The ANC and the PAC were no longer banned.
- Nelson Mandela and his fellow political prisoners would be released.
- He was going to work towards equal rights for all South Africans.

In April 1994, the first fully democratic elections were held in South Africa. The ANC gained 62.5 per cent of the vote and Nelson Mandela became the new President of South Africa.

Factor 10: The end of the Cold War

During the Cold War the white apartheid government had been an enemy of communism and had given free access to South Africa's ports to Western warships. In return it had received weapons and support. The ANC on the other hand had been seen as friendly to the Soviet Union. Once the Cold War ended in 1991 the naval bases lost their importance and the West withdrew its support for the apartheid regime.

What happened after apartheid ended? Did Nelson Mandela's vision of a better South Africa become a reality?

In 1999, Nelson Mandela retired from politics. New elections were held, with the ANC winning nearly two-thirds of the vote. Thabo Mbeki became the new President of South Africa. Apartheid had left South Africa with many problems. There were enormous inequalities in wealth and black South Africans had suffered from years of poor living conditions, poor education and lack of health care. How well did Nelson Mandela and the democratically elected governments that followed deal with these problems?

ACTIVITY

1 Read Source 21.
  a) What evidence does F.W. de Klerk give to show that South Africa is now a better place since the end of apartheid?
  b) What problems does he argue still exist?
  c) To what extent does he think that South Africa has improved since the end of apartheid?

2 Carry out your own research to check the arguments put forward in Source 21. Are the arguments still accurate? Use a range of sources to find out about South Africa today.
  a) Do you agree with F.W. de Klerk that 'the new South Africa is a far, far better place' than the country that existed under apartheid? Can you add to the examples that F.W. de Klerk gives with evidence from your own research?
  b) Do you agree that 'much still remains to be done'? If so give examples from your own research.

SOURCE 21 *F.W. de Klerk, from an article in the* Guardian, *23 April 2007. F.W. de Klerk was President of South Africa 1989–1994. In 1993, along with Nelson Mandela, he was awarded the Nobel Peace Prize.*

Fortunately, Nelson Mandela did not die for his ideals. After 27 years in prison, he lived to lead his people to the non-racial democracy that he had envisioned – surely one of the most inspiring political sagas [stories] of any age. And so Nelson Mandela's vision was broadly fulfilled. He became the first president of our non-racial democracy and worked tirelessly for reconciliation. The indignity of apartheid has gone. We have enjoyed prolonged economic growth. Tourism is booming. A new black middle class has emerged and South Africa is again a highly respected nation.

Yet aspects of Mandela's 1964 vision remain frustrated. Half the black population still live below the poverty line. Crime is at unacceptable levels and six million South Africans are HIV-positive. Sadly, political divisions are still based on colour. Whites remain economically privileged, but have virtually no say in the government. Many Afrikaners believe they are subject to new forms of racial domination – and 20 per cent of the white population has emigrated.

Despite all this, the new South Africa is a far, far better place than the bleak scene of repression, discrimination and poverty depicted by Nelson Mandela in his speech [see pages 174–175]. Much of the vision that he portrayed in his speech has been achieved – but much still remains to be done.

◀ SOURCE 22 *Nelson Mandela and F. W. de Klerk receive the Nobel Peace Prize, December 1993.*

THE BIG STORY: Power Part Four

Rights/Protest

The three case studies you have studied in this section of the book tell a very important story. They show how 'Rights' have often had to be fought for, as equal rights have rarely been given to all members of a country. People have always resisted being repressed and having their rights abused. Think back to what you studied in Years 7 and 8. Anti-slavery campaigners and Chartists had to make similar decisions to suffragettes and civil rights campaigners in the United States about **how to protest**. As we have seen there are many different ways that individuals or groups can protest.

ACTIVITY

1 Look back at the political protest spectrum that you produced for the campaign for equal civil rights in America on page 163. Where would you place the following groups or individuals from this enquiry on the spectrum?
   • Sol Plaatje
   • Nelson Mandela
   • Steve Biko
   • COSATU (The Confederation of South African Trade Unions)
   • Archbishop Desmond Tutu
   • Stompie Moeketsie
   • The British anti-apartheid movement

2 Can you think of other protest groups or individuals that you have studied who have used similar methods? Place the following individuals on the political protest spectrum:
   • Boudicca
   • Wat Tyler (leader of the Peasants' Revolt)
   • Henry Hunt (speaker at Peterloo)
   • William Lovett ('moral force' Chartists)
   • Feargus O'Connor ('physical force' Chartists)
   • Thomas Clarkson
   • Toussaint L'Ouverture
   • Gandhi
   • Millicent Fawcett (Suffragist)
   • Sylvia Pankhurst (Suffragette)

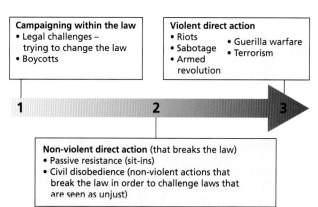

Campaigning within the law
• Legal challenges –
   trying to change the law
• Boycotts

Violent direct action
• Riots
• Sabotage   • Guerilla warfare
• Armed   • Terrorism
   revolution

1   2   3

Non-violent direct action (that breaks the law)
• Passive resistance (sit-ins)
• Civil disobedience (non-violent actions that break the law in order to challenge laws that are seen as unjust)

3 Is there any link between the way people protested and the success or failure of their methods? For example:
   • Does the use of violence tend to achieve more than non-violent campaigns?
   • How important is direct action?

When did life really improve for ordinary people?

The last 100 years are often seen as the period when life really improved for ordinary people living in Britain. Since 1900 there has been a dramatic increase in life expectancy, the government has taken greater responsibility for living conditions and many people have benefited from improvements in science and technology. In this enquiry you will investigate the pace of change since 1900. Is it a story of constant and uniform progress over the last 100 years or is the story a bit more complicated than that?

THE BIG STORY

The Big Story so far …
The graph below tells the story of ordinary life across 1000 years. Diagrams like this provide useful overviews of change over a long period of time.

DISCUSS

1 Look at the graph. Can you remember the reasons for the dips in the graph?
2 Why did life improve for many ordinary people after 1850?

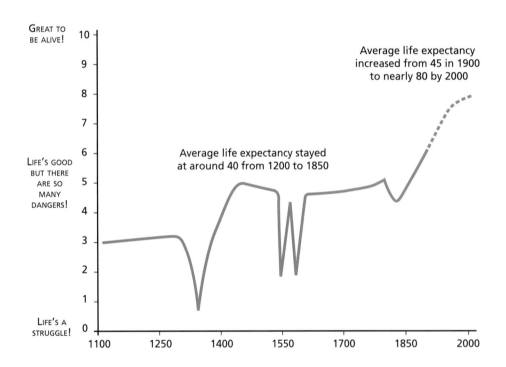

GREAT TO BE ALIVE! — 10

LIFE'S GOOD BUT THERE ARE SO MANY DANGERS! — 5

LIFE'S A STRUGGLE! — 0

Average life expectancy increased from 45 in 1900 to nearly 80 by 2000

Average life expectancy stayed at around 40 from 1200 to 1850

x-axis: 1100, 1250, 1400, 1550, 1700, 1850, 2000

The graph shows that life has improved for ordinary people over the last 100 years. During the late nineteenth century local councils and governments began to improve working and living conditions but there was still a great deal of poverty, and life expectancy for many people remained low.

At the start of the twentieth century workers tended to do a six-day week with no paid holidays. The majority of people started work when they were twelve. Workers were paid low wages, factory conditions were harsh and there were many accidents. Servants made up more than 10 per cent of the employed population.

During the twentieth century life expectancy increased dramatically. There was a sharp decline in the number of people dying from infectious diseases. This was a result of improvements in living conditions and vaccinations. Working conditions also improved during the twentieth century and people benefited from increased educational opportunities. Your task is to investigate when life really improved for ordinary people. Do you think the key changes took place in the first or second half of the twentieth century? Which period in the twentieth century saw the most dramatic changes? Were there periods of stagnation when little change occurred?

Puzzle 1: Who was most likely to win the 1945 General Election?

Winston Churchill (Conservative)

- Had taken over as Prime Minister of Britain during the Second World War, heading a government of all parties.
- Played an important role in Britain's victory – in particular his inspirational speeches helped to maintain morale at home.
- Represented the Conservative Party which had governed many times before.
- Two Conservative leaders had been Prime Ministers in the 1930s: Stanley Baldwin and Neville Chamberlain.

Clement Attlee (Labour)

- Had served under Churchill in the war as Deputy Prime Minister.
- Represented the Labour Party, which had governed briefly only twice before.
- Limited skills as a public speaker.
- Had distinguished himself at Oxford University and was seen as a great intellect.
- Churchill described Attlee as 'a modest little man with much to be modest about'.

Puzzle 2: What was causing the Mysterious Queues of 1942?

In 1942 Britain was used to queuing. People were forced to queue on a daily basis for rations of food and clothing. Generally, the queues were orderly, but people were sick of queuing. They would only queue if they felt they had to. Yet in 1942 queues began forming outside some of the country's bookshops.

What do you think they were queuing for?

How are these queues linked to the result of the 1945 General Election?

ACTIVITY

1 Look at the graph opposite. It suggests that the pace of change during the twentieth century was one of uniform progress. Form a hypothesis – do you think that this is what the pace of change was like since 1900? Draw a graph from 1900 to the present day showing how you think life has changed for ordinary people.

2 Compare your graph to those drawn by other students. Are they a similar shape?

3 Suggest answers to the two puzzles on the left. They might seem like odd questions for us to ask at this stage of your investigation but their link to the key enquiry questions and your hypothesis will become clear later.

185

Why did Winston Churchill lose an election after winning a war?

This is the document that was the object of the queue in 1942.

It was not the release of a new novel – it was the publication of a government report! How many of you know people who have queued for hours to get a copy of a government report? These publications don't normally attract great interest among the general public. Government publications are not written to entertain. The language used is very dry and the front covers are usually very simple. The report that created so much interest in 1942 was the report on 'Social Insurance and Allied Services' written on request of the government by Sir William Beveridge. It soon became known as 'The Beveridge Report'.

Beveridge's report sold 630,000 copies – unheard of for a government publication. This report would become so significant that the achievement of every British government after the war would be measured by it. Even though the war raged on in 1942 and Britain's survival was far from certain, Beveridge's report was nothing to do with war on a battlefield. However, it did outline a plan for a mighty struggle. During the Second World War, William Beveridge was asked to produce a report recommending what should be done to improve people's lives when the war was over.

Beveridge's report had a big influence on the outcome of the 1945 General Election. To the surprise of many people, including Winston Churchill, Clement Attlee's Labour Party won an overwhelming victory. Both the Conservative and the Labour Party accepted the basic aims of the report. They agreed that more needed to be done to improve the lives of ordinary people after the war. However, Churchill and his fellow Conservatives were worried about the cost of Beveridge's proposals. In contrast, Attlee promised to implement the Beveridge Report in full. The promise of the future proved stronger than gratitude to Churchill for his war leadership, and Attlee won the election. A new war began: the war on the Five Giants.

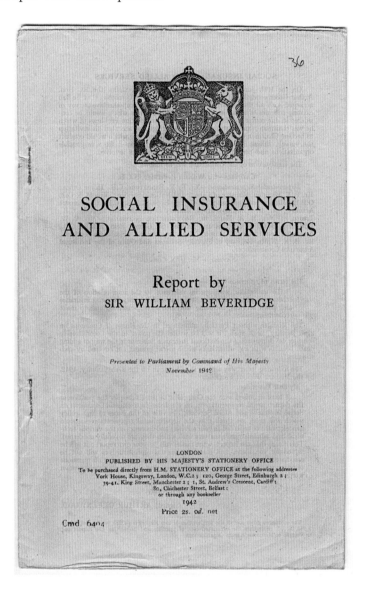

SOCIAL INSURANCE
AND ALLIED SERVICES

Report by
SIR WILLIAM BEVERIDGE

Presented to Parliament by Command of His Majesty
November 1942

LONDON
PUBLISHED BY HIS MAJESTY'S STATIONERY OFFICE
To be purchased directly from H.M. STATIONERY OFFICE at the following addresses
York House, Kingsway, London, W.C.2 ; 120, George Street, Edinburgh 2 ;
39-41, King Street, Manchester 2 ; 1, St. Andrew's Crescent, Cardiff ;
80, Chichester Street, Belfast ;
or through any bookseller
1942
Price 2s. 0d. net

Cmd. 6404

What can Beveridge's Five Giants tell us about life in Britain before the Second World War?

Beveridge's report identified 'Five Giants' that needed to be defeated if life in Britain was going to be better than it had been during the first half of the twentieth century. Beveridge's Five Giants were:

**Want (Poverty)   Ignorance (Lack of education)
Idleness (Unemployment)
Squalor (Poor housing)   Disease (Illness)**

The Labour Party was elected because many people thought that they would do more than the Conservatives to tackle the Five Giants that Beveridge identified. As you can see in the information box (left), governments had introduced some measures to try to improve life for ordinary people during the first half of the century.

Beveridge felt that these measures had done little to destroy the Five Giants. Do you agree?

ACTIVITY

1 Use the 1930s Memory Scrapbook (pages 188–189) to investigate life in Britain in the 1930s.
   a) Record evidence of Beveridge's Five Giants.
   b) Which Giant do you think would have had the most damaging impact?
2 Does this evidence suggest that life improved for ordinary people during the period 1900–1939? Re-draw your ordinary life graph (page 185) from 1900 to 1939.
3 What label would you choose for this period?
   a) How appropriate is each label below?
   b) Choose a label for the period. You can select from the list below or invent your own.

**The Age of Progress –
life improves for ordinary people
The Age of Stagnation –
the same old story for ordinary people
The Age of Regression –
life gets worse for ordinary people**

The 1930s memory scrapbook

How strong were the Five Giants in the 1930s?

In 1935 the average height of a working-class boy going to an ordinary council school was 58 inches (127.6 cm). A middle-class boy attending a grammar school averaged 61.1 inches (134.2 cm). A boy from a wealthy family averaged 63.7 inches (140 cm). This difference was almost certainly due to variations in the amount of nutrition each received. The poorer one was, the less well one ate. In 1937, one working-class person in ten was below the poverty line.

PAWNBROKER CASHES IN

Many families were forced to use the pawnbroker to make ends meet. (A pawnbroker lent money against the security of a family's possessions. If they couldn't repay the pawnbroker then the possessions were sold.)

In Great Britain in 1930, nearly one person in five was unemployed. Unemployment peaked in 1933 at 2,950,000 but was still almost two million in 1939.

Jarrow Crusade 1936

Workers marched 280 miles from Tyneside to London, most of it in the pouring rain, to protest about the high rate of unemployment. The north of Britain was severely hit by unemployment. Jarrow on Tyneside had 70 per cent of its adult males unemployed. Wigan had an unemployment rate of 33 per cent.

Slums Disgrace

In 1936 11 per cent of the working-class population of York lived in slum houses. Scotland had well over 400,000 dwellings without an inside toilet. Nationally in 1936, 3.8 per cent of houses were found to be overcrowded. Much Victorian slum housing remained across the country. Big cities such as London, Glasgow, Manchester, Liverpool and Newcastle still contained poor slums without proper sanitation – in some cases with no gas and electricity. It was rare for a newly married working-class couple to rent a house of their own. Most moved into one room of their parents' house.

QUARANTINE
SCARLET FEVER

In the 1930s, health insurance usually meant that only the chief wage earner of the household could get free medical treatment. Only about half the population were covered by health insurance. Doctors and hospitals charged fees to patients. Most people not covered by health insurance could not afford these charges. So many people did not benefit from new treatments or the medical advances that had been made.

Average life expectancy for a boy born in 1931 was 58.7 years. In the 1930s, dangerous infectious diseases such as TB, scarlet fever and diphtheria were common. An infected cut or wound could kill in the 1930s. Once infection took hold there was no real cure.

Education Scandal

Four out of five children received no secondary education and gained no qualification. State secondary schools did exist but they charged a fee. Also a child at school brought no income into the family home. This meant that a working-class child had very little chance of education beyond the age of fourteen. Free places at secondary school could be gained through excellent performance in exams but there were far too few to go round.

The Privileged Few

University was unheard of for working-class children.

189

DOING HISTORY: Change and continuity

So far in your study of history you have learnt that:

- At any one time, there are usually things that are changing and things that are staying the same (continuities).
- Some changes happen quickly. Some happen slowly.
- A key change in a pattern of events is called a turning point.

It is also important that we think carefully about the *right words* to describe the nature of change during a period. By using more precise words we can give a better picture of how life was changing at the time.

· · · · · · · · · · · **ADVICE BOX** ·

Bringing change and continuity to life!

Try and avoid simply labelling the nature of change as either 'quick' or 'slow'.

Use a variety of words and try to explain the nature of change.

You could use words and phrases such as:

- *rapid* – to suggest that change happened at a very fast pace.
- *gradual* or *non-existent* – to suggest that change was far slower or did not happen at all.
- *consistent progress* – to suggest that things improved at an even rate.
- *inconsistent* – to suggest that at times things changed at speed and at other times the pace of change slowed down.
- *total change* – to suggest that change affected everyone or occurred in all areas.
- *partial change* – to suggest that not everyone was affected by the changes.
- *significant* or *relatively insignificant* – to describe how important the changes were.
- *revolutionary* – if you think the period marked a crucial turning point in history.

It may help to imagine change during a period *as a person*. How would they appear as a person: enthusiastic, weary, confused, reluctant, sleepy, etc.?

ACTIVITY

1. What words would you choose to describe changes in ordinary people's lives during other periods of history? For example, the Middle Ages (1000–1500) or the Industrial Revolution.
2. What three words would you use to describe the nature of change during the period 1900–1940? Add these words to your ordinary life graph (page 187).
3. Use the Evidence Files and sources on pages 191–193 to complete your graph for the period from 1940 to the present. For each period make sure that you choose three appropriate words to describe how life was changing for ordinary people at the time.

DISCUSS

Reflect on what you have learnt so far about the lives of ordinary people in the first half of the twentieth century. Can you find examples of the following:

- Continuity (similarities with other time periods you have studied, for example, the nineteenth century)?
- Change happening slowly?
- Change happening quickly?

EXTRA RESEARCH

In groups, carry out interviews with people who remember what life was like in either the 1950s, 1960s, 1970s or 1980s. How do they describe life during this period? You can use these interviews to help you to complete your ordinary life graph. Think of some good words to describe how life was changing during each decade.

190

To what extent did life for ordinary people improve in the late 1940s?

After winning the 1945 election the Labour government set about tackling the Five Giants identified in the Beveridge Report. Two measures (the 1944 Education Act and the 1945 Family Allowances Act) had already been introduced. The Labour government had to put these into practice as well as introduce other changes.

Evidence File

Education Act 1944
- Provided compulsory and free secondary school education up to the age of fifteen.

Family Allowances Act 1945
- Gave every family five shillings (25p) per child per week.

Slum Clearances
- After the Second World War slums were demolished and new estates of council houses were built. These houses were supplied with running water and proper sanitation.

National Insurance Act 1946
- Made it compulsory for *all* workers (except married women – who had the option) to pay part of their wages in National Insurance. The government and the employer also made contributions.
- In return, workers received benefits if they no longer earned money as a result of illness, unemployment or old age.
- People were paid a state pension on reaching the age of 65 (men) or 60 (women).
- National Insurance also provided maternity benefits. Mothers received a lump sum on the birth of each child. Also, if they had been paying National Insurance they received an allowance for eighteen weeks.

National Assistance Act 1948
- Established National Assistance Boards to help those who were not working and so not paying National Insurance contributions.

National Health Service 1948
- The National Health Service Act of 1946 brought the whole population into a scheme of free medical and hospital treatment.
- The NHS was set up in 1948 and provided health care for all. Over eight million people who had never seen a doctor now received free care.
- Existing hospitals were taken over by the government and made free to all. The building of new hospitals began and millions of people benefited from free hearing aids, dentures and glasses. The NHS invested in the latest technology and surgical operations became more complex.
- Local authorities provided maternity care, health visitors, ambulances and vaccination programmes (protecting children from whooping cough, measles, diphtheria and tuberculosis). Poor people gained access to a range of treatments that they had previously been unable to afford.

DISCUSS

1 Look at the measures in the Evidence File on the left that the government introduced during the 1940s. Match each measure to one of the Five Giants.
2 Which measure do you think was the most important?
3 The 1940s have been labelled a 'social revolution'. Why could this period be seen as a revolution or turning point in the lives of ordinary people?

The late 1940s – another picture

By the end of the 1940s the government was playing an important role in improving the lives of ordinary people. However, the war had only recently ended and people still faced many problems. If a time machine took you back to Britain in the 1940s you would be confronted by a very unfamiliar place.

SOURCE 1 Austerity Britain, 1945–51 *by David Kynaston*.

No supermarkets, no motorways, no teabags, no sliced bread, no frozen food, no flavoured crisps, no lager, no microwaves, no dishwashers, no CDs, no computers, no mobiles, no duvets, no Pill, no trainers, no hoodies, no Starbucks.

Shops on every corner, pubs on every corner, cinemas in every high street, red telephone boxes. Trams, trolley-buses, steam trains.

No laundrettes, no automatic washing machines, wash day every Monday, clothes boiled in a tub, scrubbed on the draining board, rinsed in the sink, put through the mangle, hung out to dry.

Central heating rare, coke boilers, the coal fire, the hearth, the home, chilblains common. Back to back houses, narrow cobbled streets, Victorian terraces, no high rises, suburban semis, the march of the pylon.

Austin Sevens, Ford Eights, no seatbelts, motorcycles with side cars. A Bakelite wireless in the home, televisions almost unknown, no programmes to watch, the family eating together.

Suits and hats, cloth caps and mufflers, no leisurewear, no 'teenagers'. Heavy coins, heavy shoes, heavy suitcases, heavy tweed coats, heavy leather footballs. Meat rationed, butter rationed, lard rationed, margarine rationed, sugar rationed, tea rationed, cheese rationed, jam rationed, eggs rationed, sweets rationed.

Make do and mend.

Evidence Files

The 1950s

- The quality of life for many people improved. Rationing ended and many had more leisure time and more money to spend on luxury goods.
- The sales of cars quadrupled and many more people were able to buy their own homes.
- In 1957 the Prime Minister, Harold Macmillan, claimed that the British people had 'never had it so good'.

- The scale and quality of treatment provided by the NHS improved. There was an increase in the number of doctors and extra funding and better technology made more complex operations possible.

The 1960s

- Governments began to invest in health education. There were campaigns to warn people about the dangers of smoking (see photo, right) and alcohol and to encourage them to take more exercise and have a healthy diet.
- A government report in 1966 found that 166,000 people were living in poverty – mainly because of low wages. Another report from the 1960s claimed that 6 to 9 per cent of the population were in poverty and up to 28 per cent were on the poverty line.

[WARNING! Remember that the meaning of the word poverty has changed over the last 200 years. In the early nineteenth century it tended to mean an inability to stay alive without help. By the late nineteenth century 'poverty' was seen as the level of income below which poor people could not afford the basic essentials of life. By the time of the Beveridge Report, 'poverty' meant poor quality of life.]

- In 1968 the government created the Department of Health and Social Security (DHSS), which introduced extra benefits to help people living in poverty.

Yes I smoke! But then I'm just another sheep... what about you?

- Working hours average: 43 (compared to 48 in 1935).
- Trade unions became more powerful. By the end of the 1970s nearly 60 per cent of workers belonged to them.
- The 1960s and 1970s saw improvements in working conditions, pay and benefits. In many jobs Saturday working ended.
- In 1972, the school leaving age was raised to sixteen.
- The standard of living continued to rise. Income stayed ahead of prices. People were now able to afford a range of goods. By 1972, 48 per cent of the population owned a colour television, 42 per cent a telephone and 66 per cent a washing machine.

- Average working hours: 42.
- Mass unemployment returned. By the mid-1980s three million workers were on benefits.
- For the majority of people the standard of living continued to rise.
- New diseases such as AIDS appeared but, overall, life expectancy continued to rise.

- By the end of the 1980s over 90 per cent of homes contained a colour television, whilst over 80 per cent had a telephone and washing machine.
- By 1991, 55 per cent of homes contained a microwave, 48 per cent a tumble drier, 68 per cent a video recorder, 27 per cent a CD player and 14 per cent a dishwasher.

Many decades have passed since the Beveridge Report. Successive governments have each had their turn at fighting the Giants but has Beveridge's dream been realised yet?

- Average working hours have crept back up to 44. The working week is growing longer again.
- Many homes now have central heating and double glazing.
- There has been a significant growth in female employment. Almost as many women as men are now employed.

- Advanced surgery now takes place and there has been a decline in the numbers of people dying from infectious diseases. This is a result of improvements in living conditions and vaccinations.
- The NHS finds itself under increasing pressure. Hospitals are struggling to cope with rising demand (because of more elderly people) and funding problems (because of the high cost of new treatments and technology).

ACTIVITY

Would William Beveridge be pleased with the progress that has been made since the 1940s?

1 Carry out further research on the condition of each of Beveridge's Five Giants today. Use websites and other up-to-date sources of information to help you.

Want   Ignorance

Idleness   Squalor   Disease

Is the Giant:

- Dead?
- Severely wounded and likely to die soon?
- Wounded but still posing a threat?
- Untouched – at least as strong as in the 1930s?
- Bigger. Actually more threatening now than in the 1930s?

2 Look at how the writer of Source 1 has described the late 1940s. The source is written in an unusual style. Using less than 200 words the author gives us a clear picture of life at the time. Use your research to write your own version of the source for the present day. Remember to keep your report to fewer than 200 words.

3 The writer uses the phrase 'Make do and mend' to sum up the late 1940s. What label would you use to sum up today?

4 What do you think will happen next? How will ordinary people's lives change in the next 100 years? What will happen to the Five Giants?

Which invention has done the most to improve ordinary lives?

You may have changed the shape of your ordinary life graph to show that the story of the last 100 years was not one of continual rapid progress. Change was relatively slow during the period 1900–1940. It was only after the Second World War that the lives of ordinary people really started to change for the better.

However, our Big Story of ordinary life is one of overall improvement over the last 250 years. New inventions and improvements in science and technology have had a major impact. In 2004, *The Times* ran a debate to find Britain's greatest invention of the last 250 years. It ended with a vote by the public and a decision made by a panel of experts. Different people used different criteria to reach a judgement.

A great invention should:
- change the way that large numbers of people live.
- have positive consequences – the invention should improve the quality of lots of people's lives.
- have long-lasting consequences – the invention should have an impact over a long period of time.

It should not:
- have unwanted consequences – these include things that the inventor may have been totally unaware of (for example – global warming).

DISCUSS

Look at the criteria on the left. Is anything missing? What would be your most important criteria?

ACTIVITY

1 Work in groups to develop a set of Top Trumps cards like the one on the right. Use the criteria in the example provided (right) or develop your own four tests to establish the most important invention. Write a brief comment to explain each score.

2 Which invention of the last 150 years do you think has done most to improve ordinary people's lives?

3 Compare your choice to the invention chosen by:

   a) the general public in the vote organised by *The Times*.

   b) the panel of experts set up by the same newspaper.

   Their decisions can be found on page 196. Did they agree with you? If not, produce a short argument that challenges their choice and supports your own.

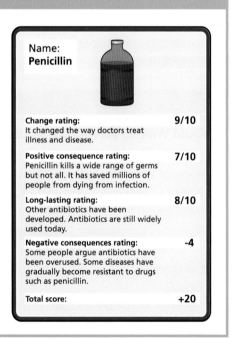

Name:
Penicillin

Change rating: It changed the way doctors treat illness and disease.	9/10
Positive consequence rating: Penicillin kills a wide range of germs but not all. It has saved millions of people from dying from infection.	7/10
Long-lasting rating: Other antibiotics have been developed. Antibiotics are still widely used today.	8/10
Negative consequences rating: Some people argue antibiotics have been overused. Some diseases have gradually become resistant to drugs such as penicillin.	-4
Total score:	+20

Vaccinations

In 1796 Edward Jenner, a doctor from Gloucestershire, immunised eight-year-old James Phipps against smallpox by infecting cuts in his arms with pus from a milkmaid with cowpox. The idea of using disease to provide protection was very important. During the nineteenth and twentieth centuries vaccinations became the main way of preventing infectious diseases. Vaccinations have been used to protect millions of people from disease all across the world.

Steam railway

Richard Trevithick built the first steam locomotive. Railways made mass public transport possible for the first time. They also played a vital role in transporting raw materials and goods during the Industrial Revolution.

Electricity

Michael Faraday developed several devices capable of generating electricity during the 1830s. Electricity is essential to modern day life, powering everything from railways to computers to life support machines. Think of what life is like during power cuts! Electricity made possible other developments too, like the growth of cinema, television and the music business.

Telephone

Alexander Graham Bell invented the telephone in the 1870s. It quickly changed the way that people communicated with each other. The telephone was used by armies to speed up communication and it changed the way that business was conducted. It also changed the lives of ordinary people. Think of how few people write letters and how many people would be lost without their mobile phone!

Electric light

Although the American inventor Thomas Edison usually gets the credit for the invention of the electric light bulb, the British inventor Joseph Swann developed a similar filament lamp in the same year. Swann and Edison merged their lighting companies in 1882 and began to sell their light bulbs in Britain. Electric light bulbs were safer and more efficient than the gas lamps they replaced.

Bicycle

The 'Penny-farthing' bicycle was first developed in the 1870s. The Rover safety bicycle was designed by John Kemp Starley a few years later. Modern day bicycles still follow the same design. The bicycle allowed men and women to travel cheaply and it provided a healthy and environmentally friendly way of getting around.

Television

John Logie Baird invented the television in the 1920s. He used a spinning cardboard disc containing sixteen lenses to create moving pictures. There was an instant demand for television and broadcasts from the BBC began during the 1930s. Today it dominates many people's lives and is often blamed for the increase in obesity!

Penicillin – a new wonder drug

In 1928 Alexander Fleming discovered that a strain of penicillium mould produced a substance that killed bacteria. By 1942 penicillin was available as a drug and was used to treat Allied soldiers on D-Day. Penicillin was the first antibiotic and led to a new type of drug that saved millions of lives.

Jet engine

Frank Whittle came up with the idea of a gas turbine jet engine in 1929. The first test flights took place in 1941. The invention totally changed all types of aircraft. The world became a smaller place as the new engine allowed aircraft to fly higher and faster. Journey times were cut significantly and it became cheap, safe and quick to fly all over the world. Journeys that had taken days or even weeks could now be completed in just a few hours.

Modern genetics

In 1953, Francis Crick and James Watson identified the double-helix structure of the DNA molecule (the basic unit of genetic inheritance). Their discovery transformed our understanding of how life works. It has led to genetic screening for disease, genetic engineering and improvements in drug design.

Medical scanners

In 1971 Godfrey Hounsfield introduced the first computed tomography (CT) scanner that, for the first time, produced accurate images of the interior of the living brain. CT and other scanning techniques such as magnetic resonance imaging (MRI) have improved the diagnosis of disease. They allow doctors to peer inside patients' bodies to trace injury and disease.

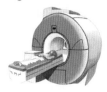

Computers and the World Wide Web

Charles Babbage invented the first computer early in the nineteenth century. Computers today affect everything from the world of work to medicine to transport to games. The first public website went online on 6 August 1991. The World Wide Web brought computers into people's homes. Today we communicate, shop and learn on the web.

Explaining change

Government action or better science and technology? What has had the biggest impact on improving the lives of ordinary people?

What invention did you choose as the most important technological breakthrough of the last 250 years? The panel of experts decided that electricity should take first place with vaccinations second. The general public disagreed, voting the bicycle as the greatest British invention.

However, new inventions, better technology and improvements in science are not the only reasons why the lives of ordinary people have improved. Government action has also played an important role.

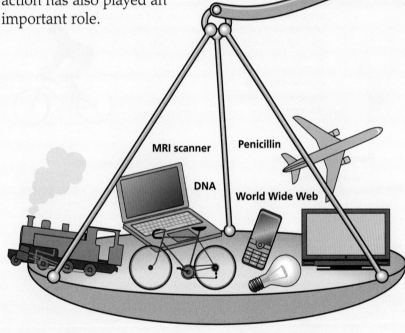

MRI scanner

Penicillin

DNA

World Wide Web

Science and technology

- New technology has changed many manufacturing jobs. New machinery has meant that many jobs are now less physically intense and demanding. It has also helped to make jobs safer.
- Vaccines developed against measles, mumps, typhoid, whooping cough and polio.
- Better science and technology has led to improvements in drug design, genetic screening and gene therapy.

ACTIVITY

1 Use pages 191–195 to add to each side of the scales.

2 Look at the list of changes introduced by the government over the last 200 years. Which change do you think was the most important?

3 Do you think that new inventions and improvements in science and technology have done more to improve people's lives than changes made by governments:

a) Over the last 100 years?

b) Over the last 200 years?

c) Over the last 1000 years?

4 What do you think will be more important in the future – government action or continued improvements in science and technology?

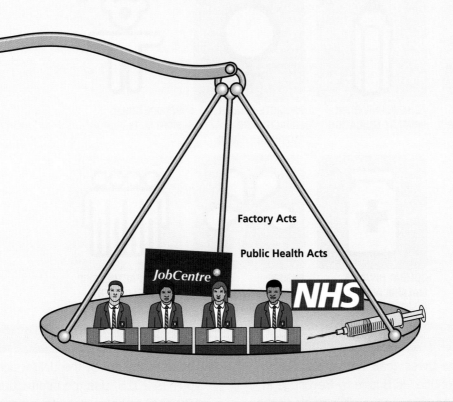

Government action

Nineteenth century:

- Public Health Acts improve water supplies, drains and sewers.
- Factory Acts shorten the hours women and children could be made to work.
- Education made compulsory until the age of eleven.
- Vaccinations introduced to protect people against infectious diseases.

Twentieth century:

- 1909 – Labour exchanges set up to help people find work.
- 1912 – School clinics set up to give children free medical treatment.
- 1940s – The Welfare State is established. The government now provides services and support to make sure that everyone has a reasonable standard of living. As part of these reforms the NHS is established.
- 1960s and 1970s – Health and safety laws made stronger. Laws introduced to stop sex and race discrimination at work.

▶ Progress for all?

As you have seen in the previous enquiry, in Britain over the last 100 years there have been major improvements in life expectancy and social conditions. The five problems identified by Beveridge in 1942 have not disappeared but the Five Giants have been reduced in size. However, is it the same in other parts of the world?

To what extent have the Five Giants been destroyed in other parts of the world?

In 2000 the United Nations set itself eight goals for the new millennium.

ERADICATE EXTREME POVERTY AND HUNGER

ACHIEVE UNIVERSAL PRIMARY EDUCATION

PROMOTE GENDER EQUALITY AND EMPOWER WOMEN

REDUCE CHILD MORTALITY

IMPROVE MATERNAL HEALTH

COMBAT HIV/AIDS, MALARIA AND OTHER DISEASES

ENSURE ENVIRONMENTAL SUSTAINABILITY

GLOBAL PARTNERSHIP FOR DEVELOPMENT

ACTIVITY

1 As you can see these goals are very similar to the targets identified in Britain by Beveridge in 1942. Match as many of the UN's goals to the Five Giants identified by Beveridge. What new problems have emerged since the 1940s?

2 The deadline set by the UN for achieving these goals is 2015. Use the information on pages 199–200 to help you write a report on how successful the UN has been in achieving its goals so far. Present your report as a newspaper article or as a school report like the one below.

Subject	Target	Grade (A–F)	Comments
Poverty	To halve poverty by 2015		
Education	Primary education for all and increase the number of girls in education		
Child and maternal mortality	Reduce the number of children who die at a young age and reduce the number of mothers who die giving birth		
Disease	Stop the spread of HIV/AIDS		
Environment	Reduce pollution and stop an environmental disaster		

What do statistics tell us?

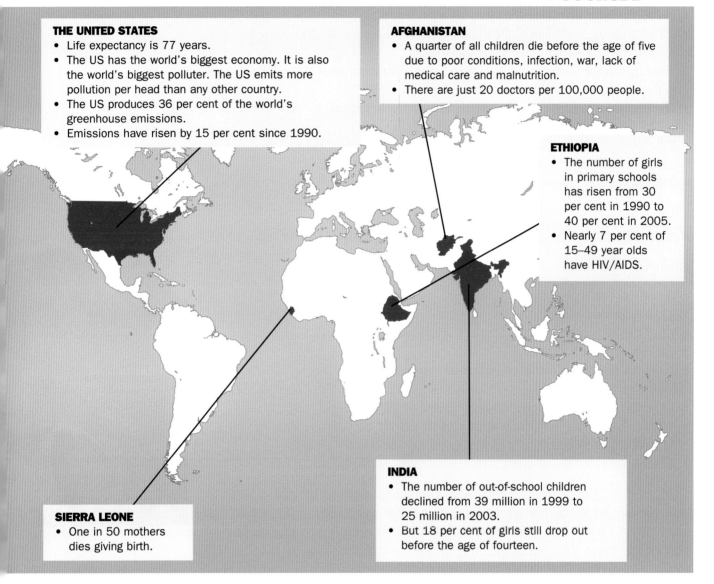

THE UNITED STATES
- Life expectancy is 77 years.
- The US has the world's biggest economy. It is also the world's biggest polluter. The US emits more pollution per head than any other country.
- The US produces 36 per cent of the world's greenhouse emissions.
- Emissions have risen by 15 per cent since 1990.

AFGHANISTAN
- A quarter of all children die before the age of five due to poor conditions, infection, war, lack of medical care and malnutrition.
- There are just 20 doctors per 100,000 people.

ETHIOPIA
- The number of girls in primary schools has risen from 30 per cent in 1990 to 40 per cent in 2005.
- Nearly 7 per cent of 15–49 year olds have HIV/AIDS.

INDIA
- The number of out-of-school children declined from 39 million in 1999 to 25 million in 2003.
- But 18 per cent of girls still drop out before the age of fourteen.

SIERRA LEONE
- One in 50 mothers dies giving birth.

	UK	India	Afghanistan	Ethiopia	Sierra Leone
Life expectancy	78	64	43	45	34
Infant mortality (per 1000 live births)	67	114	165	114	165
Adult literacy	99	61	36	41.5	36
Children enrolled at a primary school	100%	83%	27%	46%	41%
Population living on less than US$1 a day	0%	34%	No figures	26%	57%
Population undernourished	0%	21%	70%	42%	50%
Population without access to clean water	0%	16%	87%	76%	43%

SOURCE 3 Poverty Injustice Disaster – *a 2007 Christian Aid report.*

- In 2007 Christian Aid calculated that every eight seconds a child dies of hunger.
- 1.2 billion people (one-fifth of the world's population) live on less than 60p a day.
- 1.1 billion people do not have clean water to drink.
- Three men in the United States have more money than the poorest 600 million people in the world.
- The US spends one billion dollars per day on defence. In just thirteen days this would pay for health and nutrition for the whole world for a year.
- Poor countries pay back (as a result of debt repayments) more money to rich countries than rich countries give to poor countries.
- 900 million people in the world cannot read or write.

SOURCE 4 The State of the World's Children, *Unicef (2005).*

Of the world's children:

- almost half live in poverty
- 1 in 6 is severely hungry
- 1 in 7 has no health care
- 1 in 5 has no safe water to drink
- 1 in 3 has no toilet or sanitation facilities at home.

- 15 million children have been orphaned because of AIDS.
- 1,700 children in the world become infected with HIV every day.
- 120 million children do not attend primary school. The majority are girls.

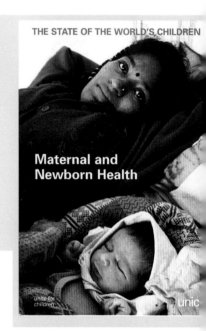

SOURCE 5 *Extract from a 2007 report showing trends in life expectancy over the last 30 years. The report showed that life expectancy in the richest countries of the world is more than 30 years higher than it is in the world's poorest countries. The gap is widening across the world.*

Area	Life expectancy (2000–2005)	Trend over the last 30 years (in years)
The West	78.8	Up 7.2
Russia and Eastern Europe	68.1	Down 0.9
Arab states	66.9	Up 14.8
South Asia	63.2	Up 13.1
East Asia and Pacific	70.4	Up 9.9
Sub-Saharan Africa	46.1	Up 0.3
Latin America and Caribbean	71.7	Up 10.6

SOURCE 6
Predictions by aid agencies and Unicef.

- By 2025, two-thirds of the world will not have enough water.
- By 2010, over 18 million African children will have lost one or both parents to HIV/AIDS.

What can Nelson Mandela's 2005 Trafalgar Square speech tell us about the inequalities that still exist in our world?

You have already used one of Nelson Mandela's speeches to find out about South Africa under apartheid (see pages 174–175). After 'retiring' from politics in South Africa, Nelson Mandela continued to campaign on issues he believed in. Mandela visited London in 2005 to speak at a 'Make Poverty History' rally. In his speech he outlined some of the problems that he thought still faced the world at the start of the 21st century.

I am privileged to be here today at the invitation of the Campaign to Make Poverty History. As you know, I recently formally announced my retirement from public life and should really not be here. However, as long as poverty, injustice and gross inequality persist in our world, none of us can truly rest.

Massive poverty and obscene inequality are such terrible scourges of our times – times in which the world boasts breathtaking advances in science, technology, industry and wealth accumulation – that they have to rank alongside slavery and apartheid as social evils. The Global Campaign for Action Against Poverty can take its place as a public movement alongside the movement to abolish slavery and the international solidarity against apartheid. In this new century, millions of people in the world's poorest countries remain imprisoned, enslaved, and in chains. They are trapped in the prison of poverty. It is time to set them free. Like slavery and apartheid, poverty is not natural. It is man-made and it can be overcome and eradicated by the actions of human beings. And overcoming poverty is not a gesture of charity. It is an act of justice. It is the protection of a fundamental human right, the right to dignity and a decent life. While poverty persists, there is no true freedom.

The steps that are needed from the developed nations are clear. The first is ensuring trade justice. I have said before that trade justice is a truly meaningful way for the developed countries to show commitment to bringing about an end to global poverty. The second is an end to the debt crisis for the poorest countries. The third is to deliver much more aid and make sure it is of the highest quality.

We thank you for coming here today. Sometimes it falls upon a generation to be great. You can be that great generation. Let your greatness blossom. Of course the task will not be easy. But not to do this would be a crime against humanity, against which I ask all humanity now to rise up. Make Poverty History in 2005. Make History in 2005. Then we can all stand with our heads held high. Thank you.

MAKE POVERTY HISTORY

PUZZLE – What links these ten images?

▲ *Westminster Abbey, London.*

▲ *Windsor Castle.*

▲ *Richard the Lionheart.*

▲ *Canterbury Cathedral.*

◀ *A pint of beer.*

▲ Traditional Christmas card.

▲ The Fens.

▲ A full English breakfast.

▲ Marks & Spencer.

▶ Dr Barnardo's.

Typically British?

To many people the images on pages 202–203 seem typically British.
However, the answer to the Puzzle is not that simple.

During the reign of Edward the Confessor, Westminster Abbey was built by his Norman Archbishop of Canterbury, Robert of Jumieges. Edward had also been brought up in Normandy.

Many castles and cathedrals were built in Britain after the Norman conquest in 1066. By the end of the century, the old Saxon ruling class has been replaced by Normans. Immigration was encouraged. Large numbers of Dutch, Italian and German merchants settled in London and large market towns. Highly skilled Flemish masons worked on the cathedrals and great castles.

In the fourteenth century during the time of the Black Death, nearly one-third of the population was wiped out by disease. This produced a gap in the labour market and England was short of workers. The gap was filled by workers from Europe. International trade expanded during the Tudor period and Henry VIII invited skilled ironworkers from Germany. During the Elizabethan age, Italian silk weavers were invited to Britain.

After the Great Plague of the 1660s, England was once again short of workers. Large numbers of Huguenot refugees (French Protestants) arrived. In France, Protestant churches had been destroyed and children had to be baptised and raised as Catholics. Huguenots worked as clock-makers, spinners, weavers and wood carvers; they improved the silk industry and set up paper mills. Within a few years, French Huguenots made up 1 per cent of the population of Britain. By start of the eighteenth century there were 20,000 Huguenots troops in the British army.

Richard I or Richard the Lionheart was brought up in France. During his ten-year reign he spent only six months in England. He was even buried in France. It was not until 1399 that England had a king (Henry IV) who spoke English as his first language.

Monarchs after Richard came from different parts of Europe. William of Orange was Dutch; his coronation attracted large numbers of Dutch immigrants who worked as engineers, clockmakers, goldsmiths and artists. Hanoverian monarchs (George I, II and III) opened close links with Germany. They were followed to England by German businessmen, bankers, scholars, musicians and artists. Many German immigrants joined the army.

Half of the early 'English' breweries were German or Dutch owned and even the English breweries relied on foreign mixers and coopers. It was the Dutch who introduced the hops to Kent from which traditional English beer is made.

The Fens were drained and turned into agricultural land by Cornelius Vermuyden, a Dutch engineer. Vermuyden was employed by Charles I to drain the Fens and the marshy Thames estuary near Dagenham.

The 'traditional' Christmas (St Nicklaus, decorated fir trees, wrapped gifts, candles and carols such as 'Silent Night' and 'Good King Wenceslas') was introduced from Germany and made popular by Prince Albert and Queen Victoria.

Queen Victoria had German ancestors and married a German prince (Prince Albert of Saxe-Coburg and Gotha).

Bacon and sausages, key parts of the traditional English breakfast, were introduced by German butchers during the eighteenth century.

During the Victorian period large numbers of Germans settled in Britain. Many came to escape war in their homeland. By 1871, Germans were the largest foreign-born minority in Britain. There were many German physicians, engineers, teachers, butchers and tailors.

In the late nineteenth century, 150,000 Jewish immigrants arrived from Eastern Europe. Most were escaping persecution. Violent attacks, called pogroms, prompted large numbers of Jews to leave Eastern Europe.

Michael Marks left a small town in Polish Russia in 1878. Like many Jews at the time he was leaving an area where Jews were increasingly being attacked and persecuted. When he arrived in Britain he spoke almost no English and had very little money. However, he saved enough money to buy his own stall at Leeds market, where all goods were sold for a penny. Marks opened similar stalls in other towns before going into partnership with Thomas Spencer in 1894. Marks and Spencer had been born and by 1903 there were 40 shops across northern England.

Other high street shops were also set up by people who settled in Britain from other countries. Burtons was set up by Montague Ossinsky, the son of a Jewish, Lithuanian bookseller. Ossinsky arrived in England, aged fifteen. He changed his name to Burton and moved to Sheffield in 1909 where he started to trade in men's clothing. By 1925 he had over 300 shops and 'Burtons' employed over 5000 people.

Dr Thomas Barnardo was a Jewish Dubliner who came to London in 1866. He became a teacher at one of the East End's 'free schools' and saw the awful conditions in which many children lived. In 1877 he bought two warehouses in Mile End and turned them into what would become one of the biggest schools in London – with over a thousand children. As well as being taught, children were given breakfast and dinner. By 1905 when he died, Barnardo's schools had educated over 50,000 children. His orphanages had housed 12,000 more.

Barnardo was one of many people from Ireland who moved to Britain during the nineteenth century. During the 1840s, 400,000 Irish people came to Britain in order to escape the poverty and hardship caused by the Irish potato famine. By the 1880s the Irish community in Britain numbered nearly one and a half million (3 per cent of the population). Many were forced to live in the overcrowded cities of the Victorian period and were victims of the poor slum conditions. However, nearly half of the Irish in Britain were able to find skilled or professional work. Famous Irish writers such as Bram Stoker, Oscar Wilde and George Bernard Shaw also came to settle in London.

The Irish also made up a sizeable proportion of the British army and by 1868 there were 55,000 Irishmen in the army.

During the nineteenth century, Indian 'Lascars', African, Caribbean, Asian and Chinese seamen settled in British ports. London was fast becoming the busiest trading centre in the world and this created a need for workers. Indian crews – the Lascars – were hired by the British merchant fleet in increasing numbers. They did all kinds of jobs working as clerks, storekeepers, engineers, boilermakers, blacksmiths, joiners, and carpenters. Lascars were often paid only a sixth or seventh as much as British sailors. On some ships up to 85 per cent of the crew were Lascars. The streets around London docks soon became home to Indians, Malaysians, Somalis and Chinese.

After the Second World War there was a serious labour shortage in Britain. Workers from overseas had to be found quickly. 345,000 workers from Europe were recruited to work in Britain. A scheme called 'Westward Ho!' brought 78,500 refugee workers and their families from the Ukraine, Romania, Bulgaria, Yugoslavia, the Baltic and Poland. These migrants were desperately needed to work on the land or in heavy industries such as coal and steel.

Migration Myths: How should the story of migration to Britain really be told?

In this enquiry you are going to explore migration to Britain. There are a lot of myths surrounding migration. A myth is a belief or story that people think is true but is actually a long way from the truth. By the end of this enquiry you should be able to shatter a few of the 'Migration Myths' and tell your own story of migration to Britain.

Pages 204–205 show us that many of the things we think of as being 'typically British' were introduced by people who settled in this country from overseas. This may surprise many people. It is often assumed that the story of large-scale migration to Britain did not begin until after the Second World War. However, this is just one of the Migration Myths that you will be challenging in this enquiry.

In May 1948 a ship called the *Empire Windrush* sailed into Kingston harbour, Jamaica. It was only half full and heading for England. A few West Indians from the RAF were in the Caribbean on leave and the *Empire Windrush* had come to collect them. However, there were spaces for a few hundred more and the skipper advertised for people to fill the ship. Eventually, 492 passengers made the trip. Nearly half had jobs or contacts in Britain. Within weeks, most had found jobs as electricians, on farms, on the railways or in hospitals. Their reasons for coming to England were mainly economic. Jamaica had been devastated by the hurricane of August 1944, the economy was in a poor state and unemployment was high. Sugar was the main export of the West Indies but the price of sugar had sunk so low that the crop was hardly worth harvesting.

Since the Second World War large numbers of people from all over the world have settled in Britain. 1948 is often seen as a turning point in Britain's history. However, is this a Migration Myth? Look at the three Migration Myths on the right. You may already feel that you have evidence that starts to challenge them.

MIGRATION MYTH 1

Large-scale migration to Britain did not start until after the Second World War

Many people believe that the arrival of the *Empire Windrush* was the start of mass migration to Britain. You need to test this myth …

• Was *Empire Windrush* really the start of mass migration to Britain?
• Is migration a relatively new story or is it one of the oldest stories in our history?

MIGRATION MYTH 2

Migrants have always moved to Britain for economic reasons.

People tend to make big generalisations about people who move to Britain. One is that migrants have always moved to Britain for the same reasons as the passengers on board the *Empire Windrush* – economic reasons. You need to explore …

• How typical were the motives of the people on the *Empire Windrush*?
• Did earlier migrants have the same reasons for moving to Britain?

MIGRATION MYTH 3

Migration before the Second World War had little impact on Britain

Because people think that mass migration started after the Second World War, they have tended to underestimate the impact that migration has had on the history of Britain. You need to investigate …

• To what extent did British economic, political, social and cultural life change as a result of migration before the Second World War?
• Did the people who migrated to Britain only have a limited impact?

Idea 1
Produce a large **myth-busting timeline** that you can display in the classroom. You can use the model below to help get you started.

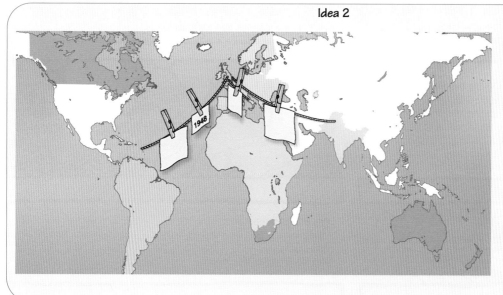

The Romans came from...

43AD

1948

People from the Caribbean came ...

The Romans changed...

These people had...

- Place dates when migrants arrived on the timeline.
- Write down who moved to Britain and where they came from next to the date.
- Above the line, record the reasons these people had for moving to Britain.
- Below the line, record the impact they had on Britain.

ACTIVITY
Read the information on pages 204–205 and 208–211.
In groups, discuss how you could use the information on these pages to challenge the three Migration Myths.

You must use at least one of the methods of presentation on the left. However, you can also use more than one method of presentation.

Idea 2

Produce a large **myth-busting map** that you can display in the classroom.
- Attach string from Britain to the countries from where large numbers of people have migrated to Britain.
- Attach to the string the date or period when the migrants arrived.
- Also attach an information sheet that summarises their reasons for moving to Britain and the impact this group had on Britain.

Idea 3
Use ICT to produce a **film** or **PowerPoint presentation** that challenges the three Migration Myths.

Who do we think we are?

When does the story of mass migration to Britain really begin?

The information on pages 204–205 shows that the migration story starts a long time before the *Empire Windrush*. However, how far back does the story really go? Look at the information on the rest of this page – you may need to stretch your timeline back a couple of thousand years! It appears that we are all immigrants; it simply depends on how far back you go.

c. 1000BC
During the Bronze Age the Beaker people arrived in boats from Central Europe. They came armed with bronze swords and were clever potters and skilled engineers. Migrants from southern Europe (the Mediterranean) also arrived.

c. 800BC
During the Iron Age the Celts fought their way into France and Britain. They came from Central Europe to find land to farm.

AD43
Romans invaded Britain. The Romans brought people from all over the Empire who settled here. The Roman army was made up of Gauls, Hungarians, Germans and North Africans.

AD410
Roman withdrawal. The Angles and the Saxons started to invade and settle in England from the fifth century. England was divided into a number of kingdoms. Saxons (from northern Germany) settled in the south and west (Sussex and Wessex). The Angles (from central Denmark) settled in the north and east. The Jutes (from the northern tip of Denmark) took control of Kent and the Isle of Wight.

End of eighth century
Viking raids began. The Vikings came from Denmark and Norway. At first they raided settlements along the coast. Later they settled here and ruled part of the country.

Ninth century
Alfred (a descendant of Saxon migrants) became King of Wessex. The Vikings conquered much of the north and Midlands. However, the Saxons, under Alfred, fought back. The country became Saxon in the south-west and Danish in the north and east.

1016
Cnut the Dane became King of all England and managed to unite the country. He became a Christian and built new monasteries. In this period London was a 'Scandinavian-style' city and the leading citizens were Danish merchants.

What can individual stories tell us about migration?

Individual stories can tell us a lot about migration. Use the stories on pages 210–211 to explore, in more detail, migration before the arrival of the *Empire Windrush*. These stories should help you destroy the three Migration Myths to an even greater extent.

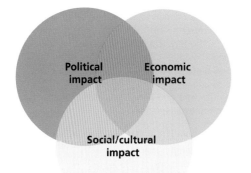

Political reasons
People who are forced to leave their own country because of their political beliefs

Religious reasons
People who are forced to leave their own country because of their religious beliefs

Economic reasons
People who come to work and improve their quality of life. A country sometimes invites economic migrants if it needs more workers

▲ *Venn diagram 1: Do people always migrate for economic reasons?*

Political impact

Economic impact

Social/cultural impact

◄ *Venn diagram 2: What impact have individual migrants had on Britain?*

ACTIVITY

1 Read the individual stories on pages 210–211. Fill in Venn diagram 1 on the left. Think carefully about why each individual or their family settled in Britain. Some individuals may belong to more than one category. Others might not belong to any of the three circles.

2 On a separate piece of paper make brief notes on the impact that each individual had when they arrived in Britain.

3 Use your notes to place each individual in Venn diagram 2. Once again you need to think carefully – some individuals may have impacted on more than one area.

4 Look back to page 205 and add the names of Michael Marks, Montague Ossinsky and Dr Thomas Barnardo to both of your Venn diagrams.

5 Write two short paragraphs challenging Migration Myth 2 – Migrants have always moved to Britain for economic reasons, and Migration Myth 3 – Migration before the Second World War had little impact on Britain.

PICTURE PUZZLE

Look at the pictures on the right. You may have studied these individuals in Year 8 or earlier in Year 9. Can you remember why they settled in Britain and the impact they had? Where would you place each individual in the Venn diagrams?

▲ *Olaudah Equiano*

▲ *Duleep Singh*

▲ *Dadabhai Naoroji*

Migration stories

Olaudah Equiano was kidnapped from his home in Africa when he was eleven, forced on a long journey to the coast and taken to Barbados as an enslaved African. Eventually, by trading and saving hard, Equiano was able to buy his freedom for £40. After many years travelling to Turkey, Italy, Portugal and even the Arctic, Equiano settled in Britain where he played a leading role in the campaign to end the slave trade. Equiano spoke at London debating societies and published several anti-slavery letters in London newspapers. He was a skilled writer and public speaker.

Equiano wrote a very important book telling the story of his own life. *The Interesting Narrative of the Life of Olaudah Equiano* was first published in London in 1789. It became a bestseller and eight editions had to be published to meet public demand. The book was even translated into German, Dutch and Russian. It was a very important part of the campaign and persuaded many people to support the anti-slavery campaign.

Mary Prince was born in 1788 in Bermuda to a slave family. She was sold to a number of brutal owners and suffered terrible treatment. In 1828 she travelled to England with her owners. Here she left her owners and worked with the Anti-Slavery Society. She became the first woman to present an anti-slavery petition to Parliament and was the first black woman to write and publish an autobiography, *The History of Mary Prince: A West Indian Slave*. The book was a key element in the anti-slavery campaign. It made people in Britain aware that although the slave trade had been made illegal, the horrors of life on the plantations continued.

William Cuffay's grandfather was an enslaved African who had been taken to St Kitts. His father became a cook on a warship and his family eventually settled in Chatham in Kent. William became a tailor. However, he became increasingly involved in politics. After he joined a trade union and was sacked for going on strike, William saw a need for MPs who would do more to help working people. In 1839 he became active in the Chartist movement. Cuffay organised protests and was a powerful speaker at Chartist rallies. In 1842 he was chosen to become president of the London Chartists. After 1845 Cuffay was seen as one of the leading figures in the Physical Force Chartists. He believed that violence should be used to get equal rights for working people. In 1848 a spy provided information to the government on a group of London Chartists. Based on the evidence given by the spy, Cuffay was arrested, charged with planning a revolt and transported to Tasmania.

Poland was invaded by Germany in 1939. Only a few days later Stalin invaded Poland from the East. More than a million and a half Polish people were transported to the East where nearly a million of them died. **Witold Urbanowicz** was a Polish fighter pilot. He was captured by the Soviet army when they invaded Poland but managed to escape to France. While in France, he and a group of other Polish pilots were invited to join the RAF. During the Battle of Britain, Urbanowicz shot down fifteen enemy aircraft and was later awarded the British Distinguished Flying Cross.

In total, the RAF accepted 14,000 Polish airmen. Polish pilots played a crucial role in the Battle of Britain, shooting down one in seven enemy aircraft. In addition, on D-Day, Polish army units formed an important part of the Allied army, whilst Polish intelligence units played a crucial role in cracking the German Enigma code. When the war ended, 120,000 Polish people stayed in Britain. The Polish Resettlement Corps was set up and members worked alongside demobilised British troops in bomb disposal, farming and rebuilding the country.

Dadabhai Naoroji came to London from Bombay in 1850 to set up his own cotton trading company. He went on to become professor of Gujarati at University College, London and later went into politics. In his writings, he demonstrated how India's poverty was, to a large extent, the result of its being drained by Britain – up to £40 million was exported to Britain every year. In 1892 he became MP for central Finsbury.

Some people settled in Britain after being driven out of their country because of their political beliefs. **Karl Schapper** was expelled from Germany and settled in England. Here he became leader of the Workers' Education Association and fought hard for better schools.

Princess Sophia Alexandra Duleep Singh was born on 8 August 1876. She was a daughter of Maharajah Duleep Singh (see pages 16–25), an Indian prince who had his lands taken from him and was forced to move to England.

Sophia was one of several Indian women who played a significant part in the Suffragette movement in Britain. Although she was born into wealth and mixed in royal circles, she stood firm in her belief that women should have the vote. Sophia was active in the Women's Social and Political Union (WSPU) and the Women's Tax Resistance League (WTRL). Sophia refused to pay taxes and sold the Suffragette newspaper outside of the palace gates when she was a guest at Hampton Court. She also supported Indian communities in Britain.

Guglielmo Marconi was the child of an Irish Protestant mother and an Italian father. He was brought up in Italy. He came to London in 1896 after being disappointed at the Italian government's lack of interest in, and support for, his work in electronics. In 1901 he sent the first radio message across the Atlantic and in 1909 was awarded the Nobel Prize for physics.

Walter Tull's grandfather had been enslaved in Barbados, whilst his father had come to Kent and worked as a joiner in Folkestone. Following the death of his mother in 1895, Tull was raised in an orphanage in Bethnal Green, where he became an outstanding member of the football team. His talent was spotted by Tottenham Hotspur, who signed him as a professional. He later moved to Northampton Town, for whom he was playing when the First World War broke out. Tull enlisted in the Middlesex Regiment and fought on the Somme and in Italy. In 1917 he was promoted to the rank of second lieutenant, thus becoming the first black officer in British military history. He died in 1918, leading an assault on a German trench in France. His fellow soldiers showed their respect for him by repeatedly trying to recover his body from the battlefield.

Between 1933 and 1939, 60,000 Jews arrived in Britain desperate to escape persecution as Hitler and the Nazi Party occupied more and more of Europe. **Ludwig Guttman**, a skilled neurosurgeon, arrived in Britain in 1939. A specialist in spinal injuries and paraplegia he went on to set up Stoke Mandeville Hospital.

Nicholas Winton's parents had left Germany at the end of the nineteenth century. He was born in England, where he was baptised a Christian and worked as a clerk on the British Stock Exchange. In 1938 he went on a fact-finding mission to Prague and was horrified by the plight of the Jews. When he returned, he set up a scheme to evacuate to England as many endangered children as possible. These *Kindertransports* first left Prague in December 1938 and continued until the start of the Second World War. In all, 669 children arrived in Britain.

Mahinder Singh Pujji was born in Simla, India in 1918. He went to school and college in Lahore and went on to study law. In 1936 he learned to fly at the Delhi Flying School. When the Second World War broke out he saw a newspaper advertisement asking for pilots to join the RAF. Pujji volunteered and came to England. He was one of the first Indian pilots to serve with the RAF, flying Hurricane fighter planes.

Over 2.5 million servicemen and women from the Indian subcontinent (present-day India, Pakistan, Bangladesh and Sri Lanka) contributed to the Allied cause during the Second World War. Most of this number served in the Indian Army. However, 55,000 joined the Royal Indian Air Force, while several airmen like Mahinder Singh Pujji came to Britain to serve with the RAF. During the Second World War the price paid by the Indian subcontinent was heavy. 36,092 people were killed or reported missing and 64,354 were wounded. Almost 80,000 had to endure captivity as prisoners of war.

Patrick James Foley's parents travelled to Leeds from Ireland in the 1830s. After he left school, Foley worked with various friendly societies, trying to help those in poverty. Foley later became one of the founder members of Pearl Assurance. By 1913 it was the third largest life assurance company in Britain. Foley also built several Catholic schools in London.

Why is it difficult to summarise the experiences of people who have moved to Britain?

You have already seen how people moved to Britain for a variety of different reasons. In this enquiry you will explore what life was like for people who settled in Britain. You will focus on one particular group – people who moved from the Caribbean during the years that followed the Second World War. How similar were people's experiences? How easy is it to write about the Caribbean experience of moving to Britain?

The people from the Caribbean who arrived on board the *Empire Windrush* in June 1948 had high hopes of building a good life for themselves in Britain. People living in Britain's colonies had been brought up to think of Britain as their 'mother country' and felt she would always treat them as part of her family. Many of those on board had already been to the UK as part of the war effort, many of them serving in the RAF.

During the Second World War, Britain turned to the countries in her empire for support. During the Second World War, 16,000 West Indians volunteered for service. In the Caribbean, money was raised for tanks, aeroplanes and ambulances. Huge amounts of raw materials and food were sent to Britain to help supply her people and the war effort.

After the Second World War, Britain was short of workers. During the 1950s and 1960s people from the Caribbean, India, Pakistan and Bangladesh were all invited to Britain to fill important jobs, especially in transport, health and the textile industry.

The British government promoted Britain as an ideal place for Caribbean people. British government ministers visited the various islands, trying to persuade people to come and settle in Britain. During the 1950s, British firms began actively advertising for workers. For example, in 1956, London Transport wanted to recruit nearly 4000 new employees and used recruitment posters containing photographs like the one on the right.

DISCUSS

What impression does the photograph create of life in Britain? Is migration portrayed as a positive experience?

Was migration a positive experience for those people who moved to Britain from the Caribbean?

Two passengers on board the *Empire Windrush* were Aldwyn Roberts and Cecil Holness. Aldwyn Roberts was a calypso singer known as Lord Kitchener. Cecil Holness had joined the RAF in 1944. He returned to Jamaica in 1947 and then came back to Britain on the *Empire Windrush*. He lived in London and worked as a mechanic.

DISCUSS

Read Aldwyn Roberts' and Cecil Holness' accounts of settling in Britain. To what extent were their experiences positive? How typical do you think these experiences were of other migrants?

SOURCE 1 *Aldwyn Roberts.*

A friend told me I can get a job in The Sunset Club. I started singing this song. Of course, the Caribbean people understood the song and they explained it to their white friends. Then it became so popular I was singing it in three clubs in one night. This went on for quite a while. After this I had no worries. I was living like a king.

SOURCE 2 *Cecil Holness.*

Just when we got married, 1949, and I saw this advert in a shop window about rooms to let and then when I phoned the lady, she say, 'Oh yes, come round, it's all here, you'll get the room.' So when I arrive, I rang the bell and this white lady she came out and I said, 'Good afternoon madam,' and the moment when she answered the door you know it's like as if she's so frightened because she didn't expect to see a black man. She said, 'No, I haven't got any room to let. I don't want black people.'

In the ten years after the arrival of the *Empire Windrush*, over 125,000 West Indians came to Britain. You need to investigate what it was really like for these people when they settled in Britain. Was migration a positive experience?

ACTIVITY

1 Draw an experiences line like the one below. Do you agree with where we have placed Aldwyn Roberts and Cecil Holness?

2 As you read Sources 3–6 on page 214, place each individual on the experiences line. Make sure you can explain every decision you make.

SOURCE 3 *Vince Reid came to Britain on the* Empire Windrush. *He was thirteen.*

When I went to school, first of all, I was a subject of curiosity, which is quite surprising when you think that you had black soldiers in England. And people would come up and rub your skin and see if it would rub off the black, and rub your hair, and, you know, it's really insulting. And of course there was always the latent violence, people wanting to fight you. I was the only black child in the school. They didn't even give me a test to see what grade I should be put in, they just put me in the lowest grade. Then they had a sort of end of year examination and I moved up into the top class. But I remember a teacher teaching Shakespeare and he said, 'Who can explain what this soliloquy means?' So I put my hand up. Of course the way I spoke then is not like I speak now, I had this Jamaican accent. And this teacher just rolled around. I felt so ashamed, that he was basically mocking me. And I really stopped going to school because I felt so angry and ashamed. It still hurts to this day. You weren't expected to know anything and they just took the mickey. That was 1949 and it still hurts.

SOURCE 4 *Berris Anderson settled in London in the 1950s (this interview was published in 1998 in* Reform, *a church magazine).*

I worked for seven weeks at British Rail and then the foreman got rid of us. This white chap was working there and he had a fire and when we went there to try to warm our hands he moved away and went to get the foreman. He called us to the office and said, 'On Friday, you finish'. All seven of us. We were treated different but that is the only place [it happened] while I've been here.

SOURCE 5 *Pearline Wynter settled in London in the 1950s (this interview was published in 1998 in* Reform, *a church magazine).*

Well, the welcome was very good for me, I didn't find any fault with it. And up to now in this country I have never had trouble with anyone. I can't give anyone a bad name for that.

SOURCE 6 *Ivan Weekes came to Britain in 1955.*

I used to feel not only frightened but wondering what's going to happen next. I could get bumped off. And people would look at you, like spears, daggers. People would spit at you. Nobody spit at me personally but I know what happened. If you went to sit down beside somebody on a bus they'd shuffle up. But then somebody would look at you, see that you're frightened as hell and say, 'Oh mate, take no notice of them, we're not all the same.' I think that's so important to say. That was my experience, 'take no notice of them, we're not all the same.' And just those few words gave me two things: hope and comfort. People were not all the same.

ACTIVITY

Write a newspaper or magazine article that summarises what life was like during the 1950s, 1960s and 1970s for people from the Caribbean who migrated to Britain. You can use information and source material from pages 213–214 and 216–217 as well as carrying out your own research into this topic.

Make sure you read the advice on the page opposite before you start.

Why is it difficult to summarise the experiences of people who have moved to Britain?

At first the activity on page 214 may appear an easy task. You have already looked at some source material and there is extra information and source material waiting to be used. However, how easy is it to summarise the experiences of migrants? Look at the experiences line you have produced using Sources 1–6. What does this show you? Did all migrants have the same experience?

During your study of history at Key Stage 3 you have already seen that:

> **People's lives are different**
> **... even if they live in the same period of history.**
> **... even if they live in the same country in the same period of history.**

Diversity is a key concept in history. Sometimes people assume that all migrants have a similar experience, especially if they all move from the same part of the world, during the same period, and to the same place. However, the experiences line that you have produced shows that this is not the case. Even within a group of people migrating from the same part of the world (the Caribbean) to the same place (Britain) at a similar point in time (the 1950s and 1960s), different people have different experiences. Compare, for example, Vince Reid's story with Pearline Wynter's.

People involved in the same 'historical event' may have different experiences depending on a number of different factors. These factors can include who they meet and where they settle. It is also important that we recognise that the experiences of one individual might vary, even over a very short period of time. Look again at Ivan Weekes' story – not everyone he met treated him the same. As he says, 'People were not all the same.'

ADVICE BOX

You have already learnt that in history we make generalisations, because they are a useful way of coming to a conclusion. However, this type of writing needs to be approached with care. As you have already seen, the story of people migrating to Britain from the Caribbean is complicated. At times the experience may have been positive, at other times negative. We must be careful not to tell a simple story that gives the impression that everyone had the same experience.

1 *New migrants started by living in a hostel until they had saved enough money to get their own place. Landlords were greedy and charged too much rent. New migrants who tried to rent houses were faced with racism from the landlords. It was hard for West Indians to find places to live. Migrants faced prejudice and were treated very badly on arrival in Britain. Migration was a very negative experience.*

2 *New migrants often started by living in a hostel until they had saved enough money to get their own place. Some landlords were greedy and charged too much rent. Sometimes, new migrants who tried to rent houses were faced with racism from the landlords. It was often hard for West Indians to find places to live.*

DISCUSS

Look at the two accounts on the left. Why is one account far more accurate than the other? Think carefully about the words that have been highlighted.

Moving to Britain: The Caribbean experience

Britain had always portrayed itself in a good light. People in the colonies were not told about the poverty of Britain's cities – all they saw were displays of wealth and power. Many migrants were disappointed with what they found. Many new migrants started by living in a hostel until they had saved enough money to get their own place. Some landlords were greedy and charged too much rent. Sometimes, new migrants who tried to rent houses were faced with racism from the landlords.

People would often save money together in a money-saving system known as 'pardner' or 'sou-sou'. This collective practice meant that they were able to obtain deposits for their own houses.

Many migrants who came to Britain were already well educated. But sometimes their qualifications were not recognised in Britain. Other times, racist employers refused to give them jobs. As a result, many people had to take less well-paid and less qualified positions, or re-train for a job they already knew how to do. More than half of the Caribbean males in London were in employment for which they were overqualified.

There was also racism directed against black communities in the form of violence and persecution. In August 1948, violence broke out in Liverpool as mobs of white people attacked hostels where the West Indians were staying. In 1958, black communities in Nottingham and in London (Notting Hill) suffered racist violence – homes were petrol bombed and there were attacks on black people and shops. After the Notting Hill riots, nine white youths were sent to prison. The judge, Lord Justice Salmon, said they had filled the nation with disgust: 'Everyone, irrespective of the colour of their skin, is entitled to walk through our streets with heads erect and free from fear.'

However, violence against migrant communities was relatively rare during the 1950s and 1960s. There was interaction between different communities in everyday life. Also, the law was changed to try and tackle racial discrimination. Race Relations Acts were passed in 1965, 1968 and 1976. The 1965 law made discrimination against black people in public places such as hotels and cinemas illegal. The 1976 law made it illegal to encourage racial hatred and established the Commission for Racial Equality (CRE).

During the 1960s, a new political party called the National Front was formed. It distributed pamphlets attacking black people and Jews. By 1974, it was fielding 44 candidates in the general election and it gained 3 per cent of the vote. The 1970s and early 1980s also saw a rise in the number of racially motivated assaults. In 1976, John Kingsley Reid of the National Front greeted news of a racist murder with the words: 'One down, a million to go.' However, anti-racists came together to combat these groups. One example was the 'Rock Against Racism' concert held in London in 1978 (right). It is estimated that 80,000 people marched six miles from Trafalgar Square to the East End of London for the concert.

The following accounts are taken from interviews with people who left the Caribbean in the 1950s and early 1960s and eventually settled in and around Ipswich.

My family thought that the education system must be better in England and therefore it would be a good idea to send me to England to join my mother. And that's what happened. I came over here but the education system was disappointing. The fact that there was no more Latin, which I had been doing in St Kitts, there was no more French after the second form. Then I found in terms of academic subjects that I just coasted, I was just able to coast for two years because of the grounding I had in St Kitts. You weren't really as a black person expected to achieve anything in this country, no one was bothered if you didn't achieve. The difference is that had I been in the Caribbean someone would have done something.

When I came here, a young teenager leaving a happy-go-lucky place – sunny, hot – you came here and it was cold. I went straight into the country, on to a farm and it was really very lonely. When I got to Ipswich we had to wait for the bus and I really felt terrible. All I could see was white people and they were looking at me and I thought, 'Gosh, am I from outer space or something?' But, nobody said anything and I couldn't understand why people didn't smile. Everybody seemed so serious and they just looked at you. All I could think of was that I'd left a lovely sunny place and come to this really dark and bleak place. But, all my life here, I can't say I've had a bad time because you know even if people were racist or anything they never showed it to me before my face.

I've got cousins and uncles who came up during the war here, had to fight for the 'mother country' as it was termed in those days. But then, when I came to England, after all that – knowing that your relatives came up to fight and to help the country, and you come up here and the way people treat you and the way people act with you, you think, 'So why did my relatives come up here to help them do anything if that's the way they carry on?' You walk in the pub and you find the landlord, you'll go up to the bar and order the drink, and the landlord will go at the other end, he'll get the glasses, not empty, but he fills them up, and gives the guys at the other end a drink for free rather than serving us.

When I came out my husband took me to this house, an English couple, and they were so friendly. She said, 'We are glad to meet you. Your husband is our friend from the time he came here.' And they said, 'I hope you have a good time in England, and we welcome you.'

You came here with a degree and you weren't going to get a job that suited. The education matched Britain because all the papers in the Commonwealth were set here. The English didn't see you, some of them not all, didn't see you as people.

Although we were taught everything about English history, the English people weren't taught anything about the West Indian people. The West Indian people felt that they should be accepted in England because we were all British citizens, we all had British passports, we thought we were entitled to be here, and then we were treated like outcasts really.

I joined the RAF. I quite enjoyed it, the travel, the people. I've been to stations where I was the only black person. I can't say I noticed any prejudice. Although it existed, it was frowned on, if anybody had any thoughts they had to keep them to themselves.

When I put in for a job, the manager told me that the reason I didn't get the job was because he didn't think a number of his senior managers would like the idea of someone like me, working with young white girls in the office. My first ever experience of racial discrimination was on the train from Liverpool Street coming to Ipswich. Four of us went in the train. There were four people sitting on the one side, and these four people just got up and walked out. I said to my friend, 'What was that all about?' And he said, 'You're going to have to get used to that. Some people just don't like us because we're black.'

They didn't know anything about us, while we had a little idea about them, you see, we were British. You'd get on a bus and if people saw you coming to sit down they'd slide up the seat before you could sit down or they'd open up their legs and put their handbags at their side so we didn't sit there. We always had to stand up.

It was hard work but I decided to work to educate my children because I missed the education part of my life. That is what I came to England for. When I was going on the plane and I looked up at the sky and I said, 'God help me get a job to educate my children.' My son went into the army and later became a barrister, my daughters became a nurse and a social worker. So my hard work paid off. I'm glad I came to England because everybody has a chance to do things.

THE BIG STORY: Movement and Settlement Part Three

Bringing the story up to date – challenging some new myths

Flooded by Immigrants

Some People Feel Swamped by Immigrants

1 in 4 Asylum Seekers Ends Up in Britain

Asylum – the Joke's on Us

DISCUSS

Look at these newspaper headlines and quotes from politicians. What impression of immigration do words such as 'flooded' and 'swamped' create?

Headlines such as these have led to the development of a new set of Migration Myths. They suggest that …

1 The number of people migrating to Britain has been far greater than those who have emigrated since the end of the Second World War.
2 Britain takes in far more refugees and asylum seekers than other countries.
3 Increases in immigration have been bad for Britain.

ACTIVITY

Examine the statistics and source material on this page and opposite. Use this information to challenge the three new myths on the left.

For much of the twentieth century figures for emigration from Britain were far higher than figures for immigration. Between 1961 and 1981 one million more people left than arrived.

In a recent survey people thought that Britain's immigrants made up 20 per cent of the population – the true figure is 4 per cent.

In 2005, the UK ranked fourteenth in the league table of EU countries for the number of asylum applications per head of population. Asylum-seeking in Europe is in decline – the number of refugees entering Europe has almost halved over the past decade.

In the ten years leading up to the 2001 census, three and a half million people had come to live in Britain; three million had left. Several million Britons live overseas today. Does anyone argue against their right to do so?

By the start of the 21st century a shortage of doctors and nurses meant that the NHS had to actively recruit from overseas. By 2003, 42,000 foreign nurses were working in the NHS.

During the 1990s, conflicts in the Balkans, the Gulf, Somalia, Rwanda, Sierra Leone and Iraq increased the number of migrants. By 2000, 19 million people were classed as refugees. In a recent survey people thought that Britain was taking in 25 per cent of the world's refugees. In fact Britain takes in just 2 per cent. The UK, one of the richest countries in the world, hosts less than 3 per cent of the world's total refugee population. The world's poorest countries take responsibility for the vast majority of refugees. Nearly two-thirds of all refugees are hosted in the Middle East and in Africa.

Britain's population could shrink without immigration. The birth rate needed to keep it at its present level is 2.2 children per woman. At present it is running at 1.7. There is also a need for young workers to support a rapidly ageing population. Many economists argue that immigration is crucial for a strong economy.

How should the story of migration to Britain really be told?

SOURCE 7   'The British', *a poem by Benjamin Zephaniah.*

The British
Serves 60 million

Take some Picts, Celts and Silures
And let them settle,
Then overrun them with Roman conquerors.

Remove the Romans after approximately four
    hundred years
Add lots of Norman French to some
Angles, Saxons, Jutes and Vikings, then stir vigorously.

Mix some hot Chileans, cool Jamaicans, Dominicans,
Trinidadians and Bajans with some Ethiopians,
Chinese, Vietnamese and Sudanese.

Then take a blend of Somalians, Sri Lankans,
    Nigerians
And Pakistanis,
Combine with some Guyanese
And turn up the heat.

Sprinkle some fresh Indians, Malaysians, Bosnians,
Iraqis and Bangladeshis together with some
Afghans, Spanish, Turkish, Kurdish, Japanese
And Palestinians
Then add to the melting pot.

Leave the ingredients to simmer.

As they mix and blend allow their languages to
    flourish
Binding them together with English.

Allow time to cool.

Add some unity, understanding, and respect for the
    future
Serve with justice
And enjoy.

Note: All ingredients are equally important. Treating one
ingredient better than another will leave a bitter and unpleasant
taste.

Warning: An unequal spread of justice will damage the people
and cause pain.

Give justice and equality to all.

ACTIVITY

1 What are the key messages in Benjamin Zephaniah's poem?

2 Produce a double page for a magazine or a newspaper exploring migration to Britain.

a) On one side of the page write a feature titled 'Ten things everybody should know about migration to Britain'. Make sure that the ten statements that you come up with destroy the Migration Myths on pages 206 and 218. You should also try to give people an idea of how migrants to Britain have been treated.

b) The other side of the page is up to you. You could write your own poem exploring migration to Britain or produce a collage, cartoon or poster that challenges the Migration Myths.

How have ideas and beliefs changed since 1900?

During the twentieth century Victorian ideas about the world were challenged by people who had very different beliefs and attitudes. How did new ideas and beliefs change the way that people saw the world?

ACTIVITY

1 Which twentieth-century visitor would be the best person to challenge each talking exhibit in the gallery?
2 What would they say to the person in the gallery they are challenging?
3 Would each visitor find anyone they agreed with?

GALLERY OPEN AT 1900

The vote for every man over the age of 21!

You must always speak out against things you do not believe in. But you should not break the law when you protest and you should never use violence. Parliament is where laws are changed and that is where you should make your case.

People should help themselves. The government should not interfere in people's lives. Why should I pay more taxes to pay for water and sewage systems for other people who are too lazy to work hard? The more you help people the softer they become.

THE POWER AND PROTEST GALLERY

THE ORDINARY LIFE GALLERY

Fergus O'Connor 1794-1855

William Wilberforce 1759-1833

THE CONFLICT GALLERY

Pierre de Coubertin 1863-1937 Founder of Olympics

Samuel Smiles 1812-1904

It is crucial to have a strong navy. Wars are won and lost at sea. The country with the most powerful army and navy will always win through.

Women should not compete in the Olympics. They have but one task, that of crowning the winner with garlands.

Lord Horatio Nelson 1758-1805

Empires are a good thing. The British Empire is the greatest force for good the world has ever seen. It has made Britain the richest country in the world and it benefits the people of India.

THE EMPIRE GALLERY

Lord Curzon Viceroy of India 1859-1925

Cecil Rhodes 1853-1902

What and who is most worth remembering?

Winston Churchill has been rated as one of the most influential leaders in history by *Time* magazine and topped a BBC poll of the 100 Greatest Britons. In this chapter you will explore why so many people think that Churchill is a significant historical figure. You will also have the chance to reflect back on other individuals and events you have studied. Why do we remember some events but forget others? Why do people argue about what and who is most worth remembering?

Why do so many people think that Winston Churchill is significant?

In late 2002, the BBC asked people to nominate who they thought had played the most 'significant part in the life of the British Isles'. The top ten figures were then put into a telephone and email poll to find the 'Greatest Briton' of all time. The results of this poll are shown below.

SOURCE 1 BBC History Magazine, *January 2003.*

1. Winston Churchill 447,423 votes (27.9 per cent)
2. Isambard Kingdom Brunel 391,262 (24.4 per cent)
3. Diana, Princess of Wales 222,025 (13.9 per cent)
4. Charles Darwin 112,496 (7 per cent)
5. William Shakespeare 109,919 (6.9 per cent)
6. Isaac Newton 84,628 (5.3 per cent)
7. Elizabeth I 71,928 (4.5 per cent)
8. John Lennon 68,445 (4.3 per cent)
9. Horatio Nelson 49,171 (3.1 per cent)
10. Oliver Cromwell 45,053 (2.8 per cent)

Churchill tops Greatest Briton poll

Remember what you have already learnt about significance:

- Being significant is not the same as being famous. Churchill did not top the poll simply because lots of people had heard of him.
- People use criteria to decide what and who is significant.

ACTIVITY

1 Look at the criteria you used to assess the significance of the Holocaust on page 140. Which of those criteria can also be used to assess the significance of an individual? Can you think of other criteria that should be used to assess the significance of an individual?

2 Write five criteria for assessing the significance of an individual. Place one criterion on each skittle in Significance Alley. How many of these significance skittles does Churchill knock over? Use pages 223–225.

Nearly forgotten? How important was Winston Churchill before the Second World War?

These words were said by Adolf Hitler in a 1942 radio broadcast. To what extent was Hitler right? Would Churchill have been an insignificant figure if war had not broken out in 1939?

> Churchill, what has he achieved in all his lifetime? Had this war not come, who would speak of Winston Churchill?

Winston Churchill was born on 30 November 1874 at Blenheim Palace in Oxfordshire. His father had been a leading politician. Winston was brought up by his nanny and did not find school easy. He never went to university and struggled to get into the Royal Military College at Sandhurst – only passing the entrance exam at his third attempt.

After Sandhurst, Churchill began a career in the army. He saw action on the North West Frontier of India and in the Sudan.

Churchill was a gifted writer. His first book, about an uprising in India, was published in 1898. He went on to write 43 books during his lifetime.

Whilst working as a journalist during the Boer War, he was captured and made a prisoner-of-war. Churchill managed to escape and returned to Britain a hero.

In 1900 Churchill became Conservative Member of Parliament for Oldham. Churchill suffered from a slight lisp. He worked hard to overcome this, visiting speech therapists and practising both words and gestures in front of a mirror until he was confident.

In 1904 Churchill left the Conservatives and joined the Liberal Party. In 1908 he entered the cabinet as President of the Board of Trade, later becoming Home Secretary and then First Lord of the Admiralty.

During the First World War, Churchill was blamed for the disastrous Gallipoli campaign, which resulted in heavy losses for Britain and her allies (see page 57). Churchill and Allied war commanders seriously underestimated the power of the Turkish army. He resigned from the government and joined the army, serving for a time on the Western Front.

In 1917 Churchill returned to a role in the government as Minister of Munitions where he supported the development of the tank as a weapon of war. From 1919 to 1921 he was Secretary of State for War and Air.

In 1922 Churchill rejoined the Conservative Party, serving as Chancellor of the Exchequer.

From 1929 until 1939 Churchill did not have an important position in government. During the 1930s, Churchill's views made him unpopular. Churchill believed that British rule of its empire should continue and he opposed Indian self-rule and independence.

Churchill strongly opposed Neville Chamberlain's policy of Appeasement towards Hitler. However, his warnings about the rise of Nazi Germany and the need for British rearmament were ignored.

DISCUSS

Look at your criteria for what makes an individual historically significant. How many of these criteria would Churchill knock down if his political career had ended in 1939?

223

How important was Winston Churchill during the Second World War?

When war broke out in 1939, Churchill became First Lord of the Admiralty. In May 1940, Neville Chamberlain resigned as Prime Minister and Churchill took his place. The war was going very badly for Britain. Hitler had invaded much of Europe, and Britain was the last remaining country in Western Europe that was able to fight back. Churchill and his government had to make sure that the morale of people throughout the British Empire remained high and that they would continue to support the war effort. Churchill played a vital role as leader of the country. He was often used in propaganda posters and cartoons.

▲ SOURCE 3 *A government poster from 1942.*

THE WARDEN OF EMPIRE

Reprinted from Punch, October 1 1941

▲ SOURCE 2 *A cartoon from* Punch, *October 1941. Churchill is dressed as an air-raid warden.*

▲ SOURCE 4 *A photograph of Churchill visiting people in Manchester whose homes had been bombed.*

DISCUSS 1

- Look at the images on this page. What impression do they give of Churchill?
- How would images such as these have helped to keep morale high?

How can words help to win a war?

Churchill's speeches were even more important. Unlike most modern politicians, he wrote them himself. They were inspirational and helped to strengthen the spirit and determination of men and women throughout the British Empire. Churchill's speeches boosted the morale of the British people and made them believe that victory was possible.

SOURCE 5 *Just three days after becoming Prime Minister Churchill delivered this speech to the House of Commons (13 May 1940).*

I have nothing to offer but blood, toil, tears, and sweat. We have before us an ordeal of the most grievous kind. We have before us many, many months of struggle and suffering. You ask, what is our policy? I say it is to wage war by land, sea, and air. War with all our might and with all the strength God has given us, and to wage war against a monstrous tyranny never surpassed in the dark and lamentable catalogue of human crime. That is our policy.

I take up my task in buoyancy and hope. I feel that our cause will not be suffered to fail among men. I feel entitled at this juncture, at this time, to claim the aid of all and to say, 'Come then, let us go forward together with our united strength.'

When he realised that France was soon to be defeated and that an invasion of Britain was likely to follow, Churchill felt 'physically sick'. However, he was able to convince the British people that they were in safe hands and that he could lead them to victory. After the evacuation of Allied forces at Dunkirk, Churchill cleverly turned a serious military defeat into a victory. He was able to persuade the British people that the evacuation had been a great success and he created what became known as the 'Dunkirk spirit', a determination to 'never surrender', to fight on until victory came.

SOURCE 6 *Churchill's speech to the House of Commons on 4 June 1940.*

Even though large tracts of Europe and many old and famous states have fallen or may fall into the grip of the Gestapo and all the odious apparatus of Nazi rule, we shall not flag or fail.

We shall go on to the end, we shall fight in France, we shall fight on the seas and oceans, we shall fight with growing confidence and growing strength in the air, we shall defend our island, whatever the cost may be, we shall fight on the beaches, we shall fight on the landing grounds, we shall fight in the fields and in the streets, we shall fight in the hills; we shall never surrender.

SOURCE 7 *Churchill gave this speech on 18 June 1940.*

Hitler knows that he will have to break us in this island or lose the war. If we can stand up to him, all Europe may be free and the life of the world may move forward into broad, sunlit uplands. But if we fail, the whole world, including the United States, including all that we have known and cared for, will sink into the abyss of a new Dark Age, made more sinister, and perhaps more protracted, by the lights of perverted science. Let us therefore brace ourselves to our duties, and so bear ourselves that, if the British Empire and its Commonwealth last for a thousand years, men will say, 'This was their finest hour'.

DISCUSS 2

Why do you think Churchill's speeches were so powerful? Look at the list below. Find examples of Churchill using the following techniques:

- Honesty – to make people believe in what he is saying.
- Using powerful images – to make people realise how serious the situation is.
- Involving the audience – to make them feel that they have a vital role to play in the struggle.
- Sounding positive and certain – in order to keep up morale and reassure the British people.
- Displaying determination and courage – to inspire people to show the same qualities.

How has Churchill been remembered?

Churchill provided the strong and inspirational leadership that was needed during the Second World War. Churchill never talked of defeat or surrender and rejected peace terms offered by Hitler. He was able to build strong relations with the United States and maintain a difficult alliance with the Soviet Union. During the war, Churchill travelled 40,000 miles in a bid to keep the 'big three' together.

Churchill lost power in the 1945 post-war election. Between 1948 and 1954 Churchill published a six-volume set of books on the Second World War, for which he was awarded the Nobel Prize for Literature. These books helped to establish Churchill's own interpretation of the conflict and reinforce his central role in leading Britain to victory. In 1951, he became Prime Minister again. He resigned in 1955, but remained an MP until shortly before his death.

Churchill died on 24 January 1965 and was given a state funeral (above). As his body lay in Westminster Hall, more than 300,000 people queued for hours in the cold and rain to pay their respects. An estimated 350 million people around the world watched the pictures of his funeral.

Churchill's reputation has remained high since his death. Some historians have questioned some of the military decisions that Churchill took during the war; however, few people would question his overall contribution to the war effort. As you have seen, in 2002, Churchill was voted the 'Greatest Briton' of all time. In addition, in 2007, the speech he gave to the House of Commons on 4 June 1940 was selected by the *Guardian* as one of their 'Great Speeches of the Twentieth Century'. Reflecting on the importance of the speech, the historian Simon Schama said:

Churchill's words went to war when Britain's armed forces seemed to be going under. They were the lifeboat and the blood transfusion. They turned the tide.

(The *Guardian*, 20 April 2007.)

Statements about significance can change over time

Statements about significance reflect the attitudes and values of the time in which they were produced. An individual (or event) who is seen as very significant in one age can seem less relevant or important in another.

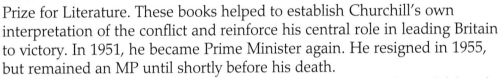

DISCUSS

Think about Churchill. Do you think he will still be seen as significant in 100 years' time?

Look once again at the list of top ten Greatest Britons. Are there any individuals in this list who you think are no longer historically significant or who may not appear so high up in future polls?

226

Significance and Interpretations

Why do people argue about who and what is historically significant?

Statements about significance are interpretations.

Different people will come to different conclusions about who and what should be remembered. The BBC's poll to find the 'Greatest Britons' caused a lot of debate and argument. A number of factors can cause disagreement. Look at the list below. Can you think of any more?

- People may argue about which criteria to use to assess significance.
- Even if they use the same criteria they may disagree about whether or not an individual meets particular criteria. This may be because of their age, sex, nationality, religion, values or political beliefs.

ACTIVITY

1 Look at the other individuals in the top ten Greatest Britons (page 222). Choose at least two individuals. Explain why some people might argue that they are historically significant. Explain why someone else might disagree.

2 What about your own opinions? Is there someone you have studied who you think should be in the list of top ten most significant Britons? Sum up, in less than 100 words, why you think they should be included. Remember to be clear on the criteria you have used to reach your decision.

3 Imagine that the poll had been to find the ten most significant individuals from *world* history. Who would be in your list? Remember that you can choose individuals from any period of history.

4 Compare your list with that of other people in your class. How does it differ and can you explain why it is different?

5 For the front cover of this book we had to choose two individuals from the twentieth century that we thought were significant. Why do you think we chose these individuals? Do you agree with our choices? Who would you choose to go on the front cover of this book?

Which events are most worth remembering?

In the UK we remember some of the most significant events in our past by holding a special day of commemoration.

11 November – Remembrance Day
To commemorate the sacrifices of members of the armed forces and civilians in times of war. It is observed on 11 November to remember the end of the First World War on that date in 1918. The first Remembrance Day was held in 1919.

27 January – Holocaust Memorial Day
Dedicated to the remembrance of the victims of the Holocaust. It was first held in 2001. The chosen date is the anniversary of the liberation of Auschwitz concentration camp by the Soviet Union in 1945.

ACTIVITY

1 Why do you think both of these days commemorate events that took place in the twentieth century?

2 Is it also important to remember key events from previous time periods?

| The Battle of Trafalgar | The ending of the British slave trade | The execution of Charles I | The Battle of Hastings |

| The end of slavery in the British colonies | The Black Death | The Peasants' Revolt |

3 Imagine that the government wanted to introduce three more days on which we remembered significant historical events. Which dates and events would you choose? Explain your answer.

Which events are most worth studying?

Planning a history course for pupils or writing a history textbook for use in schools is very difficult. With history, you can study anything that happened at any time in the past, to anybody, anywhere in the world. As authors we have had a number of arguments about what should be included and what should be left out of this book.

> We should include more pages on the Second World War. This was the most significant event in our history. Just think what Europe would be like if Hitler had won. We need to include some more information on the Eastern Front and the role that the Soviet Union played in opposing Hitler. This was one of the key turning points in the war. Twenty million people from the Soviet Union were killed in the conflict. Even Churchill admitted that it was the Russians who 'tore the heart out of the German army'.

> I disagree, history textbooks are too full of conflict and war. There are other important events to study – like the way that ordinary people had to struggle for civil rights. I want to include more pages on the struggle to achieve civil rights in South Africa and how women in our country had to fight to win the right to vote. These events changed the lives of millions of people. They also show how ordinary people have the power to change the world in which they live.

ACTIVITY

Imagine that a new edition of this book is being produced but it only contains 100 pages. Look at the Contents pages at the front of this book. Which key events would you keep and which would you cut? Explain your reasons.

In the end we decided to make cuts to the conflict section of this book and include more pages on the struggle to achieve equal rights. Do you think we made the right decision?

Are there any other key events from the last 100 years that you think we should have included in this book?

The book with no name!

You are now going to sum up some of the big ideas from this course by making improvements to our book cover.

The title

This book has no descriptive title so it's up to you to choose one. Think of a title that
- grabs people's attention
- sounds intriguing
- but also sums up what you think are the important changes in this period.

The pictures

You might not agree with our choice of pictures so you can choose your own if there are people who you think better represent the period.

Once you have created your covers (you can get a template to work with on the computer) you can then take a class vote on which one best conveys the period.

Here are one person's covers for the Year 7 and Year 8 books that you used:

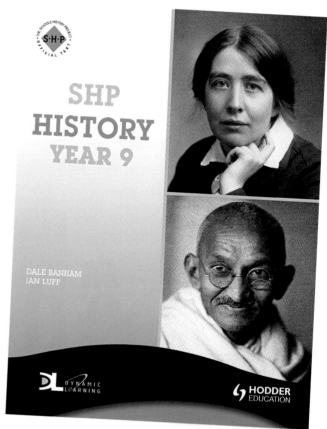

Speed interviews

During your study of history you have met lots of fascinating characters from the past. Your final challenge is to try to recall what they did and why they should be remembered. You also need to think about how these individuals might react if they had the chance to meet characters from different periods of history. Would there be arguments between people about what they did and how important it was?

ACTIVITY 1

Preparation for the speed interviews

Imagine that you could bring some of the characters you have studied at Key Stage 3 back to life in your classroom! What would they say to each other during a speed interview? You will become one of the characters in the diagram. For your character, think about how they would respond to the following key questions:

1 What did you do? (Aim to sum this up in under 100 words.)
2 What are you most proud of?
3 What would you do differently if you had the chance again?
4 Why should you be remembered? (Try to sum this up in a sentence.)

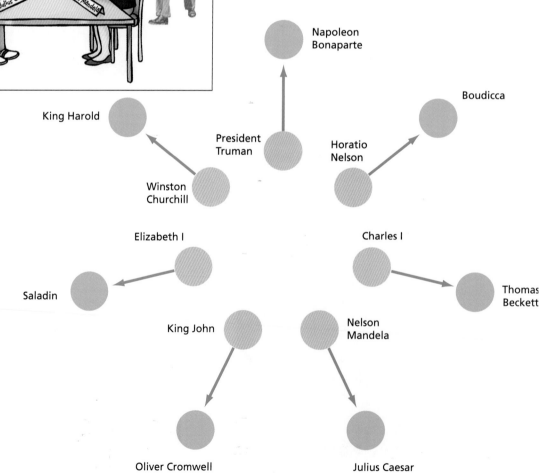

King Harold

Napoleon Bonaparte

Boudicca

President Truman

Horatio Nelson

Winston Churchill

Elizabeth I

Charles I

Saladin

Thomas Beckett

King John

Nelson Mandela

Oliver Cromwell

Julius Caesar

ACTIVITY 2

The speed interviews

- Start in the position shown in the picture below. Each character has one minute to talk through their answers to the four key questions.
- You then have one minute of open debate between the two characters. How would the characters react to each other? Would they get on or start arguing? How important would they think each other was?
- When the time is up, the characters in the inner circle stay where they are. The individuals on the outer circle move one place clockwise and the speed interviews begin again.

ACTIVITY 3

Battle of the circles!

After the speed interviews are finished it is time to make a decision as a group on who you think has the strongest case for being remembered. Each of the two speed interview circles should choose a character to represent it. These two individuals should then meet, introduce themselves and argue about who should be remembered the most. They can be helped by other members of their circle.

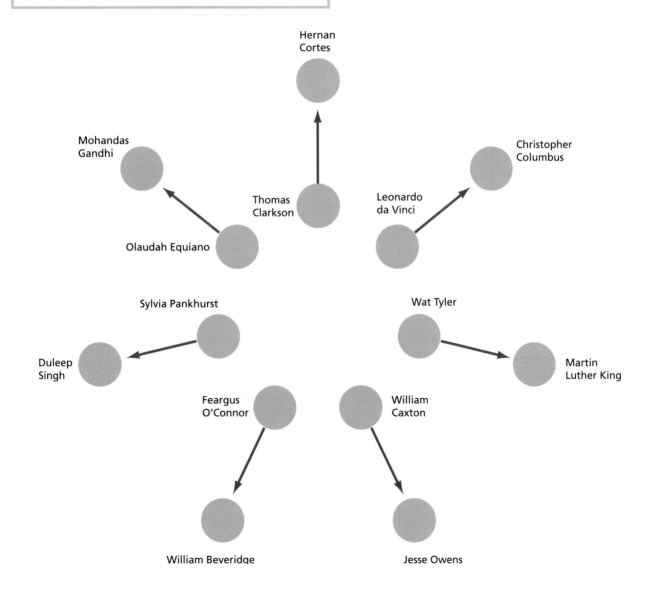

Hernan Cortes

Mohandas Gandhi

Christopher Columbus

Thomas Clarkson

Leonardo da Vinci

Olaudah Equiano

Sylvia Pankhurst

Wat Tyler

Duleep Singh

Martin Luther King

Feargus O'Connor

William Caxton

William Beveridge

Jesse Owens

Index

Acknowledgements

Cover t Hulton Archive/Getty Images, b Dinodia Images/Alamy; **p.3** tl Bob Thomas/Getty Images, tr & cl Central Press/Getty Images, bl Hulton Archive/Getty Images, br Keystone/Getty Images; **p.4** IOC Olympic Museum/Allsport/Getty Images; **p.5** tl Getty Images, tr IOC Olympic Museum/Allsport/Getty Images, b Popperfoto/Getty Images; **p.6** t Rolls Press/Popperfoto/Getty Images, b Ronald C. Modra/ Sports Illustrated/Getty Images; **p.7** tl Paul Popper/Popperfoto/Getty Images, tr © Corbis, b Craig Prentis/Allsport/Getty Images; **p.8** Roger Viollet Collection/Getty Images; **p.9** t Jed Jacobsohn/Getty Images, b Odd Andersen/AFP/Getty Images; **p.10** t Popperfoto/Getty Images, b Keystone/Hulton Archive/Getty Images; **p.11** t © Hulton-Deutsch Collection/Corbis, bl Tony Duffy/Getty Images, br © London 2012/Handout/Reuters/Corbis; **p.12** London Stereoscopic Company/Getty Images; **p.13** London Stereoscopic Company/Getty Images; **p.16** Private Collection/Mark Fiennes/Bridgeman Art Library; **p.19** Image courtesy of Norfolk County Council Library and Information Service – to view thousands of images of Norfolk's history visit www.picture.norfolk.gov.uk; **p.20** Mansell/Time Life Pictures/Getty Images; **p.22** Ian Luff; **p.24** Peter Jordan/PA Archive/Press Association Images; **p.25** Hulton Archive/Getty Images; **p.26** t Popperfoto/Getty Images, b Margaret Bourke-White/Time & Life Pictures/Getty Images; **p.27** © Sean Sexton Collection/Corbis; **p.28** t Reinhold Thiele/Getty Images, b Hulton Archive/Getty Images; **p.32** Indo-British/Int Film Investors/The Kobal Collection; **p.34** Mansell/Time Life Pictures/ Getty Images; **p.36** PA/PA Archive/Press Association Images; **p.37** © British Library Board (566/(4)); **p.38** Popperfoto/Getty Images; **p.39** Dinodia Images/Alamy; **p.41** Margaret Bourke-White/Time & Life Pictures/Getty Images; **p.48** © Bettmann/Corbis; **p.49** Harry Benson/Getty Images; **p.51** Kimimasa Mayama/AFP/Getty Images; **p.52** t Seapix/Alamy, b Gareth Cattermole/Getty Images; **p.53** t cupra images/Alamy, b Brian Harris/Rex Features; **p.58** Imperial War Museum, London; **p.59** t & b Imperial War Museum, London; **p.60** tl, bl & br Imperial War Museum, London, tr TopFoto; **p.63** Mary Evans Picture Library/Illustrated London News; **p.64** Imperial War Museum, London; **p.65** Paul Popper/Popperfoto/Getty Images; **p.66** t Paul Popper/Popperfoto/ Getty Images, b Central Press/Getty Images; **p.67** t The RAMC Muniment Collection in the care of the Wellcome Library, b TopFoto; **p.68** © Corbis; **p.69** t ullsteinbild/TopFoto, c Fox Photos/Getty Images, b United Artists/The Kobal Collection; **p.70** Solo Syndication/ Associated Newspapers Ltd. (photo: The British Cartoon Archive, University of Kent); **p.71** t Imperial War Museum, London, c © Corbis, b ullsteinbild/TopFoto; **p.72** t Hulton Archive/ Getty Images, cl Popperfoto/Getty Images, cr © Bettmann/Corbis, b AFP/Getty Images; **p.77** t Fred Morley/Fox Photos/Hulton Archive/ Getty Images, b ullsteinbild/TopFoto; **p.78** l, c & r Ian Luff; **p.79** Hulton Archive/ Getty Images; **p.80** reproduced by kind permission of Alma McGregor; **p.81** © Corbis; **p.82** tl Keystone/Getty Images, tr Imperial War Museum, London, bl Topical Press Agency/Getty Images, br M. McNeill/Fox Photos/Getty Images; **p.84** Alinari/ TopFoto; **p.85** reproduced by kind permission of Nora Lang; **p.86** ullsteinbild/ TopFoto; **p.90** © Corbis; **p.91** From *Hiroshima Diary: The Journal of a Japanese Physician, August 6 - September 30,1945* by Michihiko Hachiya, translated and edited by Warner Wells, M.D. Copyright © 1955 by the University of North Carolina Press, renewed 1983 by Warner Wells. Foreword by John W. Dower © 1995 by the University of North Carolina Press. Used by permission of the publisher.; **p.94** t © Bettmann/Corbis, c Pfc. James Cox/US Army/ National Archives/Time Life Pictures/Getty Images, b © Bettmann/Corbis; **p.95** t © Corbis, c © John Van Hasselt/Corbis Sygma, b RIA Novosti/TopFoto; **p.96** © Jacques Pavlovsky/Sygma/ Corbis; **p.100** © Leif Skoogfors/Corbis; **p.104** l Spencer Platt/Getty Images, r Stan Honda/AFP/Getty Images; **p.106** l Henry Guttmann/ Getty Images, r Hulton Archive/Getty Images; **p.107** © Bettmann/ Corbis; **p.109** © Corbis; **p.110** b © David King; **p.111** l, tr & br © David King; **p.112** t © David King, b RIA Novosti/TopFoto; **p.113** tl RIA Novosti/TopFoto, tr © David King, c Popperfoto/Getty Images, b The Granger Collection/TopFoto; **p.115** l Süddeutsche Zeitung Photo/Scherl, r © Bettmann/Corbis; **p.116** t The Art Archive/Private Collection/Marc Charmet, b TopFoto; **p.117** t ullstein bild - W. Frentz, c © Corbis, b ullsteinbild/TopFoto; **p.118** tl akg-images, tr Yad Vashem, c ullstein bild - W. Frentz, b Keystone/ Getty Images; **p.119** t ullsteinbild/ TopFoto, b TopFoto; **p.120** t Institut für Stadtgeschichte Frankfurt am Main, b Bundesarchiv, Koblenz, Germany (Plak 003-002-046/Grafiker: Rene Ahrle); **p.121** Süddeutsche Zeitung Photo/Scherl; **p.123** Yad Vashem; **p.124** t & br reproduced by kind permission of Frank Bright, bl Yad Vashem; **p.125** t & br reproduced by kind permission of Frank Bright, bl Roger-Viollet/ Topfoto; **p.127** t Keystone/Hulton Archive/ Getty Images, bl USHMM, br TopFoto/AP; **p.130** t Willy Georg/Rex Features, bl Yad Vashem, br Rex Features; **p.132** tl & bl Yad Vashem, r ullsteinbild/ TopFoto; **p.133** t & bl Yad Vashem; **p.134** t TopFoto, b Robert Harding Picture Library Ltd/Alamy; **p.135** t © dpa/ Corbis, b © epa/Corbis; **p.138** t USHMM, courtesy of Samuel Gruber, b Keystone/Getty Images; **p.142** tl © Wilberforce House, Hull City Museums and Art Galleries/ Bridgeman Art Library, tr Alisdair Macdonald/Rex Features, cl Mansell/Time Life Pictures/Getty Images, cr USHMM, courtesy of Samuel Gruber, ctr Hulton Archive/ Getty Images, cbr © Bettmann/ Corbis, br © Jon Hursa/epa/Corbis; **p.144** Topical Press Agency/ Getty Images; **p.146** l & r © Museum of London; **p.149** l Mansell/ Time Life Pictures/Getty Images, r Mary Evans Picture Library; **p.150** British Library, London/Bridgeman Art Library; **p.151** Hulton Archive/ Getty Images; **p.153** © Museum of London; **p.154** t & b © Bettmann/ Corbis; **p.155** Hulton Archive/Getty Images; **p.156** New York Times Co./Getty Images; **p.157** l & r © Bettmann/Corbis; **p.159** t Danny Lyon/Magnum Photos, b Leonard Freed/Magnum Photos; **p.160** tl Elliott Erwitt/Magnum Photos, tr Arthur Fellig/International Centre of Photography/Getty Images, b © Bettmann/Corbis; **p.161** © Bettmann/Corbis; **p.162** t © Bettmann/ Corbis, b Gjon Mili/Time Life Pictures/Getty Images; **p.163** TopFoto; **p.164** tl © Corbis, tc, tr & b © Bettmann/Corbis; **p.165** t Donald Uhrbrock/Time Life Pictures/Getty Images, c © Bettmann/Corbis, b Gene Herrick/AP/Press Association Images; **p.166** tl, tr, c & b © Bettmann/Corbis; **p.167** t AP/Press Association Images, c © Hulton-Deutsch Collection/Corbis, b © Corbis; **p.168** t & b © Bettmann/ Corbis; **p.169** t Hulton Archive/Getty Images, cl & cr © Bettmann/ Corbis, b Michael Ochs Archives/Getty Images; **p.171** © Michael Czerwonka/epa/Corbis; **p.172** l Sipa Press/Rex Features, r Walter Dhladhla/AFP/Getty Images; **p.173** Alexander Joe/AFP/Getty Images; **p.177** l © Dave G. Houser/Corbis, r TopFoto/AP; **p.178** t TopFoto, bl Eli Weinberg, UWC Robben-Island Mayibuye Archives, br © Bettmann/ Corbis; **p.179** t Keystone/Getty Images, b Jurgen Schadeberg/Getty Images; **p.180** t Mark Peters/ Getty Images, c TopFoto/AP, b © David Turnley/Corbis; **p.181** t © Louise Gubb/Link Picture Library, b Central Press/Getty Images; **p.182** Gerard Julien/AFP/Getty Images; **p.186** The National Archives (PREM 4/89/2); **p.188** tl William Vanderson/Fox Photos/Getty Images, tr J. A. Hampton/Topical Press Agency/Getty Images, c Popperfoto/Getty Images, b Keystone/Getty Images; **p.189** t Richards/Fox Photos/Getty Images, b Fox Photos/ Getty Images; **p.192** The National Archives (INF 13/255(9)); **p.193** Keystone/Getty Images; **p.198** © UNDP Brazil; **p.201** © Andy Aitchison/Corbis; **p.200** © United Nations Children's Fund (UNICEF), December 2008; **p.202** tl © Angelo Hornak/Corbis, tr © Fridmar Damm/Corbis, cr JTB Photo/ Photolibrary, bl kpzfoto/Alamy, br Mick Rock/Photolibrary; **p.203** tl Mary Evans Picture Library, tr David Wootton/Alamy, cr © Joe Gough - Fotolia.com, bl Chris Cooper-Smith/Alamy, br Robert Convery/Alamy; **p.204** tl © Fridmar Damm/ Corbis, tr © Angelo Hornak/Corbis, ctl & bl Mary Evans Picture Library, cr kpzfoto/Alamy, cbl Mick Rock/ Photolibrary, br David Wootton/Alamy; **p.205** tl © Joe Gough - Fotolia.com, tr Chris Cooper-Smith/Alamy, bl Robert Convery/ Alamy, br Reinhold Thiele/ Getty Images; **p.206** NMeM Daily Herald Archive/Science & Society Picture Library; **p.209** l British Library, London/© British Library Board. All Rights Reserved/Bridgeman Art Library, c Private Collection/Mark Fiennes/Bridgeman Art Library, r Hulton Archive/ Getty Images; **p.210** l Imperial War Museum, London, tr British Library, London, UK/© British Library Board. All Rights Reserved/ Bridgeman Art Library, cr National Portrait Gallery, London (NPG D13148), br Hulton Archive/Getty Images; **p.211** tl Topical Press Agency/Getty Images, tr © Hulton-Deutsch Collection/Corbis, ctl Bob Thomas/Popperfoto/Getty Images, cbl PA/PA Archive/Press Association Images, bl Family Handout/PA Archive/Press Association Images, br TopFoto/UPP; **p.212** London Transport Museum; **p.213** Barratts/S&G Barratts/EMPICS Archive; **p.216** t © Hulton-Deutsch Collection/Corbis, c © Daily Express (photo: John Frost Newspapers), b PA/PA Archive/Press Association Images; **p.224** t TopFoto, bl Punch Ltd., br Keystone/Getty Images; **p.226** Fox Photos/Hulton Archive/ Getty Images; **p.227** Diana Bier Westminster Commemorate Dead/Alamy.